# CHELSEA CLINTON

It's **YOUR** World

Get Informed

Get Inspired

&Get Going!

PUFFIN BOOKS

*For Charlotte*

PUFFIN BOOKS
An imprint of Penguin Random House LLC
375 Hudson Street
New York, New York 10014

First published in the United States of America by Philomel Books,
an imprint of Penguin Random House LLC, 2015
Published by Puffin Books, an imprint of Penguin Random House LLC, 2017

Library of Congress Cataloging-in-Publication Data is available.
ISBN 9780399176128 (hc)

Puffin Books ISBN 9780399545320

Printed in the United States of America

10 9 8 7 6 5 4 3 2 1

Edited by Jill Santopolo. Design by Semadar Megged.
Charts, graphs, and infographics by Siobhán Gallagher.

# CONTENTS

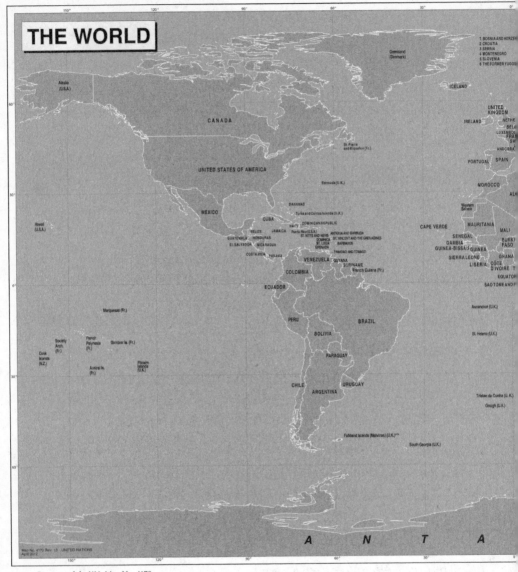

# THE WORLD

1. BOSNIA AND HERZEGOVINA
2. CROATIA
3. SERBIA
4. MONTENEGRO
5. SLOVENIA
6. THE FORMER YUGOSLAV

Greenland
(Denmark)

ICELAND

Alaska
(U.S.A.)

CANADA

UNITED
KINGDOM

IRELAND                    NETHE

BEL
LUXEMBO
FRA
SW

ANDORRA

St. Pierre
and Miquelon (Fr.)

PORTUGAL   SPAIN

UNITED STATES OF AMERICA

MOROCCO

Bermuda (U.K.)

AL

Hawaii
(U.S.A.)

MEXICO

BAHAMAS

Western
Sahara

CUBA          Turks and Caicos Islands (U.K.)

CAPE VERDE        MAURITANIA

HAITI    DOMINICAN REPUBLIC

BELIZE        JAMAICA    Puerto Rico (U.S.A.)

GUATEMALA   HONDURAS            ST. KITTS AND NEVIS    ANTIGUA AND BARBUDA

SENEGAL            MALI

DOMINICA   ST. VINCENT AND THE GRENADINES

EL SALVADOR   NICARAGUA                ST. LUCIA   BARBADOS

GAMBIA                   BURKI
GUINEA-BISSAU   GUINEA       FASO

COSTA RICA   PANAMA                GRENADA

GRENADA   TRINIDAD AND TOBAGO

SIERRA LEONE            GHANA

VENEZUELA   GUYANA

LIBERIA   CÔTE
D'IVOIRE   T

COLOMBIA             SURINAME
French Guiana (Fr.)

EQUATOR

ECUADOR

SÃO TOMÉ AND P

Marquesas (Fr.)

PERU

Ascension (U.K.)

BRAZIL

BOLIVIA

St. Helena (U.K.)

Society
Arch.
(Fr.)

French
Polynesia
(Fr.)

Gambier Is. (Fr.)

Cook
Islands
(N.Z.)

PARAGUAY

Austral Is.
(Fr.)

Pitcairn
Islands
(U.K.)

Tristan da Cunha (U.K.)

CHILE       URUGUAY

Gough (U.K.)

ARGENTINA

Falkland Islands (Malvinas) (U.K.)**

South Georgia (U.K.)

A       N       T       A       R

Map No. 4170 Rev. 13   UNITED NATIONS
April 2012

150°          120°          90°          60°          30°

Courtesy of the UN, Map No. 4170

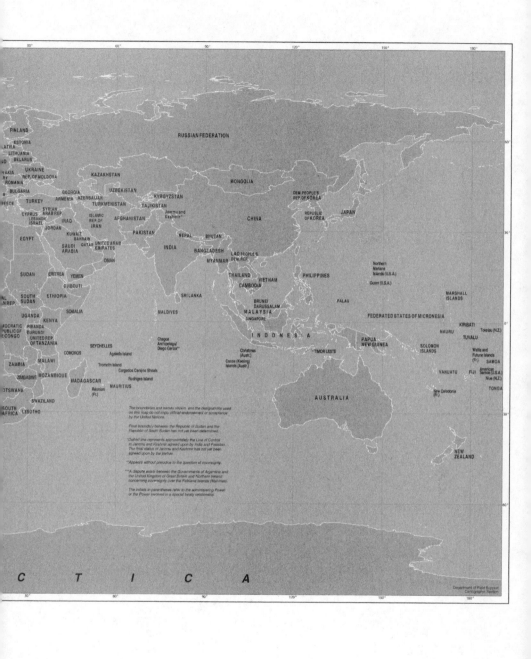

FINLAND
ESTONIA
LATVIA
LITHUANIA
BELARUS
UKRAINE
REP. OF MOLDOVA
ROMANIA
BULGARIA
GREECE
TURKEY
CYPRUS
LEBANON
ISRAEL
SYRIAN
ARAB REP.
JORDAN
IRAQ
EGYPT
KUWAIT
BAHRAIN
QATAR
SAUDI
ARABIA
UNITED ARAB
EMIRATES
OMAN
SUDAN
ERITREA
YEMEN
DJIBOUTI
SOUTH
SUDAN
ETHIOPIA
UGANDA
SOMALIA
KENYA
DEMOCRATIC
REPUBLIC OF
CONGO
RWANDA
BURUNDI
UNITED REP.
OF TANZANIA
ZAMBIA
MALAWI
ZIMBABWE
MOZAMBIQUE
BOTSWANA
MADAGASCAR
MAURITIUS
SWAZILAND
SOUTH
AFRICA
LESOTHO

RUSSIAN FEDERATION

KAZAKHSTAN
GEORGIA
ARMENIA AZERBAIJAN
UZBEKISTAN
KYRGYZSTAN
TURKMENISTAN
TAJIKISTAN
ISLAMIC
REP. OF
IRAN
AFGHANISTAN
PAKISTAN
Jammu and
Kashmir**
MONGOLIA

DEM. PEOPLE'S
REP. OF KOREA
REPUBLIC
OF KOREA
JAPAN

CHINA
NEPAL
BHUTAN
INDIA
BANGLADESH
MYANMAR
LAO PEOPLE'S
DEM. REP.
THAILAND
VIETNAM
CAMBODIA
SRI LANKA
MALDIVES

PHILIPPINES

BRUNEI
DARUSSALAM
MALAYSIA
SINGAPORE
INDONESIA

PALAU

Northern
Mariana
Islands (U.S.A.)
Guam (U.S.A.)

MARSHALL
ISLANDS

FEDERATED STATES OF MICRONESIA

KIRIBATI
NAURU
Tokelau (N.Z.)
TUVALU

SEYCHELLES
Agalega Island
Chagos
Archipelago/
Diego Garcia**
Tromelin Island
Cargados Carajos Shoals
Rodrigues Island
COMOROS
Réunion
(Fr.)

Christmas
(Austr.)
Cocos (Keeling)
Islands (Austr.)

TIMOR LESTE
PAPUA
NEW GUINEA
SOLOMON
ISLANDS

Wallis and
Futuna Islands
(Fr.)
SAMOA
VANUATU
FIJI
American
Samoa (U.S.A.)
Niue (N.Z.)
New Caledonia
(Fr.)
TONGA

AUSTRALIA

NEW
ZEALAND

The boundaries and names shown, and the designations used
on this map do not imply official endorsement or acceptance
by the United Nations.

Final boundary between the Republic of Sudan and the
Republic of South Sudan has not yet been determined.

*Dotted line represents approximately the Line of Control
in Jammu and Kashmir agreed upon by India and Pakistan.
The final status of Jammu and Kashmir has not yet been
agreed upon by the parties.

**Appears without prejudice to the question of sovereignty.

***A dispute exists between the Governments of Argentina and
the United Kingdom of Great Britain and Northern Ireland
concerning sovereignty over the Falkland Islands (Malvinas).

The initials in parentheses refer to the administering Power
or the Power involved in a special treaty relationship.

C T I C A

Department of Field Support
Cartographic Section

# INTRODUCTION

What's the first thing you remember reading? The first thing I remember reading on my own was the local newspaper, the old-fashioned kind that left ink stains on my hands. I probably read *Corduroy* or a Curious George story first, out loud to my parents, but it's the newspapers I pored over as I ate my morning Cheerios that mark the line in my mind between not-reading and reading. The newspaper is probably what I remember most because it's what enabled me to be a part of my parents' conversations about what was happening in our hometown of Little Rock, Arkansas, and the broader world. Those conversations happened around the dinner table every night and intensely after church on Sunday over lunch. They happened on the way to school and on the way home from ballet class, before Brownies meetings and after softball games. In other words, they happened all the time.

Knowing what was in the newspaper meant I didn't have to wait for my parents to explain everything to me. I could ask questions to start conversations about the world too. Best of all? The newspaper helped hide how much honey I poured on top of my Cheerios. My mom wouldn't let me have sugary cereal growing up (more on that later) and so I improvised, adding far more honey than likely would have been in any honeyed cereals. Thankfully, my mom never caught on.

I was very fortunate growing up. My main worries were things like trying to get my mom to relax her ban on sugary cereals, figuring out how to stick a clay honeycomb or papier-mâché Jupiter or clay-and-Popsicle-stick coral reef to poster board for various science projects, how to sell more Girl Scout Cookies than I did the year before and whether my best friend Elizabeth and I would sleep at her house or my house Saturday night. I never doubted I would have a roof over my head, a school to go to, enough to eat, books (and newspapers) to read, a safe neighborhood to play in and a doctor to see if I got sick.

My parents and grandparents made sure I knew I was lucky. I don't remember a time not knowing the life story of my mom's mom, my grandma Dorothy. By the time she was eight, my grandma Dorothy's parents had abandoned her twice, often leaving her hungry and alone in their Chicago apartment. The first time was when she was three years old. Ultimately, they sent her to live with her grandparents in California. When she became a teenager, her grandparents told her she was no longer welcome in their home and that since she was old enough to get a job and support herself, she had to leave. If she hadn't found a job working in someone else's home, she would have been homeless. If her employers hadn't supported her determination to go to school, she would have had to drop out. As a teenager, she constantly worried about whether she would have a roof over her head, be able to go to school or have enough to eat.

My grandmother always talked very matter-of-factly about her memories of being hungry and scared as a child. Knowing her story helped me be aware that some of the kids I knew at Forest Park Elementary, Booker Arts Magnet School or Horace Mann Junior High likely had to worry about whether there would be enough to eat that day and whether it would be safe to play outside when they got home. Less than twenty-five years before I was born, Horace Mann was a school only for African American students. Back then, schools were segregated by race in Arkansas—as they were across much of the South until the late 1950s—and the schools white kids went to had more and better resources, like nicer classrooms, more books, newer desks and fancier playgrounds. The wounding legacy of segregation and growing up knowing adults who had worked

*My grandma Dorothy as a kid in 1928.*

Courtesy of the Author's Parents

for civil rights and equal opportunities for African Americans was part of what made me understand that many kids in my community and around the world were still treated differently because of the color of their skin. My mother's work on behalf of girls and women first in Arkansas and later around the world helped me understand how being born a girl is often seen as reason enough to deny someone the right to go to school or to make her own decisions, even about who or when to marry.

Long before I turned eighteen and started voting, really for as long as I can remember, my parents expected me to have an opinion or point of view about everything. Truly, everything. What I experienced, what I learned in school and what I saw or read about in the news. They also expected me to be able to back up my views with facts and evidence—and, if I could, to work to change things that frustrated me. It never seemed to matter how old—or young—I was. And it wasn't just my parents; my grandparents felt the same way. As my grandma Ginger, my dad's mother, often told me before she passed away when I was thirteen, "Chelsea, you've been blessed and you need to always be thinking about how to expand the circle of blessings." My grandma Dorothy repeatedly told me, "You'll never know until you try."

Reading the newspaper and knowing what was happening was only a first step—making a positive difference, or at least trying to, was what mattered most. Those expectations were one of the greatest gifts my parents and grandparents gave me.

It felt important, and exciting, to know I could make a difference, or, again, that at least I could try. I wrote a letter to President Reagan when I was five to voice my opposition to his visit to the Bitburg cemetery in Germany, because Nazis were buried there. I didn't think an American president should honor a group of soldiers that included Nazis. President Reagan still went, but at least I had tried in my own small way. In elementary school, I was part of a group that helped

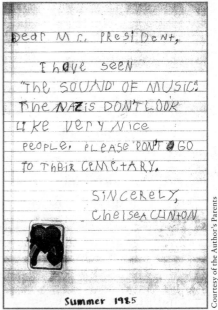

*This is a photocopy of the letter I sent to President Reagan in 1985. I included one of my favorite stickers as a sign of respect (and hoped it might help the president take my letter more seriously).*

start a paper-recycling program. Through my church in Little Rock, I volunteered in park cleanups, helped with food drives and worked in soup kitchens. There was always more to do, but seeing bags fill up with trash, barrels fill up with canned food and people eating meals all taught me that a group of people working together could have a real impact—and that such work could even be fun.

Supported by my grandparents, while in elementary school, I joined organizations like Greenpeace, the World Wildlife Fund and Conservation International because I believed in their work and wanted to be part of it, even if it was being done far from Arkansas. All were dedicated to protecting our environment and protecting animals—whales, elephants, giant pandas— that I had seen only in our local zoo or on television but felt a connection to. I wanted to play even a minor part in ensuring their futures. I talked about issues I cared about to anyone who would listen and hoped I wasn't too annoying, because if I wasn't annoying, and I was making a good argument, then maybe one more person would care about whales or elephants or giant pandas than before I'd started.

What I didn't realize when I was younger was how much of what I read, thought about, debated and tried to make a difference on were issues that arguably had even more of an impact on kids my age than on grown-ups. That's still true. Some things, like certain infectious diseases, are more dangerous for kids, while other things, like global warming, affect kids more because you will live with the consequences for longer (unless we stop climate change). A good part of what I worry about now, I first started worrying about when I was a kid. This is a book about some of the big issues our world and particularly kids face. It's also a book about some of the solutions young people (and a few adults) have created and supported to help make their families, neighborhoods, cities and our world healthier, safer and more equal.

This book is not exhaustive, meaning it does not address every single issue around the world today. Far from it. It also does not come close to tackling every detail of the issues I do talk about. In the same way, the solutions I describe represent only a small part of what has been tried and what has worked, for example to help people be healthier or to get more kids in school. Throughout, it draws on facts and research. Hopefully the data makes the issues more interesting—and feel as urgent to you as they do to me. I hope the little history I include has a similar effect. Understanding why a problem exists and whether it recently has gotten better or worse is important in figuring out the best solution. This book is not political, in the sense that it does not take a political position, or tell people to vote a certain way. It does recognize how the people who get elected and hold office in the U.S. and around the world influence the issues we most care about.

The issues I talk about in this book are all connected. A family living in poverty is more likely to confront hunger than one living comfortably. One type of inequality that girls face around the world is being denied the right to go to school, and so there are more girls, particularly older girls, than boys not in school. Patterns of infectious disease are changing as the climate changes and the earth grows warmer. And those are just a few examples.

Not surprisingly then, solutions are also often connected. Having equal numbers of girls and boys in school sends a powerful message to those students and to younger kids that all people have an equal right to an education and an equal right to their own dreams. Halting climate change so that we have more stable weather removes some uncertainty around the next disease outbreak; that means health systems, hospitals, clinics, doctors, nurses and others can be better prepared to save more lives. And, again, those are only a couple such examples. Throughout this book, you'll meet amazing young people (and a few older ones)—some of whom I'm lucky enough to call my friends, and many I've never met—who are working on solutions to individual issues and at these very intersections. I admire all of their work and, if nothing else, I hope their stories are as inspiring to you as they are to me.

I'm excited that you've agreed to come on this journey—after all, it's your world!

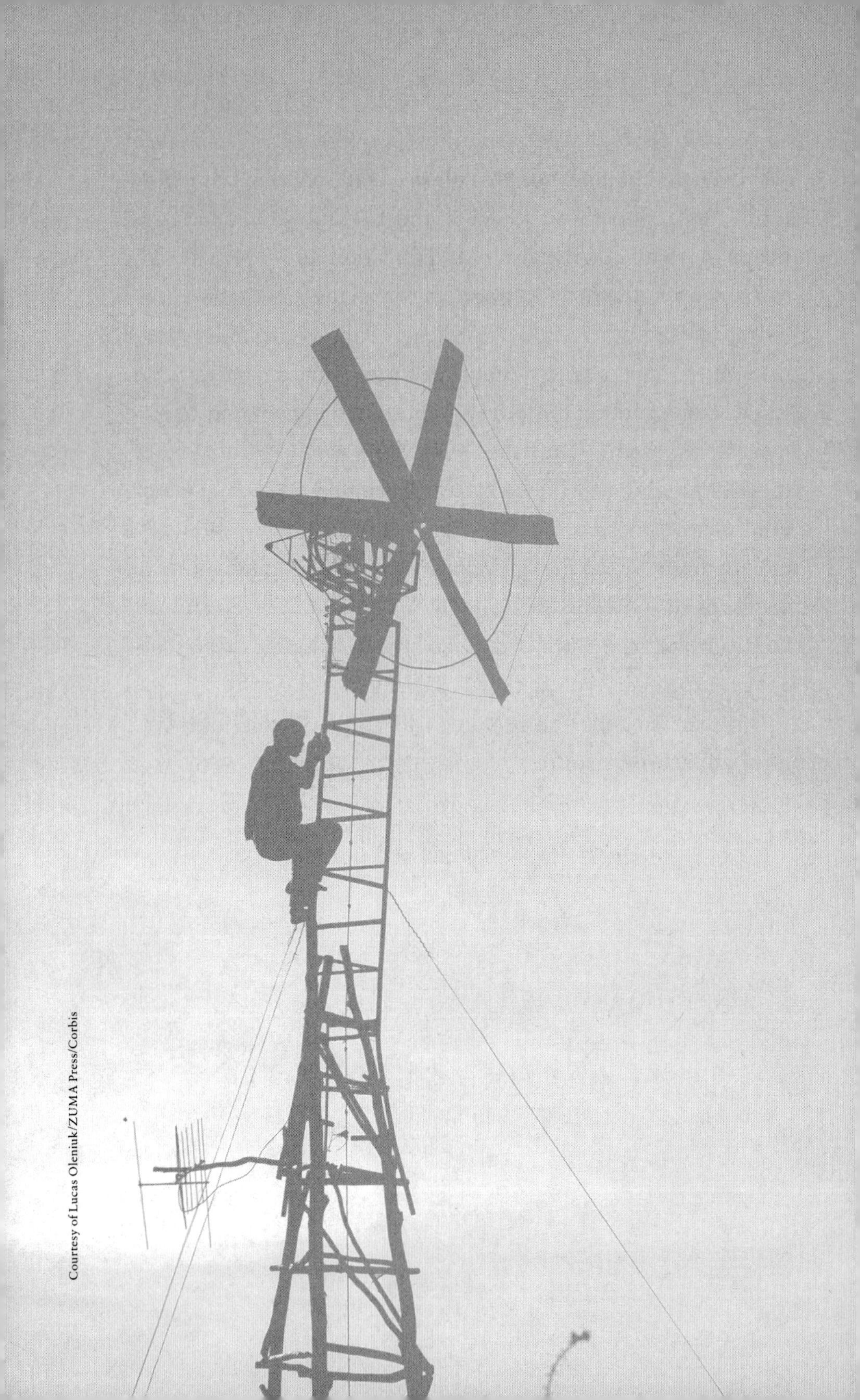

Courtesy of Lucas Oleniuk/ZUMA Press/Corbis

# PART I

# It's Your
# ECONOMY

Courtesy of Dave Anderson, Heifer International

CHAPTER ONE

# $1.25 A DAY
## POVERTY AROUND THE WORLD

When I was fifteen, I was lucky enough to travel with my mother to South Asia. We visited Pakistan, India, Bangladesh, Nepal and Sri Lanka. I remember being so excited. I couldn't wait to see the majestic Taj Mahal in Agra, India, the beautiful citadel of the Lahore Fort in Lahore, Pakistan, and the almost mythical Boudhanath Stupa in Kathmandu, Nepal. I hoped to see elephants in Sri Lanka, and I couldn't wait to share it all with my mom. Throughout the trip, I learned, saw and experienced even more than I'd imagined possible.

Our first stop was Pakistan, where we visited schools and mosques, centuries-old temples, bustling markets and parks. What I remember most are the people we saw and met, including then–prime minister of Pakistan Benazir Bhutto, the first woman prime minister or president I'd ever met. But the people who made the greatest impression on me were girls my own age and even younger who I saw

*My mom and I at the Taj Mahal in Agra, India, in 1995.*

working in fields and on streets, and those I talked to as we walked around their school or shared a soda. What struck me most from our conversations was how much we had in common and how our most enthusiastic smile-inducing moments involved talking about our favorite subjects in school, our favorite books and what we wanted to be when we grew up. I wanted to be a doctor, or at least do something related to health when I was older. Different girls I met at the girls' school we visited in Islamabad shared their dreams too. One wanted to be prime minister like Benazir Bhutto, another a doctor, one a teacher and one girl I will never forget told me she wanted to climb all the tallest mountains in the Himalayas in each country— Pakistan, India, Nepal, China and Bhutan—to conquer the mountains and to help build relationships across countries and cultures. I was in awe of her, but I was equally in awe of the girls I met who were determined to succeed, particularly those from poor communities in Pakistan and elsewhere on our trip where most kids, especially girls, didn't even go to school at the time. They were determined that the hardships that too often come with poverty—widespread disease, fewer opportunities to go to school, hard work for little pay or no work at all—were not going to be the beginning and end of their stories.

The second country we visited was India. In Ahmedabad, as we drove, we saw what seemed an endless patchwork of tin, tarp and what looked like giant garbage bags serving as roofs for thousands of homes built of metal, wood and mud. It was the first slum I'd ever seen that stretched over a horizon, and it was an overwhelming sight. It was heartbreaking to think about people who would lead their whole lives entrenched there. When we were in Mumbai, we saw the Dharavi slum, one of the largest in the world, where it's estimated 1 million people live. As we left India, I knew I would never forget the soaring splendor of the Taj Mahal, the serenity of Gandhi's ashram (more on that in a bit), the beautiful traditional dancing I'd seen—or the slums.

Courtesy of david pearson/Alamy

*This is what the Dharavi slums look like from the sky.*

In Dhaka, the capital of Bangladesh (a country the size of Wisconsin with more than 100 million people then, and even more today), the slum and

5

city seemed even more intertwined; we could see a slum not far from our hotel room's window. Seeing the slums, whether from a road or a room, and walking through different ones in different cities, it was hard to fathom that the people living there were only miles (sometimes less—only across the street) from clean water, flushing toilets, health care, schools, roads and electricity. It felt like another world—but it wasn't. The main difference? Poverty.

*Sharing a soda in Pakistan with some girls around my age.*

I've now visited slums and poor villages in Asia, Africa and Latin America. There's no difference between the dreams and dignity of people living under a tarp, in a shack or in a rural mud hut to your dreams and mine, to you and to me. As I've heard my parents say my whole life, and couldn't agree more, "Talent and intelligence are equally distributed across the world, but opportunity isn't."

What do you think is a good definition of poverty? Many different definitions exist. Poverty can be calculated based on how much money someone has, how much money someone makes or how much property and how many things someone owns or can buy with the money they have. Sometimes the definition of poverty is based on the answers to certain questions like: Is someone homeless or hungry? Do they have clean or safe water for drinking, washing and cooking? Can their kids go to school?

The World Bank, an international organization that gives loans to the world's poorest countries to help fight poverty, defines poverty according to the average amount a person lives on per day, or the average money a person spends each day. It's the most common definition and so it's the one we'll use.

When someone is living in poverty, it's harder to get a good education, have enough to eat, find clean drinking water or stay healthy, which makes it harder to find and keep a good job. And all of those things make it harder to escape poverty. The challenges are all connected, so the solutions have to be too. I hope that's something that will be clear by the time you finish this book. If you are drawn to the issue of poverty and how it impacts people around the world, you'll need to decide which definition makes the most sense to you and is most useful in thinking about which part of the poverty challenge you want to tackle and help solve.

This chapter focuses on the poorest people in the world, many of whom live in what's known as the developing world, a group of countries stretching across the globe, with average per capita incomes below a certain level. (The average per capita income is the number you get when you take how much money a whole country makes and divide it by how many people live there). I don't love the term "developing world." It seems to imply (even though I know it's not meant to) that people who live in relatively poorer countries are somehow less developed as thinkers, dreamers and doers. It also seems to discount the important contributions people from the so-called developing world have made to science, medicine, economics, literature, art and other fields. And it's a very wide category, grouping together, for example, India and Liberia, despite their different histories and geographies, not to mention populations or average per capita incomes. India has more than 285 times as many people as Liberia! And, in 2014, India's average per capita income was more than $5,000. In Liberia, it was less than $900. That's a big difference. And there's still a big difference if we look at another measure, the median per capita income. (The median per capita income is the midpoint in a country's per capita income, meaning half the population makes more money and half makes less.) It's an important measure because when calculating an average, a few very wealthy people can move an average up, making it look like a whole country has gotten wealthier when it's really just a few people. The median per capita income is a lot lower in both India and Liberia, but India's is still more than five times higher. India's median per capita income is $616. Liberia's is $118.

So, while "developing world" may be a very wide category, it's

ONE TAKE ON THE "DEVELOPING WORLD," 2015*

*As discussed in this chapter, there are many different ways to define "developing world" and each definition yields a slightly different map. If you look up "developing world," you'll see what I mean.

☐ "Developed world"    ▦ "Developing world"

Information source: USAID and World Bank

the term still most commonly used to describe countries in which people on average are not yet as well off as people in the so-called developed world, including the United States (U.S.), Canada, parts of Asia and the Middle East and much of Europe. Because of that, I'll use it . . . but not happily. Meanwhile, I hope someone comes up with a more respectful term soon (maybe you!). Also, too often in the news, in movies and television shows, poverty is equated with Africa. There is poverty in Africa, which is a huge continent made up of fifty-four different countries, but there are people struggling against poverty in every country on earth. Poverty is everywhere. So too is growth. In 2012, seven out of the ten fastest-growing economies in the world were African countries.

## HOW IS POVERTY MEASURED AROUND THE WORLD?

The World Bank defines people living on $1.25 a day or less as living in extreme poverty. You might be thinking $1.25 probably buys a lot more in Papua New Guinea or Ghana or Guatemala than in the U.S., and you'd be right—but the World Bank takes that into account. People living on $1.25 a day spend that much (or less) to survive on what $1.25 a day would buy in the U.S. Nowhere on earth is $1.25 a day enough to cover all costs related to housing, food, clean water, transportation, improved sanitation (systems to separate poop and water), education, health care and other things people need to live a decent, safe life. Just to put that in perspective, $1.25 is about how much it costs to buy a package of trail mix in a vending machine—not enough to live on, anywhere. Extreme poverty may also be called absolute poverty—whatever it's called, it's the reality for many people across the world. In 2011, just over 1 billion people across the world lived on less than $1.25 a day—most on a lot less than $1.25. The average income among the world's poorest 1 billion people is an astonishingly low seventy-eight cents a day.

Sometimes people living on less than $1.25 a day are referred to as the "bottom billion," because they make so much less money than people at the top of the economic ladder or pyramid (pick your favorite shape). This is another image I don't like, as it seems to suggest that poor people are somehow less than or below everyone else. The money you have—or don't have—says nothing about your character, your dreams or who you are. But it's a term you might read in news stories or hear in conversations about people living in absolute poverty, and one you may end up feeling comfortable using given what a powerful image it is. And even though just over 1 billion people on the planet are living on less than $1.25 a day, another billion are living on less than $2 a day. That's less than the cost of a box of Kraft Macaroni & Cheese (my favorite food when I was your age). Many economists argue that, as is true for $1.25 a day, nowhere on earth is $2 a day sufficient for someone to afford the basic necessities and lead a safe, healthy and long life.

Some developing countries, notably China, have had more success than others in reducing extreme poverty over my lifetime (though no developing country, including China, has eradicated it). In Burundi, the Democratic Republic of Congo, Liberia and Madagascar, four out of every five people live in extreme poverty. Think about that as you look around at your neighborhood. Imagine what life would be like if almost everyone around you was hungry, thirsty and had little reason to hope tomorrow would be better than today. That's life for people living in places where almost everyone is very poor, whether that's your country, your city or your neighborhood.

### MAP OF EXTREME POVERTY*

Information source: Kaiser Family Foundation, Accessed 2015

N/A or no data

<1% of the population

1–10% of the population

10.1–25% of the population

>25% of the population

*Data based on years 1994–2011.

And it's not just life for adults. Children are even more likely to live in absolute poverty. Around the world, about 400 million children live on less than $1.25 a day. That means almost one out of every five children on earth lives in absolute poverty. Although more children are surviving into adulthood than ever before, for many children in the developing world, absolute poverty can be a death sentence. In sub-Saharan Africa—the three-quarters of the African continent mainly or entirely below the Sahara Desert (or Africa minus Egypt, Libya, Tunisia, Algeria and Morocco)—more than one in ten babies born do not live to see their fifth birthday in the poorest countries. Every country can do better, and in general the world has made tremendous progress in helping children lead healthy lives. But in far too many places, being very poor can mean an early death.

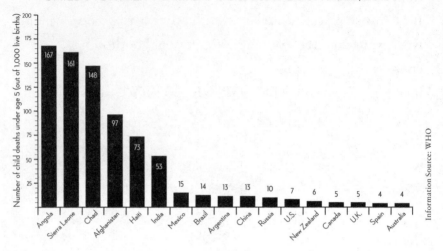

CHILD MORTALITY IN A SAMPLING OF COUNTRIES, 2013

Information Source: WHO

# THE FACE OF $1.25 A DAY

One of the places we visited on our trip to South Asia was Mahatma Gandhi's ashram in Ahmedabad, where Gandhi lived and worked for more than a decade while he led India's struggle for independence from the United Kingdom (U.K.). His nonviolent approach to resistance was crucial in helping his country finally gain independence in 1947 and influenced peaceful protesters throughout the world—including America's Dr. Martin Luther King, Jr. When we toured the ashram, it looked much as it had when Gandhi left it in 1930, pledging not to return until after independence (which tragically never happened, as Gandhi was assassinated after India gained independence but before he could return). My mom and I walked through sparsely decorated rooms and it was easy to imagine Gandhi sitting there with his spinning wheel, inspiring young men and women to join in India's march toward independence.

As was also true in Gandhi's time, the ashram is much more

than a physical space. It continues Gandhi's work in educating and empowering Indians, including through teaching women skills they can use to earn a living to support themselves and their families. One of the women we met at the ashram gave me the most beautiful hand-made paper. She shared her story of being able to

*Here my mom and I are learning about Gandhi's work at his ashram.*

support herself and her family because of the ashram's skills training and their help in selling her paper. She didn't look that much older than I was, and she already had children. She also had confidence that her children would have a better life than she did, in large part because of the income she earned from selling her paper at the ashram and elsewhere. I had read *Freedom at Midnight*, a history of Indian independence, before the trip and I remember thinking that the woman's craft and confidence were both a fitting legacy for Gandhi.

Think about that woman making paper in India but with a few crucial differences—she lives in a rural village, hasn't received any job training and she doesn't have a safe place where her paper is sold at a fair price. So she's on her own. Making paper uses a lot of water, and women living in Africa and Asia have to travel on average 3.7 miles to get water for drinking, cooking and cleaning (and for making paper). Too often, that water's not safe or clean, so she or her kids might get sick drinking it, and even die. But let's assume the water is safe to drink—that doesn't mean, however, that getting to the water is safe or that getting her finished paper to the closest market is safe.

In many places, it's not safe for a woman to walk alone anywhere. So she waits until someone can travel with her, or faces a very real risk of being attacked or even killed. Or she could pay someone to get water for her or take her paper to market for her. No good choices—waiting means losing possible business because it takes longer to make paper and get it to market, paying someone to get water or take her paper to market means losing a portion of hard-earned income and being attacked is just plain horrifying.

But let's assume she makes it safely home with water, makes her paper and then makes it safely to market, all without having to pay someone else to take her paper there for her. The closest market is probably full of people like her who live in extreme poverty and cannot afford to spend much on paper, even beautiful paper. If she could get to a market farther away, where people with more money to spend go shopping, she could charge more for her paper. But that's unlikely. So even if she works hard, makes wonderful paper, avoids getting sick or attacked and sells her paper, she may only earn just enough to help send her kids to school (if there is a school—more on this challenge in Time for School). It will be very hard for her to make enough money to never have to worry about her kids' schooling, let alone clean water, good food, reliable shelter or safety. While this picture is a little different in a city—markets filled with all different kinds of people are likely easier to get to, so she may earn more money over time—it's not likely she'll earn enough to remove all worries about food, water, safety or school. It's very hard to be very poor—and to get out of poverty—anywhere.

Poverty resembles an endless loop, where the causes bleed into the effects and go around and around . . . and around. This is what is known as the cycle of poverty. Think of our paper maker—it's unlikely the water she uses is clean, so it's likely her kids regularly get sick from dirty water. Taking care of her sick kids prevents her from being able to work more, make more paper and then sell more to earn more money to lift her family out of poverty.

THE CYCLE OF POVERTY

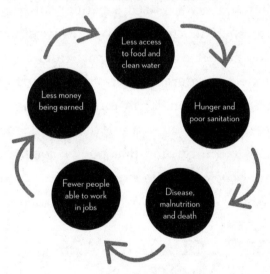

Less access to food and clean water

Hunger and poor sanitation

Disease, malnutrition and death

Fewer people able to work in jobs

Less money being earned

Understandably, economists and other people who study extreme poverty have a hard time separating out causes and effects. Like our paper maker, most people living in extreme poverty do not have access to clean water. More than three out of four people living in extreme poverty live in rural farming areas, farther from better-paying jobs and markets where people with more money shop and farther from schools to learn new skills (or even learn to read). More than half do not have access to electricity. Are people caught in extreme poverty because they're sick a lot due to dirty water (and other things)? Or because they don't have access to the greater educational and job opportunities that often come with living in a city or a wealthier country? Or are they often sick because they're so poor? These questions are thought-provoking, but I hope you won't let them distract you from the ultimate goal: to help people live to their fullest potential everywhere in the world.

We know that to help people—and countries—get out and stay out of poverty, more needs to be invested in cleaner water, quality schools, quality health care, better roads, improved sanitation and so, so, so much more. For many wealthier countries, those investments came at least in part from the government over decades, even centuries. Most poor countries haven't had the resources to make similar investments (or haven't had the leaders who've made doing so a priority). While that's starting to change, it's not surprising that poorer countries are more likely to have people living in extreme poverty than wealthier countries. What can you do? We'll get to that soon.

## WHY SOME COUNTRIES ARE POORER THAN OTHERS

While it's hard to separate out poverty's causes and effects, it's fair to wonder why some countries—and people in those countries—are poorer than others. Why is the per capita annual income just above $600 in the Central African Republic and more than 100 times that amount in Singapore and Norway? Or more than eighty-five times that amount in the U.S.? There are many complex reasons. Those discussed below are just a few highly generalized ones.

## Where You Are and What You Eat

Most historians, economists and social scientists—academics who study people and societies over time—agree that geography matters. Places that have more extreme climates and more extreme weather events—like hurricanes or droughts—are more likely to have more people living in extreme poverty. This is partly because extreme climates, particularly very hot, dry places, and places with frequent extreme weather events, like hurricanes, make it harder to grow crops. They get washed away if there's too much water one year, and too much salt water from storms can change what, if anything, farmers can grow. All of that makes it more difficult for families and communities to have a reliable source of healthy, nutritious food, which is particularly important for kids.

Worldwide, an estimated 165 million children under five are malnourished and suffer from stunting, meaning their bodies and brains are not developing at a normal, healthy rate because they don't get enough food and enough of the right kinds of food to eat. Their physical and intellectual growth is stunted because of a lack of the vitamins, minerals and nutrients every child needs to grow and develop (think of all the things you see listed on a cereal box, like Vitamin A, Vitamin D, calcium— many kids don't get any of those, much less all of them, in the amounts they need).

Poverty and stunting are deeply intertwined. Parents living in extreme poverty are more likely to have children who suffer from stunting. Children who are stunted generally grow up less physically and mentally strong, less able to learn and succeed in school (if they're in school) and less able to work as productively as people who were not malnourished as young children. Adults who were stunted as children are more likely to be poor later in life.

Notice how similar this map is to the earlier one of the developing world. It's also arguably another depiction of the cycle of poverty.

## COUNTRIES WITH HIGH RATES OF (MEANING LOTS OF KIDS SUFFERING FROM) STUNTING*

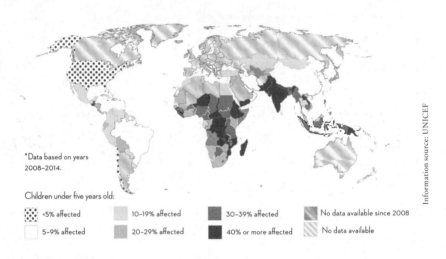

*Data based on years 2008–2014.

Children under five years old:

| | | | |
|---|---|---|---|
| <5% affected | 10–19% affected | 30–39% affected | No data available since 2008 |
| 5–9% affected | 20–29% affected | 40% or more affected | No data available |

Information source: UNICEF

A country's economy is the sum total of all activity that involves money and resources. This includes what individuals and companies make, what consumers buy and what people are paid. A strong economy depends on the strength of all these parts. The more money people earn from what they make or do, the more they can later spend. If someone has more money to spend at the market on her neighbor's paper, that neighbor will then have more money to buy food. The farmer whose food she buys will have more money to invest in seeds for next year's crops and to send her children to school and so on. If an economy has a lot more stunted workers, or workers held back by illness (that they may have gotten from dirty water) or illiteracy (because they likely never went to or stayed in school for long), none of that can happen on a large scale. Countries with fewer educated and healthy workers and fewer healthy kids in school are less likely to see their economies grow and poverty shrink.

It's also hard for a country's economy to grow if it's persistently battling extreme weather or earthquakes, and not just because of the effects on crops. Imagine if you lived in a place where hurricanes, floods or landslides occurred regularly, washing out roads and bridges, wrecking your home, your school and where your parents work and knocking out power lines (though there probably isn't power—more on that below). You'd miss days of school waiting for the damage to be repaired. Your parents would miss days of work, needing to restore your home and waiting for the roads to be fixed so they could get back to work. It's hard to build for tomorrow if you constantly have to repair damage from yesterday.

It's impossible for a country's economy to grow if there isn't enough healthy food available that people can afford. This too is not just about crops. It's also about milk, eggs, meat, fish and more. Heifer International is an organization that provides animals to poor families around the world. Not just any type of animal, but animals like cows, buffalo and goats. Why those animals? Because they—like the goat with the boy in the photo at the start of this chapter—provide both food and a way to earn money. All produce milk that can help strengthen a family's nutrition, and excess milk that can be sold to increase a family's income and help the families who buy it improve their nutrition too. Heifer also gives families animals like chicks, ducks and geese, which produce eggs families can both eat and sell. Critically, Heifer provides families with the training they need to properly care for their animals. And Heifer asks families who receive animals to give their first female offspring (because she'll later produce milk or eggs) to another family in their community; Heifer calls this "Passing on the Gift."

My family has a few ties to Heifer. In the last few years of her life, my grandmother Dorothy gave Heifer animals to all of her grandchildren for Christmas. Well, not the *actual* animals, but a certificate saying our grandmother had given animals to families in need in our names. Although I wondered why I always seemed to get a buffalo (and my cousins goats), I thought the life-giving gifts were the perfect Christmas presents. My mom wrote the foreword to a wonderful book called *Beatrice's Goat*, which tells the story of Beatrice from Uganda. Heifer gave a goat to Beatrice's family that Beatrice helped take care of. After less than three months of selling the goat's milk, Beatrice's family had saved enough money to send Beatrice to school (before, they couldn't afford the school fees, a challenge we'll talk more about in Time for School).

Beatrice worked hard and

*Beatrice graduating from the Clinton School of Public Service.*

did well in school, and as a result, received a scholarship to go to college in the U.S. She went on to graduate school at the University of Arkansas Clinton School of Public Service (started by my dad). And Heifer is based in Little Rock, right across from the Clinton Presidential Library. I am proud my dad's library is Heifer's neighbor.

There are lots of ways for kids and families to participate in Heifer's work, including by giving a goat to a family like Beatrice's. For $10 or $20, you can help send a goat, cow or flock of chicks to a family like Beatrice's. Another way to participate is through Heifer's Read to Feed program. You find a sponsor for yourself or your class who pledges a set amount of money for each book you read in a defined period of time (you can even do it by chapter or page if you want). However many books you've read at the end gets multiplied by the amount pledged and then donated to Heifer to support their work. For more on Heifer, including Read to Feed, visit heifer.org.

## Water, Water, Water

Water is another important element in understanding why extreme poverty exists in some places and not others. Of course, water is essential to life—for drinking, cooking, cleaning and bathing—but it's also vital to economies, because waterways, like rivers, seas and oceans, are used to transport products and workers. Rivers and ocean ports that are part of important trading routes are more likely to be centers of business and will have more jobs for people with different talents, skills and levels of education. It's not an accident that some of the biggest and most prosperous cities in the world—from London to Los Angeles—are around rivers or on the ocean. It's also not an accident that most of the biggest economies on earth—the U.S., China, Japan, Germany and the U.K. are the top five—have significant coastlines (or are surrounded by water). Countries without easy access to an ocean are known as "landlocked," and it's more expensive for those countries to sell or buy goods (because they have to travel longer to or from the ocean, and those travel costs get built into the price people have to pay). Many of the poorest countries are landlocked. But while places with easy water access tend to be less poor on average, it's no guarantee that poverty isn't sometimes near the water. The slum I mentioned in Ahmedabad? It's on a river. So are parts of the Dharavi slum and many slums and poor villages around the world.

It's not only proximity to water for ports that's important. As previously mentioned, people in the developing world (usually women and girls) often have to walk far to get water. That time getting water is time not spent in school, not working in a job and not building a business. And parents (generally moms) spend days taking care of children who are sick from dirty water, days they're not working and their kids aren't in school. All of that means lost income for families and lost economic growth for countries, which means not

*Here's a picture of a kid who is using a well drilled by Living Water International, which is committed to bringing wells closer to people who need them.*

Courtesy of Living Water International

getting out of poverty. We'll talk more about how diseases and poverty are connected in a bit.

One way you can help kids keep healthy and stay in school, plus help more women have time to work and earn money (both important to helping families escape poverty), is by supporting efforts to drill and maintain water wells and other water systems. Clean water flows underground all over the planet—but it often takes real work to reach even the closest underground water. People have been using wells for thousands of years, and in many places (including some in the U.S.) wells are the easiest, most reliable and safest way to access clean water. Different types of wells are best suited to different environments and it's not safe to dig a well just anywhere.

Three organizations working in partnership with local communities across the world to build, finance and drill better, safer and just plain more wells and water systems are Living Water International, charity: water and Water.org. You can support any of their work through walk-a-thons, bake sales or any creative way you can think of to raise money. In 2013, then ten-year-old Matti, along with friends and family, organized a 3.7-mile fund-raising walk in her hometown of St. Joseph, Missouri, after she learned that was the average distance women, and children travel-

*Matti and her friend Sam preparing for their Walk for Water.*

Courtesy of Tammy Flowers

23

ing with them, in Africa and Asia walk to get to water. Matti wanted to help Living Water International, an organization she first learned about through her church, in its work to build more wells so women didn't have to walk so far. Initially hoping to raise $100, Matti and her group raised $5,600, enough to cover the cost of drilling one new well for a community. To learn more about Living Water International, charity: water and Water.org, and what you can do to help build a well like Matti did, you can check out their websites: water.cc; charitywater.org; and Water.org.

## Energy

Another common challenge confronting poor people in poor countries is a lack of electricity, what's known as energy poverty. Across the developing world, more than 1 billion people lack access to electricity and another 1 billion lack access to reliable electricity (meaning they might have it sometimes, but likely not often). Across Africa alone, nearly 600 million people lack access to reliable electricity and power. That means no light after dark to read or study by, no refrigerator to keep food cool and fresh, no electric or gas stoves to cook on. There are no computers to turn on, phones to charge or TVs to watch. Imagine what your life would be like at home or at school if you didn't have power, if you couldn't do anything after dark except sleep or talk to your family. If you couldn't go outside at night because you couldn't see . . . anything. Safe, reliable energy is essential for escaping poverty, because it means kids will be able to spend more time in school (not just when it's bright and sunny) and study at home, women will be able to spend less time preparing food (cooking is easier and food can be kept in refrigerators instead of made fresh each day) and adults will be able to work more hours (again, not just when it's bright and sunny) and so much more.

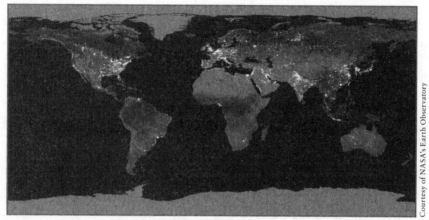

*Snapshot of the earth at night showing where there's electricity and where there's not.*

Getting energy and electricity to everyone is a logistics challenge (how to do it) and a cost challenge (is it affordable). But there's another challenge too—getting more people energy and electricity quickly and cheaply may mean electricity is generated in a way that adds more pollution to the environment. And not just a little more pollution, but a lot more. While we don't want that, we do want everyone everywhere to have the same chance we do in the U.S. to learn, study, work and play—and that requires electricity.

It's important that the world's leaders in government and business find the right balance to empower people today—literally with more power and electricity—and protect people tomorrow from the pollution that still too often comes with more power and electricity. This is something currently being discussed in global conversations on climate change. Let's hope world leaders find the right answers to help people in poverty today get electricity and to help everyone tomorrow not be burdened with even more pollution to clean up. We'll talk more about the relationship between energy and pollution later in the book.

While world leaders debate what the right solution is to energy poverty, we can support organizations and people who are solving their own energy challenges. Barefoot College teaches illiterate and semiliterate women how to make, install, use and care for household solar units. These help convert sunlight into electricity without adding pollution to the environment. Barefoot's main students? Grandmothers (just like you're never too young to make a difference, you're also never too old)! They're known as Solar Mamas and they generally work in teams of two. Every pair of grandmothers Barefoot College trains helps electrify up to 150 homes in their local village, bringing light to an average of 800 people. Solar Mamas help maintain the solar units forever, which is great for the people who get electricity and for the grandmother who has a real (and very cool) job.

Inspired by Gandhi and started by Bunker Roy, Barefoot College and its grandmother alums have helped more than 500,000 people in India and around the world access electricity—without adding tons of pollution to

Courtesy of Barefoot Photographers

*A Barefoot College Solar Mama working on a solar panel.*

the atmosphere. That's amazing. Bunker is one of the happiest and most inspiring people I've ever met. I like to think that if my grandmothers had lived in the communities where Barefoot College works, they would have been among Bunker's grandma graduates! To learn more about the work Barefoot College does and what you can do to help, please visit barefootcollege.org.

## Diseases That Won't Go Away

When someone is sick a lot or is constantly worried about getting sick, everything is harder. A sick person generally can't work as hard in a job or in school as someone who is healthy, or they might not even be able to get a job or go to school because they're sick. There's also a hopelessness about the future that constant illness can bring, a sense that it's not worth getting an education or a job—in other words, investing in the future—because death is just around the corner. More diseases live in warmer places than colder places, for all sorts of reasons. As just one example, mosquitoes that carry malaria can't survive in colder climates, so neither can malaria, a disease that infected almost 200 million people in 2013 alone.

Malaria is expensive—very expensive—for families, communities and countries. If adults are sick, they're at home, not working and not contributing to the country's economy. If kids are home sick with malaria, they're not in school learning what they need to know to later get a good job and contribute to their country's economy in the future. Academics have shown that, quite simply, more malaria means less growth for a country. Less growth year after year leads to a much smaller economy over the longer term. In other words, a poor country with malaria is likely to remain a poor country with malaria until malaria is defeated. Partly because of the relationship between hotter places and more disease, where countries are on the globe and where people live has a lot to do with whether or not extreme poverty is the norm or the exception. Sadly, malaria is only one example of what diseases can do to an economy and a country. We'll meet some other examples of diseases that are dangerous to both people and economies later in the book, and hear about what's being done to make them history. We'll talk about malaria more in Bugs and Bacteria.

## History and Neighbors

Many of today's poorest countries were colonized, or forcibly taken over, by foreign powers and only became independent from their colonizers sometime after World War II (like India did in 1947). Particularly those in Africa were ravaged by the slave trade; from the 16th–19th centuries, people were snatched and shipped off to be slaves in places like Brazil and the United States rather than building healthy productive lives in the places they were born. The history of a country's neighbors matters too. Countries surrounded by other countries with similar stories of colonization are more likely to be poor. The opposite is also true—countries surrounded by neighbors that were never colonized are less likely to be poor.

And back to food. Economists have found a relationship between longer histories of more formal farming (think of rows and rows of wheat or peas and irrigation) and wealth today. In other words, more rows of wheat for a longer time mean a country's more likely today to be relatively better off. And by a longer time, I mean a really long time. People living in the Middle East began more formal farming as long as 11,000 years ago, and in Europe about 8,500 years ago. In sub-Saharan Africa, formal farming began "only" around 2,000 years ago. Ancient and more recent history aren't the only things that matter, but both influence how wealthy or poor countries are in the 21st century—the 2000s.

Bad and good neighbors alike matter for more than just their history. Countries surrounded by relatively peaceful and stable neighbors are more likely to be peaceful and stable. Can you imagine what your neighborhood would feel like if all of your neighbors were always fighting with each other? If fighting could break out at any time and overrun your home, your school, your streets, where you shop, where you eat, where you play? Instability and insecurity often spread like viruses. Countries surrounded by unstable, insecure or violent neighbors are more likely to have to deal with spillover violence.

Wars that start in one country can also affect another country even if the violence itself isn't infectious. Countries trying to avoid getting drawn into violent conflict have to spend more resources—money, time and effort—on their own defense (militaries) than on their schools, factories or science labs—which would help their economies grow and people move out of poverty. Refugees fleeing violence at home and seeking a safer haven in another country often need things like food, shelter, clean water and clothes (all of which cost money) provided by their host country before international help arrives (and often even after it does). Countries with violent or unstable neighbors end up spending a lot of resources responding to one crisis after another and trying to stop the violence from spilling into their own land, instead of planning and investing in a better future with more opportunities for their people.

During my trip to South Asia with my mom, one of the stops we made was in the state of Gujarat in India to visit with women who were involved in an organization called the Self-Employed Women's Association (SEWA). Created by Indian activist Ela Bhatt, SEWA helps poor women get the skills, support and money they need to sustain and grow their own businesses. One of the unique things about SEWA is that it brings together Muslim and Hindu women in a part of the world where fighting between people from different religious backgrounds has cost countless lives, both between countries and within India. Today, SEWA has more than 1.9 million members.

I remember arriving at a large tent and sitting down in the audience, surrounded by hundreds of women, all of us listening as SEWA women shared their stories with my mom. They spoke about their individual experiences and their collective story through SEWA. Women from all different backgrounds told us how they'd learned how much more they had in common than they'd first thought because of their different religions. Their support for each other gave them the confidence to stand

*Learning more about SEWA from one of the women I met in Gujarat, India.*

up to bullying and harassment, and the relationships they'd built helped prevent violence between Hindus and Muslims, because they saw each other as friends and real people, not only as representatives of different religions. The SEWA women also found they could earn more money when their communities weren't fighting with one another and when they worked together. I felt deeply honored and more than a little overwhelmed when I was introduced to the audience as "a potential future member of SEWA." If you're inspired by SEWA's story and want to get involved, you can learn more at sewa.org.

## The Value of Trust

The women of SEWA learned to trust each other with their lives and their families' futures—the SEWA program helped them pool their savings and lend that money to other women who needed it to invest in their businesses, their kids' educations and more. If you think that sounds like a bank, you're right, SEWA is a bank too. SEWA borrowers repaid almost 100 percent of their loans (96 percent to be exact!) and the women who pooled their savings knew they could take their money back if they needed it.

Now imagine if you didn't know if you could open a bank account or if after you'd opened a bank account and made a deposit, you didn't know whether your money would be there when you needed it or even just the next time you went to the bank. Imagine you didn't know whether or not the money you earned or invested today would be worth 100 or 1,000 times less in a year (because of something called inflation, where money can lose value quickly if people lose trust in a country). Imagine you bought a piece of land to farm or to open a business on and you didn't know whether or not you would own that land—or the business—in a year because a government official could take your property and you couldn't do anything about it (because the police and courts weren't honest). Imagine if to avoid that fate, you had to pay a big bribe to the same government official threatening to take your property away, trading your hard-earned money just to keep your business going. You wouldn't want to participate in corruption, but to not pay the bribe would mean all your hard work would be for nothing. Imagine you didn't know if the president in office today would still hold office tomorrow or have been forcibly removed from power (what's called a military coup). Imagine if you read the newspaper or listened to the radio and you couldn't trust what you were hearing—not because of a difference of opinions, but because the facts themselves were literally made up to serve the purpose of whoever owned the newspaper (often the government), not the public. This roller coaster of uncertainty is what people face in many countries around the world.

Why is it important to trust in the reliability of what we participate in—whether putting money in a bank, running a business or voting? If people can't rely on their money having consistent value and being in the bank when they want to make a withdrawal, or if people are worried their country may tip into civil war at any point, there's arguably little reason for working hard today. The thinking goes, why bother, if it could all be gone tomorrow? If people aren't working hard and coming up with new ideas, investing in and expanding croplands and businesses, economies don't grow. But if people know that their governments aren't going to topple, that their governments aren't corrupt, that bribes aren't necessary to do business, that banks are going to be around tomorrow, that their money won't be worthless and that everyone is treated fairly and equally by the legal system (the police and courts), economies are more likely to grow and more people likely to move out of poverty.

The different experiences of South Korea, a well-functioning democracy, and North Korea, a brutal dictatorship, demonstrate this contrast, as seen in the chart. Being near the bottom of Transparency International's corruption index means that in North Korea, bribes to officials, whether in the government, the army or otherwise, are a common, even expected, part of doing business. Those who do have access to the Internet in North Korea often work for the government (and seem to spend a lot of time targeting the United States and U.S.-based businesses). In South Korea, the more than 90 percent of people who have access to the Internet also enjoy the fastest average Internet connection speeds in the world.

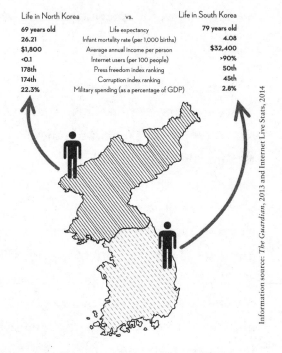

### NORTH KOREA VS. SOUTH KOREA

| Life in North Korea | vs. | Life in South Korea |
|---|---|---|
| 69 years old | Life expectancy | 79 years old |
| 26.21 | Infant mortality rate (per 1,000 births) | 4.08 |
| $1,800 | Average annual income per person | $32,400 |
| <0.1 | Internet users (per 100 people) | >90% |
| 178th | Press freedom index ranking | 50th |
| 174th | Corruption index ranking | 45th |
| 22.3% | Military spending (as a percentage of GDP) | 2.8% |

Information source: *The Guardian*, 2013 and Internet Live Stats, 2014

In recent decades, hunger and famine have repeatedly struck North Korea but not South Korea. Before World War II and the Korean War, which effectively ended in 1953, Korea was one very poor country. The main differences since then? The types of systems—political, legal, business, education—that each built over time and what each invested in (or didn't). After the Korean War, South Korea's government invested in building water, sanitation, electricity, education, transportation and health care systems and watched its economy expand and most South Koreans move well out of extreme poverty. North Korea didn't make any of those investments in a serious way that would benefit most North Koreans. Where would you rather live? It's not a hard question to answer when it's between North and South Korea. Sometimes, it's a less obvious answer, particularly when we think of beautiful places blessed with diamonds, oil or other precious natural resources.

## The Resource Curse

You may have heard of what's often referred to as the "resource curse" or "resource trap." Some of the poorest countries on earth have precious stones like diamonds and emeralds, rare metals like gold and silver, energy sources like oil or natural gas and other minerals you may not have heard of but that play an important role in our lives, like bauxite, which is used to make aluminum for soda cans, tinfoil, utensils and parts of airplanes. In many countries with these extraordinary natural resources, a few people have gotten very rich, while many people have stayed very poor and thousands—in some places millions—have died in the fighting over resource wealth. The tens of thousands who died and millions who became refugees after the Sierra Leone civil war of 1991–2002, a war largely over diamonds, is a tragically perfect example of the resource curse.

To be clear, resource wealth doesn't always lead to civil war and chaos. Botswana has diamonds. Lots and lots of diamonds. For decades, Botswana's leaders have invested much of the money made from diamond sales in building roads, bringing electricity to more people and improving education at all levels, in other words, investments to help an economy grow and people move out of poverty. From independence in 1966 through the 1990s, Botswana's economy grew faster than any other in the developing world, even South Korea's. Making smart investments was only part of the story. Botswana also established clear property rights (so that everybody knows what they own and what they don't own), the rule of law (creating a police force and court system that treats people fairly at least much of the time), a commitment to transparency (about where the diamond wealth was being invested) and a democratic election system (though one party has dominated). Who governs and how they lead—called governance—matters, particularly when thinking about addressing complex challenges like poverty. Botswana still struggles with extreme poverty and inequality. Too many people in Botswana still live on less than $1.25 a day, while some people have gotten very rich off diamonds—but it's much better off than it would have been if its leaders had kept all the diamond wealth for themselves.

More countries and more people—including in Sierra Leone—are determined to break the resource curse. And yet, many countries still need leaders more interested in the collective future of all their people and making long-term investments in things like schools, hospitals, energy and Internet connectivity. When countries don't make long-term investments like those, aren't transparent about where money is being spent, don't have clear property rights and don't have a fair legal system, that's often referred to as "poor governance," regardless of whether a country has mineral wealth or not. Countries with poor governance (like North Korea) also rarely have freedom of press (reporters who are free to report on any stories they choose), because people in power don't want any criticism. They also rarely have freedom of assembly (people able to meet when and where they want), because people in power don't want citizens to be able to gather together, organize and work for better governance. Some academics think poor governance is what best explains why some countries are poor. Others think geography and disease—lack of access to water, higher temperatures, more malaria—are the main reasons why some countries are poorer than others. Still others think extreme weather is the main culprit—relentless hurricanes, floods or monsoons. Most think it's a combination of all those things, and most agree all have to be tackled to help countries and people escape poverty.

## COMBATING POVERTY IN THE DEVELOPING WORLD

While there are similarities about the challenges people living in extreme poverty face around the world, every community is unique. As we think about how best to help countries and people move out of poverty, we have to start with and listen to the actual people we want to help, as Heifer, Barefoot College, the various water well programs and countless others do in their work. This may sound obvious—but it isn't to everyone and it doesn't always happen. Imagine how you would feel if an outsider came to your community to tell you the right answer—instead of asking you what you thought the problems were and what you wanted to see happen to make life safer, healthier and wealthier. While it's clear that clean water, improved sanitation, more and better educational opportunities, better health care, better roads, more jobs and more honest and competent governments are all crucial to combating extreme poverty, any solution has to reflect what each community wants. Clearly this is easier in places that are safe and stable than in places embroiled in war or where there are corrupt governments.

And sometimes it's not about talking with governments so much as recognizing and supporting individuals who are already lifting themselves and their communities out of poverty. You may have heard of "the boy who harnessed the wind," William Kamkwamba. Born in 1987 in Malawi, William grew up in a village with no electricity or running water, and in a family that barely survived on the food it grew with a little left over to pay for school. After a terrible drought in 2001, William had to drop out of school because his family could no longer afford his school fees. He kept educating himself by going to the library and reading everything he could. One day, he found a book on windmills and determined he'd build one. So he did. Starting with scrap parts he found in light bulbs and radios, William built the first windmill he or his village had ever seen. And it worked, generating electricity for his family and his neighbors. So he built more windmills, including the ones in the picture at the start of this section; that's William's cousin standing on one of the windmills. William also built a solar-powered water pump so his village could have clean accessible water. His family and community are a lot better off because of William's ingenuity and entrepreneurship. To learn more about William's story and to support his work, check out williamkamkwamba.com.

The world knows some things that work to fight poverty, but not nearly enough about how to help more kids (and adults) have stories like William's, particularly from afar. How do outsiders help in a way that is respectful of local people and culture today and empowering for people tomorrow? There are many different ways that wealthier countries, foundations, charities, companies and private citizens are trying to combat extreme poverty, and lots of different views about what the best approaches are. Some are focused on bigger investments like schools, hospitals and roads, while others concentrate on combating poverty one person at a time, similar to Heifer's approach with animals.

Sometimes money is loaned or given directly to individuals and families living in extreme poverty to enable them to buy better food, cleaner water, pay school fees or to start or even expand their business. These small business loans are known as microloans or microfinance. You may have heard of Kiva, one of the biggest online microloan platforms. Through Kiva, individuals anywhere can make loans directly to people living in poverty, many of whom are living below or barely above $1.25 a day. As of early 2015, more than 1.3 million people (including my husband, Marc, and me!) have helped fund loans for more than 1.6 million borrowers across the world. The average loan size is about $400. But many lenders lend $25, meaning Kiva brings together a group of people to support one loan. Kids can and do participate in Kiva's lending process—and in applying for loans to go to school or start their own businesses in the developing world. To learn more, visit KivaU.org.

While microloans and microfinance (as well as goats, cows and buffalo) are powerful tools to help individual people and families move out of poverty, large investments are needed alongside those programs. Even in very poor countries, it costs a lot more than $400 to help build a school, fill it with books and make sure there are good teachers to teach classes. Or to build a hospital and train the doctors, nurses and staff, as well as buy the equipment, medicines and tools needed to provide good health care.

*These kids loaned money to people all over the world through KivaU.org.*

Courtesy of Diana Williams

Similarly, it costs more than $400 to build and maintain a road, cell phone tower or banking system, all of which are important in helping economies grow and countries move out of poverty.

Remember our paper maker? A microloan could be really helpful to her to buy paper-making material, but it doesn't help quite as much if she still doesn't have a good road to take to get clean water or to travel on to the local market. That's generally where wealthier donor countries like the U.S., the U.K., Germany, Japan, Norway and Australia, or big institutions like the World Bank that pool together money from wealthier countries, come in. They can help developing countries build health systems, school systems, roads and other things that require more investment over longer periods of time. Sometimes the money from wealthier countries or the World Bank is given outright to countries and sometimes it's loaned to them.

Big foundations, charities and what are often called nongovernmental organizations (NGOs) play a role too. They build schools, health clinics and hospitals and help to train teachers and nurses, ideally working in coordination with one another, developing countries' governments and local community groups. NGOs in particular often provide crucial assistance after natural disasters like hurricanes, floods or earthquakes. One such organiza-

*A girl in Bulgaria in 1948 with an early CARE package.*

tion is CARE. You've probably heard of a care package, what you might send a friend or relative who's away from home. Care packages got their name from CARE and its very first program, sending boxes of food from the U.S. to Europe after World War II to help prevent mass hunger. CARE still does crucial work in nutrition, disaster relief and more to help people and communities escape poverty. If you want to learn more about the original CARE packages or CARE's work today, please visit care.org.

The business sector around the world can also have an impact on our paper maker. Companies that buy products from the developing world (whether paper or something else) can pledge to pay a price that provides enough income for her to support her family and over time, if she's successful, expand her business, while also enabling the companies to still make a profit when selling paper to consumers like us. Increasingly, companies also are committing to ensure there is no slave labor or forced labor in their supply chains, meaning no one was made to pick coffee or cotton or cocoa beans, and no one was made to work in a factory. These efforts are often known as responsible or ethical sourcing. When consumers (or shoppers) in the developed world buy products from companies who've adopted those practices, we're showing our support with our wallets. On most big companies' websites, you can find out if their products are sourced responsibly (such information may be listed under "supply chain"). To find out whether that's true of your favorite brand of paper, chocolate, clothing or shoes, check online before you next go shopping.

Aid and assistance, whether from wealthier governments, charities or NGOs, are not without controversy, even the types of assistance I just talked about like microloans for individuals or bigger loans for countries. Some people just don't believe in any aid or assistance—but they're in the minority. Most people believe wealthier countries and people who want to help should do something, but debate heatedly about what aid should be used for or how much should be given. Some people think that countries that have natural resources should receive no help from outside donors. Others believe that aid is simply the moral and right thing to do for poor people, wherever they live and whatever their governments are (or aren't) doing.

Healthier and wealthier countries are more likely to be good trading partners—which means we can sell more of our goods to them (which is good for our economy and workers) and they can sell their goods to us (which hopefully gives us more choices in what we buy while not hurting our economy or workers). Healthier and wealthier countries are also generally thought to be less welcoming to terrorists (though terror and terrorists are challenges in wealthier countries too).

Some people believe aid should go to the leaders of developing countries to use as they think best for their countries, while others think that money should flow directly to clinics, schools, businesses and entrepreneurs. And there are debates on whether more aid should be given to health, agriculture, education or something else and how to judge whether any aid program is effective or not (in other words, does it deserve an A, B, C or F as a grade). You'll have to make up your own mind about what aid you think is most important, how it should be measured and where it should—or shouldn't—go.

While you think about what the right answers and approaches are, you can help raise awareness of the fact that about one out of every seven people on earth lives on less than $1.25 a day, and why you think it's important that everyone care about poverty. In 2004, when he was nine, Dylan from New Hampshire started something called Lil' MDGs, a program to educate young people about the Millennium Development Goals (MDGs). Dylan knew that in 2000, world leaders had created the MDGs to help the world combat poverty and hunger, and to help more mothers and children lead healthier lives, among other priorities. The purpose of Lil' MDGs was to use the web and later social media (because social media wasn't common in 2004) to inform and inspire young people to take action and help us reach the MDGs by 2015. Over various campaigns, Lil' MDGs rallied over 4 million kids from forty-one countries to do things like raise money for tsunami and hurricane relief and send school supplies to students in Iraq. But Dylan started by recruiting just two people. Sometimes, we just have to start, hoping we'll make a difference in someone else's life and in our shared future. We never know how much of an impact we might have once we get going.

# Get Going!

- Help raise awareness that worldwide more than 1 billion people live on less than $1.25 a day by sharing with your family and telling at least three friends, asking each of them to tell family and friends too

- Send a cow, a goat or a buffalo (or chicks, ducks or geese) to a family who needs it through Heifer International

- Participate in Read to Feed through Heifer International to help raise funds to support their work

- Support Barefoot College so more grandmas can bring more solar energy to more places

- Share SEWA's story and work

- Help drill a well or build a water system through Living Water International, Water.org or charity: water

- Make a loan (or encourage other people to make a loan) on KivaU.org

- Start an effort like Dylan and his Lil' MDGs to raise awareness about the challenges people face living in poverty and what the world's trying to do to solve them

- If you're at least thirteen, use social media to follow organizations (like CARE) combating poverty and celebrities (like Alicia Keys) raising awareness about poverty as a way to show your interest and support for their work

- Do any of the things listed in other chapters (and there are lots more Get Going suggestions at the end of the other chapters)— helping fight climate change, helping girls have an equal chance in life and helping people get and stay healthy are all part of helping countries and people—particularly kids—overcome poverty

CHAPTER TWO

# $32 A DAY
## POVERTY IN AMERICA

When I was a kid, on Sundays my mom and I would go to church at First United Methodist Church in downtown Little Rock. My father went to Immanuel Baptist Church. After church, my mom and I would meet my dad for Sunday lunch at home or at a local restaurant. Sometimes, my mom and I would get out of church earlier than my dad. On those Sundays, before lunch, my mom and I would walk from First United Methodist to the nearby public library and I would pick out a book or two (and return the books I'd checked out the week before). Some weeks, my mom would need to go to her office downtown on a Saturday, and we'd stop by the library on the way. The best weeks were those when I got to go to the library on Saturday and Sunday. I know that sounds very nerdy! I loved (and still love) history and historical fiction, and I was always trying to convince my mom it was time for another library trip. Thankfully, she almost always said yes.

*My mom and I outside First United Methodist Church in Little Rock.*

Courtesy of the Author's Parents

I would see the same couple week after week, in the library reading, picking up a snack from our church kitchen or wheeling around their overburdened bicycles outside. She was an older white woman and he an African American man. Interracial couples were not common in the mid-1980s in Arkansas, but they seemed to attract attention more for all of the bags and blankets piled on top of their bikes than anything else.

One Sunday as I was walking into the library to return a book and check out a new one, I saw the couple curled up asleep under the library canopy. It was the first time I realized they were around all the time because they probably had nowhere else to go, and that they relied on places like our church for meals, at least on Sundays. I was ashamed I hadn't understood earlier that they were probably homeless, just like I knew my grandmother Dorothy had almost been at various points when she was a child.

I had some vague belief that my grandma had been close to being homeless because it was the Great Depression and her grandparents were cruel. Looking back, I think I viewed homelessness as dated, or something that only happened long ago. Sadly, I was very wrong. Seeing a woman around my grandma's age at the time sleeping outside the library gave me a lump in my throat. It made me realize how lucky I was to have a home and food to share with my family beyond a church kitchen and how blessed I was not to worry that one day I'd wake up and lose both.

We've talked about extreme poverty around the world, but the U.S. and other wealthier countries are not immune to poverty, even if at first glance it may look less severe. In the U.S., we don't have millions of people living in slums without sanitation, running water or electricity. We do have millions of Americans worried about losing their homes, losing a safe place to raise a family and grow old. We have millions more Americans worried about where their next meal will come from. Poverty is just as real in the U.S. as anywhere, and American kids are hardest hit. In a recent survey, the U.S. ranked thirty-fourth out of thirty-five developed, or wealthier, countries in the percentage of kids living in poverty.

Poverty, hunger and homelessness affect kids today and long into their futures. Children in the U.S. who grow up in poverty are more likely to end up poor, hungry or homeless as adults, partly because they are less likely to get the education necessary to find a good, well-paying job later in life. Kids who grow up hungry have a harder time developing physically, intellectually and mentally than those who don't, making it more likely they'll stay in poverty or fall into poverty later in life. Young people who don't see their parents actively manage money, stay within a budget and save for the future—in large part because there's no money to manage, spend or save—don't grow up understanding how important managing money (as well as actual money) is to staying out of poverty. It's hard to imagine what you don't see, particularly in your own family.

As noted in the last chapter, the causes and effects of poverty for any country, community and family are connected and deeply complex. How much poverty we have in the U.S. at any point in time depends in part on how many good, well-paying jobs there are. It depends in part on whether or not enough people have the right education and training to get hired for those jobs and to succeed in them. It depends on whether inequality between the wealthiest Americans and poorest Americans is growing—as it is in 2015—or shrinking—as it did after World War II and into the 1970s. Poverty today is also in part the product of poverty yesterday, of the year before, even the generation or century before.

In the U.S., as is true anywhere, our country's history, our communities' history and even our families' history are all relevant to understanding poverty. Broadly speaking, poor neighborhoods, whether in cities or rural areas, are more likely to have been poor historically, partly because state or local governments haven't had the resources (or sometimes the interest) in building better schools, better roads and other things that bring more businesses and jobs—and more money—to those areas. Children born into poor families are more likely to grow up and grow old living in poverty. This is partly because they're more likely to live in poor neighborhoods. The nearby jobs that do exist generally pay less, local schools tend to be worse and crime rates are often higher than is generally true in wealthier neighborhoods.

NUMBER OF FAMILIES IN THE U.S. OFFICIALLY LIVING IN POVERTY, 1959-2013

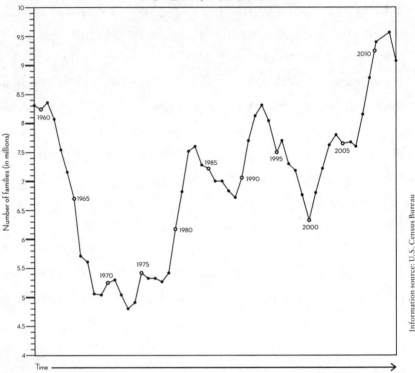

Our nation's history of racism and discrimination also helps us understand why African Americans, Native Americans and Hispanic Americans are more likely to suffer poverty. For generations, racial discrimination was legal and even encouraged to keep minorites, particularly African Americans, out of certain schools and jobs. Even after laws changed, prejudices remained in mind-sets and practices. As a result, over time, there have been fewer good schools, fewer jobs and fewer good housing options available for African Americans, Native Americans and Hispanic Americans, making getting out and staying out of poverty harder. What's in this paragraph and the one above are only a few highly generalized explanations for poverty in the U.S. History also teaches us that if different institutions—government, businesses, schools, religious groups, charities and families—all work together, we can help protect millions from the worst ravages of being poor in America, like homelessness and hunger. We can also help millions of people move out of poverty, like after World War II with more manufacturing jobs (in factories to build things like cars), and in the 1990s with more technology jobs (to work on things like computers).

## TAXES AND GOVERNMENT PROGRAMS

You may have heard about Social Security, a government program created by President Franklin Delano Roosevelt in the 1930s that gives some money to Americans over the age of sixty-five—not necessarily enough to live on by itself, but enough to keep millions of seniors officially out of poverty (which is exactly what it was created to do). The money seniors get comes from taxes the government collected on wages they or their spouses earned while they were working. It's basically an insurance program from one generation to another aiming to protect seniors from poverty.

Other government programs are specifically designed to help poor people access basic necessities—food, home heating, medical care. How much money the federal and state governments raise in taxes from people and businesses determines how much money can be used for those and other programs, like on schools, roads and bridges, scientific research, the military and much, much more. Most big programs designed to assist poor people are joint federal and state efforts, which work alongside efforts from cities, religious organizations, charities and others, as we'll talk about later in the chapter. There are very different views about what the government's role (whether federal, state or local) should be in combating poverty through programs like Social Security. You'll have to make up your mind, particularly when you're old enough to vote, about what you think government's role should—or shouldn't—be in things like fighting homelessness and hunger.

## HOW IS POVERTY MEASURED IN THE U.S.?

In 2013, more than 45.3 million Americans, including approximately 14.7 million kids, officially lived in poverty. For a family of two adults with two children, this meant they had a yearly household income of less than $23,550. For a single adult, it meant less than $11,490 a year. That works out to a little less than $32 a day—which is where I got the name of this chapter. These are known as the federal poverty guidelines, or the federal poverty line, and they're updated every year to account for changes in how much things, like food, cost. Although they are the official definition of poverty, no one seriously believes that the poverty guidelines cover all the costs to house, feed, clothe and generally care for and support a person, much less a family with kids. In many places across the U.S., $32 would buy about two large pizzas. So while $11,490 a year or even $32 a day may sound like a lot of money to you, it actually isn't enough to cover the basics for life in America. Since most people don't think the official definition of poverty captures how many people in America struggle on what they earn to provide a good, healthy, safe home and life for their families, "low-income" is often used to describe poor families. Low-income families earn up to twice as much money as those who live on the poverty line. About one out of every three Americans, or 106 million people, live in low-income families.

While it's good to be aware of these different definitions, it's important to not get too caught up in them. What's important to recognize is that in the U.S. today, tens of millions of kids start life on an uneven playing field. Imagine having to try to run a race if you started ten yards behind everyone else, hadn't eaten

### PERCENTAGE OF CHILDREN IN THE U.S. LIVING IN LOW-INCOME FAMILIES, 2013

Information source: National Center for Children in Poverty

breakfast that morning, or maybe even dinner the night before, had slept in your third homeless shelter that month and didn't have shoes that fit right. Catching up would be really, really hard. With almost 32 million American kids living in low-income families, that means four out of ten runners are starting far back. There's a lot that all of us can do to make a difference in the lives of low-income kids and their families. This is not an area where we have made nearly enough progress and it's one I think we should all feel a moral urgency to address.

# POVERTY ISN'T EQUAL

Poverty is far from limited to people of a certain race or from a certain family structure. Poverty in America looks like America. But poverty does not affect Americans equally, particularly not Americans of different races and ethnic backgrounds. Almost two out of three African American kids live in or near poverty.

PERCENTAGE OF CHILDREN IN THE U.S. OFFICIALLY LIVING IN POVERTY BY RACE/ETHNICITY, 2013

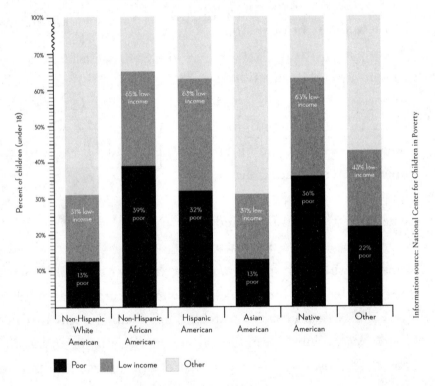

Information source: National Center for Children in Poverty

Poverty also does not equally affect women and men. More women than men live in poverty no matter their race or ethnic background or whether they live in cities or rural areas. Almost three out of five children in poverty live in households headed by a woman—a mother, grandmother, older sister or other female caregiver.

## THINGS PEOPLE THINK ABOUT POVERTY THAT AREN'T TRUE

One thing people think is true about poverty is that people who are not officially poor have enough money to support themselves and their families. While they may be able to scrape by, life is often really difficult for low-income families even if their struggles are not obvious to lots of people. Imagine having shoes, but they don't fit, because your parents could only afford to buy one pair for the whole year so they started off too big, they fit for a while and then they were too small. Or that you didn't get to play sports because uniforms and registration fees were just too expensive. Or imagine you never got to have a snack after school and there were never second helpings at dinner. Or video games? You only ever saw them advertised on TV.

Another misconception is about whether or not people in poverty work. It is true many people in poverty don't work because they're sick or disabled or because they can't find a job, or maybe because they've gotten so discouraged they stopped looking for a job. What is also true is that millions and millions of people in poverty work; at least 10 million adults who are living in poverty work.

The minimum hourly wage, or the minimum amount of money that employers have to pay most workers, in the United States is currently $7.25. The U.S. Congress sets the minimum wage for the country, adjusting it every so often. Various states or cities can raise the minimum wage in their areas, and many have, but often not by much. People who work full-time at forty hours a week for the federal minimum wage earn just over $15,000 a year. If a single mother with two kids makes that much working in a store, her family falls below the poverty line for a family of three. This helps explain why a diverse group including economists, religious leaders and activists point to raising the minimum wage as core to fighting poverty. How?

Well, similar to what we saw in the last chapter, the more money the mother working in the store earns, the more she has for spending. When she buys a new dress or a book, the shopkeeper she buys from then has more money to buy nutritious food from the grocery store for his kids. The grocery store owner then has more money to invest in expanding her store, hiring people to help with the construction and then more people to work in the store, who then have more money to take their kids to the movies, and so on . . . Other people think this isn't a good idea, arguing that higher wages would mean employers would hire fewer people. There's a wide variety of views on the minimum wage, if it should be raised, and if so, by how much. This is another area where you'll have to make up your mind about what you think the right answer is, especially when you're a voter, as more and more states and cities are putting minimum wage increases on the ballot (meaning you'd get to directly vote in favor or not).

There are countless books, articles and other materials about what people think the major causes of poverty in the U.S. are and what the best solutions to poverty are. Most are written for adults, and many are written by experts in the field for other experts in the field (meaning they're harder for anyone who is

## MINIMUM WAGE IN THE UNITED STATES, 2014–2015

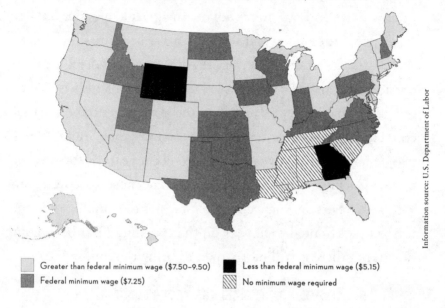

Information source: U.S. Department of Labor

Greater than federal minimum wage ($7.50–9.50)
Federal minimum wage ($7.25)
Less than federal minimum wage ($5.15)
No minimum wage required

not an expert—most of us—to read). There are some exceptions to this, like Poverty USA, an initiative of the United States Conference of Catholic Bishops. It has an excellent website for teachers, families and kids to learn about poverty in the U.S. and how to combat it, which you can find at povertyusa.org or pobrezausa.org for their all-Spanish site. Eliminating poverty is something we all have a stake in. The United States is one of the wealthiest countries in the world, yet poverty remains painfully persistent, trapping millions of kids into their adult lives, with the threat of homelessness and hunger never far away.

# HOMELESSNESS

We don't know exactly how many people are homeless in America on any given night (except the one night a year when the government organizes an effort to count). That's pretty shocking.

We know how many people are using Twitter at any moment or how many kids are in school on any given day—but not how many people are living and sleeping in a church mission, a public shelter, a bus station, a car, a park, on a street, under a bridge or outside a library, like the couple I often saw on Sundays. On the one night in January 2013, when the government and partners counted homeless people across the country, they found 610,042 people had nowhere to call home. In recent years, efforts to help people get into more stable housing, like those specifically for veterans, have seen some good results, and the number of homeless people counted each year on that one night has been going down, but there is still more to do to bring that number to zero.

## NUMBER OF HOMELESS PEOPLE IN THE U.S. COUNTED ON ONE NIGHT EACH YEAR, 2005-2013 (NOT THE WHOLE STORY)

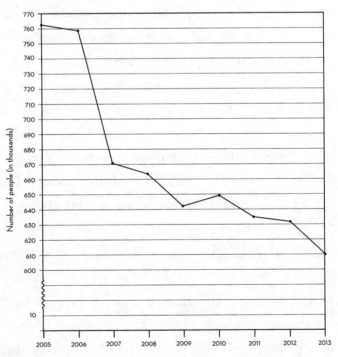

Information source: National Alliance to End Homelessness

In addition to not knowing how many people are homeless in America most nights of the year, we also don't know how many people are homeless throughout a year. This is in large part because homelessness for many people is a temporary—though terrifying—reality, meaning most people who are homeless over a year wouldn't be homeless on any single night. In 2012, an estimated 7.4 million people at some point during the year had no home and lived doubled-up with family and friends or in temporary housing or shelters. That's more than ten times the number of people counted the following January. Fewer people sleeping on the street on one night doesn't necessarily mean more people have found a home. Some recent studies estimate that as many as one out of every thirty American kids are homeless for at least one night a year, and for many, it's not just one night. In other words, if you have twenty-five kids in your class, on average, almost one kid in every class at some point in a year is homeless. And that night in January 2013? Almost one in four of the homeless counted were kids under eighteen. More needs to be done until all people have roofs over their heads at night and every kid has a home to go to after school.

In fourth grade, I was in Mrs. Porter's class—she remains one of the best teachers I ever had. There was another fourth grade class across the hall. Given the neighborhoods around my school, odds are that at least one of my classmates was homeless at some point over the school year. I don't say that so that you look around to try and figure out who is homeless. In fact, I think it's only your or anyone's business if classmates choose to share whether or not they slept in their home or a shelter the night before. But I want you to know how likely homelessness is so that you and all of us can be sensitive to what anyone may be going through on a given day, including the person sitting next to you in math class or standing ahead of you in the lunch line.

It may sound obvious, but the main reason people are homeless is because they cannot find affordable housing, meaning they can't find a home that they can afford to rent or buy within their budget. A budget is a plan for how families will spend the money they have and the money they earn. Families with more money can worry less about how much things cost, particularly when it comes to necessities like food, water, rent, heating, clothes and transportation, whether for a car, subway or bus fare. And there's money for things like vacations. People on a tight budget, who don't have a lot of money and rely on their modest paychecks, don't have a lot of wiggle room—most money they earn will be spent on necessities and it's hard to save money for a vacation or an emergency period. In the case of poor families, what they earn often doesn't cover even the basics.

The most expensive item in most family budgets is housing, so thousands of families end up homeless because they simply cannot afford their rent or mortgage. One in ten American households spends more than half of its income on a place to live. If people get sick and then are stuck with high medical bills or they have to take time off work to care for a loved one (and then aren't earning a paycheck), that's a huge strain on an already-tight budget. That can be stressful for any family, and for some families, it could mean losing their homes. There are also very real reasons why people sometimes choose to leave their homes, particularly women who are being abused or hurt by men they're living with. Too often, abused women have to choose between living with the people hurting them and being homeless. If these women are moms, their children have to live with one heartbreaking and dangerous choice or another.

## HOMELESSNESS: MYTH VS. REALITY

| Myth | Reality |
|------|---------|
| Homelessness is a permanent state. | Only one in six homeless people is chronically without a home. |
| Only certain people are homeless. | Anyone can be homeless. |
| Homeless kids don't attend school. | An estimated 1 million kids at school are homeless at some point in the year. |
| Homeless people are mentally ill. | Anyone can be homeless. |

Information source: National Law Center on Homelessness & Poverty and ThinkProgress

There are many myths and misconceptions about homelessness that are important to correct. For most individuals and families, homelessness is a temporary state between jobs or even paychecks, but too often it's a temporary state that repeats itself over and over again. But that's not true for everyone. In 2013, an estimated one in six homeless Americans at any point (like that night in January) was chronically homeless.

Another misconception is that the homeless in America look a certain way. If you think of a homeless person, what do you see in your mind? In reality, homelessness in America, like poverty, looks like America. Homelessness affects Americans of all ages, all racial, ethnic and religious backgrounds, in cities, rural areas, north, south, east and west. It is true that you are more likely to see African Americans, Native Americans and Hispanic Americans suffer from homelessness, for many reasons, including relatively higher rates of poverty and unemployment as well as the legacy and still-present ugly reality of housing discrimination. Housing discrimination can take many forms, some more obvious than others. People or businesses that own or rent homes may refuse to sell or rent to people because of their race, their religion, where they're from, whether they have children or whether they're disabled. Or they raise the sale price of a home for an African American family (but not a white family), or refuse to negotiate the monthly rent with a Hispanic family (but not a white family), or tell a Native American family all the apartments have been sold when there are still plenty of available units (for a white family). All of that is illegal and wrong, yet all still happen far too frequently, an estimated 2 million times a year across the U.S. As one example, in 2013, African Americans in Boston were denied mortgages at three times the rate of white applicants.

Our military veterans are also disproportionately represented in the homeless population, meaning that the number of homeless veterans is an unexpectedly large number compared with the percentage of all Americans who are veterans. That night in January 2013, nearly one in ten of the homeless were veterans. Why are there so many homeless veterans? It's another complex question, but one reason is that many veterans suffer from post-traumatic stress disorder (PTSD), an effect of being exposed to violence, extreme situations and war, which may make it harder to find and keep a job. The good news is that there has been a dramatic drop in homeless veterans since 2005—a 70 percent drop. But close to 58,000 veterans in 2013 without reliable roofs over their heads is far too many, so while progress has been made, more still needs to be done to help veterans get the housing and support they need.

Yet another misconception is that homeless kids aren't in school. As discussed earlier, they are in school—and some of the kids you likely know and sit next to have at some point faced the frightening prospect of not knowing where they'll sleep at night. Homelessness doesn't only affect kids' lives outside of school, it also affects how kids do in school. If you, like me, have been fortunate enough to never worry about where you spend each night, think about where in your home you do your homework, maybe in your room or maybe at the kitchen table (where I did mine). Imagine what it would be like if you had to move often and some days didn't know where you'd be doing your homework or where you'd be sleeping. Imagine how stressful that would be, how hard it would be to pay attention in class or to concentrate on taking a test.

Homeless kids are twice as likely as non-homeless kids to fall behind in school and have to repeat a grade. I can't even imagine how hard it would be to focus on homework when you're also trying to help your parents figure out where you'll sleep that night, or to take a test if you've slept in a different place every night the week before. Yet another misconception is that homeless Americans sleep only on the streets, and sadly, some do, but the majority, particularly kids, sleep inside shelters, missions or shared homes.

When Jade's family fell on hard times and lost their home, she had a tough time as her family worked to stay out of shelters and off the streets. She said, "It was the beginning of my freshman year [in high school]. We bounced around from couch to air mattress relying on family members and friends for months. I found myself killing time after school or in the library so I would be out of the way for as long as possible. When I was in someone else's home I wanted to be silent and invisible. Very often I went to school exhausted and completely stressed out. I'd be sitting in algebra or French and would start crying because the level of stress was unbearable. I no longer felt ready to take on the world. Instead it was like my world was falling apart."

Thankfully, Jade was part of an amazing organization called Girls Inc., which works to empower girls to succeed in school and in life. Through Girls Inc., trained mentors and volunteers build lasting relationships with girls in safe, girls-only spaces. They help girls set their own goals and work to give them the skills and knowledge needed to reach those goals. Girls Inc. mainly works with girls from low-income families. Jade's Girls Inc. mentor helped her stay positive and even helped her family get a storage unit for their stuff while they moved around. Today, Jade is at Boston University, and she's committed to helping other kids stay in school even if they lose their homes. She wants to be there to help someone else like her Girls Inc. mentor was for her. To learn more about Girls Inc. and find a local Girls Inc. chapter near you, visit girlsinc-online.org. The site also has resources to help girls (as well as boys) and their families think about setting goals, budgets, finding the right school (like Boston University for Jade) and much more.

*Jade at a Girls Inc. event helping to inspire other girls.*

Courtesy of Girls Inc., Photo Credit: Alan Perlman Photography

The story of Jade's family is pretty typical for families who are homeless. Some people might believe that everyone who is homeless is living with serious health challenges and struggling with mental illnesses. That's not true, and it's particularly not true for homeless kids. But it is true that many adults who are homeless suffer from a serious mental illness or medical condition. Some surveys say as many as one in four homeless adults in the U.S. suffer from some form of mental illness. That's a lot of people who are not getting the medical care they need to manage their illnesses. This is important to solve; it's also important to remember that the most likely reason a family is homeless is a lack of affordable housing (or housing that's within a family's budget).

The recent decline in homelessness as counted on that night once a year tells us something about what's working to help people stay in their homes or quickly find new housing if they lose their homes. The persistently high numbers of people who are forced to live with family and friends (like Jade's family was) tells us more still needs to be done. Federal and local governments have successfully stopped some people from losing their homes through programs that help pay part of the rent for poor families (these are called vouchers) and by encouraging the building of more affordable housing. Addressing homelessness protects human dignity—all people should have a home—and it also protects lives. In 2014, in Washington, D.C., on an unseasonably cold spring day, two people who had been sleeping outside died from hypothermia, or from being too cold. They were just blocks from the White House, where the president lives and I had the privilege of living when I was a teenager.

It may sound simple, and on one hand it is: ending homelessness in America would require everyone to have access to housing that is safe, affordable and large enough for each family. Making that happen is not easy, even for families in which at least one person is earning an income. I am a big believer in supporting what's been proven to work. Current research shows we need more affordable housing to prevent homelessness in the first place. A "housing first" approach has proven to help people who are already homeless move back into and stay in homes so that parents can find and keep stable jobs and kids can go to the same school regularly from a place they can reliably call home. "Housing first" also means helping those with mental and physical illnesses get the treatment and care they need from trained medical professionals. This approach generally depends on different groups working together, including the government, hospitals, clinics, religious groups, community centers, veterans' advocates and others.

It's also important to keep houses safe so that people never have to leave their homes because of concerns that a roof or wall may collapse. In high school, I went on a church mission trip with the Appalachia Service Project (ASP) to Breathitt County, Kentucky. We worked with one family for a week, using hammers, nails, plywood and more to strengthen their home's foundation, walls and porch. That enabled the family to stay in their home. Without those improvements, they'd expected to have to leave soon, without anywhere to go, because they thought their house would literally have fallen apart. Helping another family have a sense of security about

*With one of the kids I met on my mission trip to Breathitt County, Kentucky.*

Courtesy of Ned Bachman

their home was one of the most rewarding experiences of my life. ASP has been matching volunteers with low-income families throughout Appalachia for more than forty-five years and welcomes volunteers fourteen or older through church youth groups. If you're interested in spending a spring break, a week in the summer or any other time repairing homes for low-income families, I hope you'll talk to your minister. You can find out

*A kid helps with painting on a Rebuilding Together site.*

more at asphome.org. ASP is a Christian group but other religious and interfaith groups do similar work so even if there isn't a minister in your life, if you're drawn to this type of work, I hope you'll talk to the religious and faith leaders who are.

Rebuilding Together does related work across the country, making homes safer and healthier for low-income Americans, and Habitat for Humanity builds new homes for low-income Americans. To work on a Habitat home, you have to be at least sixteen, but you can check with your local chapter to see if there are ways for you to help out at any age. Some Rebuilding Together affiliates accept volunteers starting at fourteen, and they also work to find meaningful ways for kids (like in the picture above) to be involved beyond working with hammers and nails. I've volunteered a few times with both Rebuilding Together and Habitat for Humanity, and like my time with the Appalachia Service Project, it's deeply rewarding to make an impact in a visible way when a wall's been put up, a garden cleaned out, a new floor put down. To learn more about Rebuilding Together and Habitat for Humanity, including work they might be doing in your community, please visit their websites, rebuildingtogether.org and habitat.org.

There are very real ways you can combat homelessness and support homeless people without ever picking up a hammer (including encouraging adults in your life to pick up a hammer!). You can raise awareness about the issue—I imagine a lot of your friends don't know how many people are homeless throughout the year in our country. I imagine too that many people you know may be shocked by how many kids have to confront the scary reality of homelessness in their own lives, like Jade did. Sometimes it helps to put a face on big challenges like this one. So, think about sharing Jade's story or others you may know like hers. If people know that fighting homelessness benefits real people, particularly kids, hopefully they'll work even harder to help.

You can encourage adults in your life to volunteer at shelters, especially to help take care of, read to or tutor kids—as just a few examples. You probably can't volunteer in shelters yourself because shelters generally require volunteers be at least eighteen years old. This is different from other parts of the book, particularly the next section on hunger. The Coalition for the Homeless is a good source for volunteer options to share with adults in your life, which you can find at coalitionforthehomeless.org.

You can also help make being homeless less scary and more bearable for kids; kids who are just like you, except that they don't have a place to dependably call their own. That's exactly what California-native Alex has been doing for years, and he's only thirteen. When Alex was six, he realized that every time he finished building a LEGO® set, there were always leftover pieces. He decided to collect his extra pieces—and extra pieces from other kids—to donate to kids whose parents couldn't afford to buy LEGO sets.

*Alex with LEGO bricks he collected!*

Alex calls his effort Brickshare, and he's already given lots and lots of LEGO bricks away, all to kids whose families are living in local shelters, so that those kids can play, build and imagine, regardless of where they are or might be sleeping. He organizes events, Brickbot Drives, where kids can build LEGO sets called Brickbots out of the donated LEGO bricks. He then donates these Brickbots to other organizations that support thousands of homeless kids in his community. You could start a similar effort in your community or support Alex's efforts by mailing LEGO bricks directly to him or by donating money to buy full LEGO sets. You can find more information on how to do both at brickshare.biz.

If LEGO sets don't excite you, the same approach could be applied to other toys, books and games you've outgrown or want to share—provided the materials are in good shape. It's important that anything you donate to a shelter be something that you'd want to read, play with, use or wear. Families in shelters need and want the same things you have at your home, and every LEGO set, book and sweatshirt matters.

Think about what you wear during the week and over a whole year. You probably wear different clothes to school; to church, synagogue, temple or mosque; to play sports in; and for special occasions and holidays. Unless you live somewhere it's warm all the time, you probably wear different clothes in December than July. Next time you outgrow a piece of clothing or a game, think about whether it's still in good condition (because no one wants something that is torn, stained or broken), and if so, talk to your parents about donating it to help a kid whose family is homeless or struggling. You can encourage your parents to do the same. If this is something you're passionate about, consider starting a clothing, book or LEGO drive at your school. To find a shelter or other program (like the Salvation Army or Goodwill) where you know your donation will make a difference, you can ask your parents, teachers and any religious leaders in your life, who will probably have good suggestions.

Since the high price of housing is a key reason for homelessness, you can organize with your families, friends, neighbors and classmates to tell your mayor, your representatives (city council member, congressperson and senators), as well as our president that you want to see more safe, affordable housing for people of all incomes where you live. Habitat for Humanity has a useful toolkit to help kids reach out to elected officials, which you can find on their website. How best to achieve the goal of enough affordable and good housing may look different—and be paid for differently—in different parts of the country. But the first step of solving a problem is making sure that your elected officials know it's a problem you think is important to solve, whether for veterans, families or all people who are homeless on any given night over a year. One way to do that is by signing petitions you agree with on the change.org platform focused on raising awareness about homelessness and the need for more affordable housing. Or you can start your own petition and ask your friends and classmates to join your efforts online. You can even collect signatures the old-fashioned way (by hand). Whatever feels right to you.

Finally, you can avoid judging people who are homeless—or people who are hungry. There's a saying: "There but for the grace of God, go I," which means if fate worked out differently, if we were born to different parents, at a different time, in a different place, any one of us could be homeless, sick—or hungry.

## HUNGER

Can you imagine being hungry all the time? Being painfully, achingly hungry, day after day? We all know what hunger feels like—as a temporary condition. One morning you woke up late and had to rush out the door to make it to school on time. Or soccer practice ran late and you hadn't eaten since lunch and you felt rumbling in your stomach (maybe you even heard it growl). But you knew you were going to be able to eat when you got to the cafeteria or home after practice. Lots of people don't know where their next meal is coming from or if they'll have one at all. That's a different type of hunger. Government officials and policymakers call this food insecurity. "Food insecurity" is a funny-sounding term for something important and serious: whether or not a person has enough healthy food to eat throughout the year. In 2012, 49 million Americans lived with food insecurity, including almost 16 million kids. Many of those kids—over 14 million—at some point had to turn to food banks. Food banks are places where food is available for free to families who cannot afford to buy what they need to feed themselves. Many more people are food insecure than are homeless, with some facing the awful choice month after month to pay their rent rather than buy food. Sometimes even that situation doesn't last. A recent study found more than one out of every ten people who'd eaten at a food bank didn't have a home.

Hunger is a threat to anyone of any age, but it's particularly harmful to kids whose bodies and brains rely on nutritious food to grow. As mentioned before, kids who don't get enough healthy food have a harder time learning in school and are more likely to get sick from colds and other bugs that kids who aren't hungry often avoid. Kids who are hungry or worried about their next meal are more likely to bully other kids. Think how hard it is to concentrate on anything at all if you're hungry—whether learning something new in math or history or trying to focus on shooting a basketball. Think how much more easily you get angry without realizing it's happening if you're hungry—or maybe you've seen other people get angry when they're hungry. Most of the time, my husband, Marc, is nice, hilarious, fun to be around—except when he's hungry. We joke that he gets "hangry" (hungry + angry = hangry, a very clever word I didn't invent) and I try to avoid that happening by having snacks with me. We're very lucky; Marc's being hungry (or hangry) is always temporary. For many people, it's not temporary.

Also, too often, hunger and obesity, or being very overweight, go hand-in-hand (I know it sounds weird, but I'll explain). Many families who are food insecure purchase the cheapest food because it's often all that's around and affordable. But the cheapest food is often unhealthy, full of fat and sugar. When people live far from affordable healthy food, that's known as living in a food desert. More than 23.5 million Americans live in food deserts, and a majority of them are in low-income families. Kids from those families are more likely to be both hungry and obese. Hungry because they're not getting enough nutrition; obese because they're eating unhealthy food, and, because they're obese, they're at a greater risk of diabetes and heart disease. It's a clear example of how connected different issues are—lack of access to nutritious food, health and poverty. We'll talk more about these connections and food deserts in Staying Healthy.

Similar to poverty, hunger in America looks like all of America, but does not impact all Americans equally. More than one-quarter of African American homes deal with food insecurity at some point in a year—that's more than twice the percentage of white American households. Looking only at kids and teenagers paints an even starker picture. More than one out of three African American kids and teenagers is food insecure, far, far higher than the national average.

Additionally, chronic hunger (or hunger that never goes away) and food insecurity are further reasons why young people who are poor are tragically likely to remain poor throughout their lives. Think about the analogy earlier in the chapter about running in a race—if you can't concentrate on your schoolwork or your homework because you're hungry, you're not going to be able to learn as well or as much as kids who aren't hungry. You're not likely to do as well on tests as kids who aren't hungry, which means you're not likely to get the same grades today or the same opportunities later in school or life. All because day after day you feel hungry and worried about whether you will have enough to eat.

### FOOD INSECURITY: MYTH VS. REALITY

| Myth | Reality |
|------|---------|
| Hunger is not a big problem in the United States. | More than 46 million people eat meals in food banks. |
| People are more likely to be hungry if they aren't college educated. | More than 40 percent of food-insecure people have some form of higher education. |
| Food-insecure parents don't work. | Millions of Americans who are hungry work full- or part-time. |
| A majority of food stamps or SNAP goes to buy alcohol and cigarettes. | 85 percent of SNAP is spent on nutritious food. SNAP cannot be used to buy alcohol or cigarettes. |

Information source: Feeding America and USDA

Like around homelessness, many myths and misconceptions abound about food insecurity. Some people think it's not a big problem in the U.S. But anything measured in the tens of millions is not a small problem. Feeding America, the largest group of food banks in the country, alone served more than 3.3 billion meals to more than 46 million people in 2014. That's about one in every seven Americans. Hunger is sadly not rare in America. And you might think that if someone works, surely there's enough money to put food on the table for every family meal. Not so. According to Feeding America, millions of Americans who are hungry work full- or part-time. The hungry are often well educated. More than four out of ten food-insecure people went to at least one more year of school after they finished high school. More than one in five food-insecure households have had someone serve in the military. Hunger in America is as diverse as America itself, with one exception. The hungry are far more likely to be poor, regardless of race, education level, military service or what part of the country they live in.

You've probably heard of food stamps and may equate them with poverty. That's not far off—though not all poor or low-income Americans qualify for food stamps. The food stamp program, now called SNAP (Supplemental Nutrition Assistance Program), is the federal government's largest program to help poor and very low-income Americans, including kids, buy food. In 2013, more than 47 million Americans received SNAP funds to help purchase food at supermarkets, convenience stores and some farmers' markets. Do you know how much you spend on a meal at the mall or your family spends if you're eating out for dinner? Probably more than what SNAP provides: an average of less than $1.40 per person per meal. Many families spend all their SNAP for the month within a couple of weeks, meaning they have to rely on places like food banks for the food they need later in the month, which helps explain why the number of Americans eating at Feeding America partners is so high.

How much money people get from SNAP varies according to where they live (because food costs more in some places), how much they earn (people who earn less get more money to help buy food) and how many people are in their family (a family of four receives more than a single person does). It's really hard using only SNAP to buy enough healthy food for each meal, every day, every week, every month. There is yet another myth that families on SNAP spend most of their funds on unhealthy food, soda, alcohol or cigarettes. Over 85 percent of SNAP funds are spent on nutritious foods and SNAP funds cannot be used—in any state, by anybody—for alcohol or cigarettes.

There is no shame in needing SNAP. When food stamps were first introduced during the Great Depression (to help people like those in the picture at the start of the chapter) and then reintroduced in the 1960s, severe hunger and malnutrition were serious problems across the United States, more so than today. Food stamps helped eliminate widespread hunger and malnutrition in many poor communities, and helped protect children from severe malnutrition, stunting and the tragic consequences associated with stunting we talked about in the previous chapter. Today, when their families use SNAP, kids have a better chance to get the nutrition necessary to grow, get stronger and be able to pay attention and do better in school.

One out of every five kids in the U.S. lives in a family on SNAP, meaning that if there are twenty-five kids in a class, on average, five of them rely on SNAP for meals at home. Yet, even though SNAP is pretty common, it's not without controversy. Some people support the government expanding benefits (so more people can have more resources to buy more food) and others advocate shutting the program down (because they don't think it's the government's job to prevent people from going hungry, but rather the job of religious groups, community groups and others). Today, the government provides SNAP funds, while most food banks

ONE IN FIVE KIDS IN THE U.S. LIVES IN A FOOD-INSECURE FAMILY AND NEEDS NUTRITIONAL ASSISTANCE, 2015

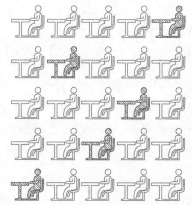

Information source: U.S. Census Bureau

and food pantries are run by religious organizations and charities or nonprofits (organizations focused on helping people, not making money). You'll have to decide what you think the appropriate role is for the government in fighting hunger in America and what roles you think religious, community and nonprofit groups should play.

Schools are another crucial part of the fight against childhood hunger because they're where kids spend most of their days. For the first time in at least fifty years, as of early 2015, a majority of kids in public school qualify for free or reduced-price lunch and breakfast at school because of their families' low-income status. On the one hand, this is terrific: we are finding a way to feed as many kids as possible at least one meal a day, hopefully making hunger less of a problem for kids, their health, their ability to learn and their futures. On the other hand, this is sad: more and more American kids live in families where hunger and food insecurity are either daily realities—or daily threats.

Some children feel ashamed about being from poor families—although they shouldn't—and those feelings stop them from using school meal programs. Students who are on free or reduced-lunch plans either pay nothing or forty cents for lunch (versus the more than $2 that is now average for school lunch across the country). Those same students also automatically qualify for free or reduced-price breakfasts at school. For many kids, the food at school may be the only real meals they will have in a day (particularly if their families have already used all their SNAP allocation for the month and there isn't a nearby food bank). Eating breakfast could make a big difference in their health, their ability to stay focused and their ability to succeed in school and life. Unfortunately, a lot fewer kids eat breakfast than qualify for it. Some kids can't get to school early because there aren't buses to take them. Others don't want to eat breakfast because unlike lunch, which everyone eats, schools only provide breakfast to kids whose families are generally considered poor or low income, and they don't want anyone to know about their families' struggles.

One thing you can do—that any kid in school can do—is to make sure none of your classmates feels badly about eating breakfast at school. Some school districts are considering making breakfast available to everyone so there's no stigma to showing up early for cereal or oatmeal. If you think that makes sense, that's something you can talk to your family about supporting in your local school district by writing your school superintendent, mayor and city council (or starting a change.org petition). Similarly, you can also work with your family, your school district and your bus drivers to expand bus schedules so that more kids can get to school in time to eat breakfast and not just for the opening bell.

Helping your school and school district offer a healthier (and tastier) school lunch is another area where you could help make a difference. This is good for all kids, particularly those who rely on school lunch as their main meal in a day. I remember most of the lunches at my junior high school consisted of pizza and sloppy joes full of mysterious ingredients—neither healthy nor terribly delicious. School kitchens are cooking for hundreds, even thousands, of kids every day during the school week, so it's important the meals are easy to make and also affordable for the district. Your school chefs and cafeteria staff are likely already working hard to figure all this out for you and your classmates. And they're not the only ones—it's an important enough question to have earned the attention of the White House and become a priority of First Lady Michelle Obama. So, if you have ideas about school lunches achieving the ideal balance of nutrition, taste and affordability, I hope you'll share them with your parents, teachers and school administrators. We'll talk more about this in Staying Healthy too.

Since so many kids rely on schools for at least one meal (lunch) if not two meals (lunch + breakfast) during the school week and the school year, more kids are likely to be hungry on the weekends and during the summer when most kids are out of school. Food banks in the Feeding America network provide backpacks full of food to more than 450,000 kids on Friday afternoons so that they can eat over the weekend. That's a lot of kids—but a lot less than the millions who are food insecure. During the summer, the federal government provides support to places where kids are likely to be—like schools, libraries and community centers—for healthy lunches. Churches and other religious organizations also work to provide food to kids during summers and on weekends. But an estimated six out of seven kids who need those meals don't get them, either because they live too far from where meals are being served and there's no way for them to get there or because they don't know they qualify for free summer lunches even if they're available at the community center or Boys and Girls Club down the street.

Like North Carolina–native William, you can do something to help kids get enough to eat when school's out. When he was just seven years old, William decided to work with the Inter-Faith Food Shuttle program to provide as many backpacks full of healthy food as he possibly could for kids during spring break. He figured his best strategy would be to talk to people outside local grocery stores, as they'd already be thinking about food and hopefully more willing to offer support. So William stood outside a store with a list of healthy food items he asked people to buy to support the backpack program. The first year he collected 1,400 pounds of food and raised $300. He thought he could do even more, so he kept raising money and

*William, "The Food Drive Kid," with food he helped collect.*

collecting food donations for the Inter-Faith Food Shuttle. This past year, when William was nine, he rallied 150 volunteers to collect 9,000 pounds of food in one day! That's a lot of food, particularly for kids who otherwise would've been hungry. He also raised $11,000 to buy even more food for kids. William isn't stopping, either. You can find out how to support William or how to start your own backpack program at thefooddrivekid.org. No Kid Hungry also has suggestions for ways to fight child hunger that don't require any money, and you can learn more at the website nokidhungry.org.

We'll end hunger in America when everyone has enough healthy food to eat every day. We know a lot about what works, specifically for kids, but we need to be doing more to make sure kids and adults have the food we all need. In addition to maybe starting a backpack program like William's, there is a lot you can do. You can help raise awareness about the millions of Americans, including American kids, who are hungry and food insecure. You can rally support for earlier buses so more kids can get to school in time for breakfast. You can start eating breakfast at school—if your school offers an open breakfast program

*Kids having a bake sale to raise money for No Kid Hungry.*

and you can get there early enough—so that no one feels singled out. You can help kids and families find summer meal programs near them (even if near is still miles away). That's actually much easier than it may sound. Anyone can text FOOD to 877-877 to find the closest summer meal site. Or you can help people look online by going to usda.gov and searching for "Summer Food Rocks" to find the closest summer meal site.

You can have a bake sale or find another way of raising money to support efforts to fight hunger, like the kids in the picture are doing for the national effort, aptly named No Kid Hungry. You can help raise money for food banks and food pantries at your local churches, mosques, synagogues, temples or community centers, as well as at local homeless shelters. You can also donate food—canned food, fresh food, cereals, vegetables, fruit and more. Some places accept all types of food and others generally prefer canned and dry foods, so make sure you check first what is needed and okay to donate. Thanksgiving and Christmas are traditional food-drive times, and it's so important no one be hungry around the holidays. It's also important to support, organize and hold drives throughout the year, because hunger doesn't disappear when we store away our Christmas and Hanukkah lights.

One person doing this work is Isaac from Keithville, Louisiana. Every morning on his way to school in nearby

*Isaac working on packages for homeless and hungry people.*

Shreveport, Isaac noticed kids who looked—and were—hungry. He went on a 4-H tour of a local food bank and saw almost-empty shelves. Isaac knew he wanted to fight hunger in his community, in part by helping food banks and other places hungry people went for food to always have full shelves. He started off supplying local homeless shelters with beef from his family's farm. Soon, he wanted to do more, so he founded Game Changers Tackling Hunger. Over time, Isaac recruited thousands of people—classmates, 4-H club members, other farmers, city leaders and more—to donate food and organize it into boxes that could be given to families and to replenish the shelves at the local food bank.

Feeding America is a great place to find local food banks and food pantries where you know your donations of money or food are going to families in need in your community. And it's where you can find partners if you want to start a program like Isaac's. To learn more, visit feedingamerica.org and type in your zip code.

Other ways to fight hunger include volunteering at a food or soup kitchen where hot food and meals are often served, or helping to sort food at a food bank into bags families can more easily take home. When I was in eighth grade and high school, I volunteered at Martha's Table, a food kitchen in Washington, D.C. Martha's Table welcomes volunteers starting at age twelve to help make and distribute meals. If you live in or near D.C., I hope you'll consider spending time volunteering there. Talk to your school or other groups

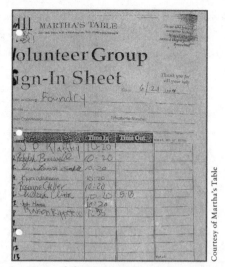

*One of the sign-in sheets from when I volunteered at Martha's Table with friends from my church youth group.*

Courtesy of Martha's Table

you're a part of to see if you can get your friends to go with you one day after school, on a weekend or over the summer. I volunteered at Martha's Table through my school and my church youth group. More information on Martha's Table can be found on its website, marthastable.org. If you don't live in D.C., you can find local food or soup kitchens by talking to your parents, religious leaders or teachers—or looking online.

Now, living in New York, I love volunteering at City Harvest, an organization that "rescues" food from restaurants, grocery stores, farms and

*Volunteering at City Harvest with Clinton Foundation colleagues.*

Courtesy of Julie Zuckerbrod/Clinton Foundation

other sources of fresh produce and groceries. We help repack bulk donations of things like fresh fruits and vegetables into family-sized bags and boxes that City Harvest then delivers to soup kitchens, food pantries and community food programs across New York City to help feed families in need. Every year in the U.S., 6 billion pounds of fresh produce is wasted. Through its members like City Harvest, Feeding America works to put more of that food on the tables of families who need it, rather than in trash bins. City Harvest welcomes volunteers fifteen and older to help sort and pack food and works with kids of all ages to organize food drives and fund-raisers, and you can learn more at cityharvest.org.

Anyone of any age can help raise awareness and support for food rescue or food donations from local restaurants, groceries and retailers. I'm proud that when my father was president, he signed what's known as the Good Samaritan law to encourage such donations by protecting donors and the groups that accept donations in case the food isn't as good or safe as they had thought. The Good Samaritan law is so named because of the parable in the book of Luke in the Bible. As you may have learned in Sunday school, the parable is the story of a traveler, presumed to be Jewish, who is robbed, beaten and left for dead. He is ignored twice by other travelers. Finally, a Samaritan traveler comes along, tends to the injured man's wounds and then helps him find shelter. The fact that historically Jews and Samaritans didn't like each other makes the story particularly powerful. It's also the context in which Jesus talks about the Golden Rule, and treating our neighbors as we ourselves would want to be treated ("Do unto others as you would have them do unto you").

You can encourage your family, when eating out, to eat at restaurants that rescue or donate extra or unused food to soup kitchens, food banks and pantries. And to shop for food at stores that do the same. You can find some of the major restaurant brands that participate in food-rescue programs at the website foodtodonate.com. If restaurants and stores you like to go to aren't participating, encourage them to get involved, starting by going to feedingamerica.org and and connecting with local food-bank partners to help more hungry people get the meals and food they need.

There are also lots of new tools that make donating food even easier for restaurants, grocery stores and others. Waste No Food is a website and free mobile app on iTunes and Android that allows places that may have excess food on any given day (like a restaurant or concession stands at a sports stadium) to post updates when they have more food than they can use. Food banks and other charities that Waste No Food has preapproved can claim the food and then are responsible for safely moving the food to shelters, food banks and other places that need it. What's really remarkable? Waste No Food started off as an idea in San Francisco–native Kiran's head when he was a seventh grader volunteering at his local church. You can learn more about how to participate in or support Waste No Food by visiting its website at wastenofood .org.

You may have read the Hunger Games series, or seen the movies. They're compelling stories about kids who believe they deserve a better world and are willing to fight for it—they're also about kids who are sometimes literally hungry. As I hope I made clear, hunger isn't only something that happens in movies set in other worlds or that only happened in America during the Great Depression (like in the picture at the start of the chapter). In 2015, hunger remains far too common a reality in the U.S. and other relatively wealthy countries. And yet, neither hunger nor homelessness rate high in what Americans are most worried about.

In a January 2015 survey asking Americans what they thought the most important problem facing our country is, dissatisfaction with the government and general unhappiness with the economy ranked the highest. This makes some sense. If you're concerned about a lot of things and you think government has a role to play in solving various problems—whether fixing potholes on your local street or fighting hunger in the U.S. or combating climate change—you might say your main worry is dissatisfaction with the government because you think it's not doing enough for what you care about. And general unhappiness with the economy could be because there aren't enough good-paying jobs for people, which directly relates to poverty, homelessness and hunger. But only 3 percent rated poverty/hunger/homelessness as the most important problem facing the United States. Whatever you're most concerned about is what you should rank first—but I worry sometimes about our ability to erase poverty, homelessness and hunger if we don't recognize them as very real problems first and then focus our energies on solving them together. This is why raising awareness about everything that is discussed in this chapter is so important and it's why we have to do what we can today while we're waiting for more people to say it's not okay for the wealthiest country in the world to have so many people hungry, homeless and poor. Churches, synagogues, mosques and temples are often found on the frontlines of fighting poverty, so if you want to learn more about poverty in your community and what you can do to raise awareness and make a difference close to home, asking the religious leaders in your life will probably give you even more information, ideas and inspiration.

As federal and state government policies have a big impact on what role the government plays in combating homelessness and hunger, you can encourage the people in your life who are over eighteen to look at what various candidates say about these issues and what their plans are. You can also help register people to vote, even though you're not yet old enough to vote, and talk about why you care about these issues and what you think the right answers are. You and your family can also support efforts at shelters and elsewhere to help homeless people register and go to vote. Just because people are homeless doesn't mean they don't have a right to vote—for mayor, for congress, for president. They absolutely do. This is another area you can draw attention to and encourage adults in your life to help with. More information can be found at nationalhomeless.org.

## OPPORTUNITY

I don't think I can write about poverty in the U.S. without also talking about opportunity, because America is at its best the land of opportunity, of hope for a better future. Yes, there are many, many hurdles that kids who are born into poor homes have to overcome. Hurdles most of us cannot even imagine. But there are also causes for celebration and optimism that we need to remember and support. One of them is that people, including young people and even kids, continue to start small businesses and become entrepreneurs.

In the last chapter I mentioned microlending—tiny loans to very poor women (and sometimes men) to help buy a milk cow or a cell phone in a remote village in Bangladesh or Burundi. In the U.S., we have more types of tools to help people start and build businesses—small business loans from banks, charities and the government, and larger investments from specialized financiers to help businesses grow. Anyone of any age can start a business. Two amazing organizations that help teach kids from low-income neighborhoods the basics about how our financial system works, how to manage money and how to start and run a business are Operation HOPE and the Network for Teaching Entrepreneurship (NFTE).

Operation HOPE helped eleven-year-old seventh-grader Princess start a baking business, Sweet Tooth Bakery, in Oakland, California. Princess wrote a business plan and pitched it (presented it) to her mentors at Operation HOPE. They were so impressed that they awarded her $300 to help her bakery move from business plan to real start-up business. Princess used the money to buy flour, sugar, tools and more. She now sells her delicious treats to a local restaurant and provides cookie dough to other kids who want to have bake sales for causes that are important to them. My good friend John Hope Bryant started Operation HOPE more than twenty years ago

*Princess with her mom, standing behind her Sweet Tooth Bakery cupcakes.*

Courtesy of Nikyea Berry

to empower poor people with the skills (like making a monthly budget) and knowledge (like how to open a bank account) necessary to getting and staying out of poverty. He had no idea when he began that he'd one day be investing in young entrepreneurs. Yet it's remarkable how many people like Princess Operation HOPE already has helped and invested in since they started focusing on entrepreneurship—more than 2,000 in about three years. It's another real testament to the idea that sometimes we just have to start, because we have no idea whose life we'll change. John started Operation HOPE before Princess was even born!

NFTE was a lifeline to Rodney Walker. A foster kid from Chicago, Rodney had been placed in multiple homes growing up. By the time he graduated from high school, he had gone to ten different schools since kindergarten. In his senior year, he took a NFTE course on how to think about starting a business and writing a business plan, and equally importantly, how to be adaptable and remain focused on his goals in the face of any obstacles. With a friend, he developed a plan for a digital video production and music business. They won $5,000 from NFTE to translate their business plan into a real business. Rodney went to Morehouse College, did well in school and kept building and expanding his business. It made money before he graduated. Now a graduate student at Yale, Rodney's future is considerably brighter, in part because NFTE gave him critical skills and confidence. Now a speaker at NFTE events, Rodney's looking to inspire other kids to dream big—and write business plans. I can't wait to see what Princess is doing when she's Rodney's age. To learn more about Operation HOPE and NFTE, visit operationhope.org and nfte.com.

Stories like Princess's and Rodney's are important to remember. All the struggles and problems I lay out in this book are big and real and have been with us a long, long time. Yes, we need big solutions to help erase poverty, from a consistently growing economy with good jobs to enough affordable housing across the country. We also have to remember that, for every kid we help feed at a food bank or at school, and for every kid (or adult) we help to start a business, we assist in fighting poverty. And in doing so, we help America become the country I believe we want it to be.

# Get Going!

- Talk to your family and at least three friends about why these issues are important—share stories of kids who were homeless, like Jade's, to help raise awareness of the people who make up the statistics
- Learn more about poverty at povertyusa.org or pobrezausa.org
- Learn more about homelessness at the National Law Center on Homelessness and Poverty at nlchp.org and more about hunger at feedingamerica.org
- Encourage adults in your life to volunteer at homeless shelters
- Start a clothing drive at school (or in your own house)
- Donate clothes to shelters, the Salvation Army or Goodwill
- Write a letter to your mayor, representative or senators telling them you think having more safe, healthy, affordable housing in your neighborhood is important
- Sign or start a petition about assisting those who are homeless, including through "housing first" approaches, at change.org
- Collect LEGO bricks and mail them to Brickshare

- Donate something you like to play with or read to a shelter near you (be sure it's still in good shape)
- Don't judge people who are homeless or hungry (and encourage others to do the same)
- Talk to your school about making breakfast available for everyone so no one feels badly about having breakfast at school
- Share ideas with your parents or administrators about how to make your school lunches healthier
- Help kids and families who need it find the closest summer meal programs, or volunteer at a soup kitchen or food pantry
- Raise money for No Kid Hungry's efforts to stop child hunger by having a bake sale at school
- Donate food to food banks and pantries in your neighborhood
- Start a food drive at your school or religious institution
- Start or support a weekend food backpack program
- Eat in restaurants that donate extra food to soup kitchens, food banks and pantries, or encourage restaurants to donate extra food
- Support Operation HOPE (and consider participating in a HOPE Business In A Box Academy and pitch event if there's ever one in your school or community) and share stories like Princess's
- Support NFTE and share stories like Rodney's
- If you're over thirteen, go on social media to follow organizations (like No Kid Hungry) and celebrities (like Mario Batali) that are fighting child hunger and/or homelessness as a way to show your interest in and support for their work

# PART II

# It's Your RIGHT

Courtesy of Nick Onken

CHAPTER THREE

# TIME FOR SCHOOL

In 1995, before my mom and I traveled to South Asia, I remember being so excited for all the new experiences ahead, the new places we would see and the new people we would meet. I read every book I could find by Gita Mehta about life in India throughout the 20th century (the 1900s). I read encyclopedia entries and old *National Geographic* articles on the countries and historical sites we would visit. By the time we left for our trip, I was so excited even though I still wasn't quite sure what to expect. I know there was at least one thing I wasn't expecting: seeing lots and lots of kids not in school. Children sitting in slums, hustling on corners, begging on roads, hanging out under trees and working—farming, cooking, carrying, cleaning—and everywhere, from cities to rural communities, not in school.

I knew some schools were not as good as others in the U.S. and I'd heard conversations on the news and at our family dinner table about improving education across our country. But until I went to South Asia, I had no idea that at that time, over 100 million kids weren't in school, either because there were no schools for them to go to or no teachers to teach them, or because they had to work, on farms, in open-air stores or as beggars on the street. Some of the kids I saw working weren't even old enough to be in elementary school.

I didn't know that in many places around the world in the late 20th century, and even still today twenty years later, kids didn't have schools to go to, teachers to teach them, desks to sit at, books to learn from and safe places to play before or after school. Many don't even have the hope of ever going to school. I didn't know how many kids had to work in a job every day instead of worrying about science class or math homework. That many kids didn't know how to read or add or subtract and weren't routinely asked, as I was by my parents and teachers, what I wanted to be when I grew up or what I'd learned in school that day. I was embarrassed I hadn't known or understood how lucky I was to have a school to go to and to have great teachers. I've had terrific teachers throughout my life, from Mrs. Minor, who taught my kindergarten class at Hall High School (yes, as bizarre as it sounds, I went to kindergarten in a high school), through Dr. Ngaire Woods, my graduate advisor at Oxford University. Millions of kids and young people aren't so fortunate.

More so than anything else discussed in this book, education is an area where I think adults should really listen to kids. After all, you're the ones who are being educated! And you're thinking about education all the time (since you spend so much time in school) so you have valuable ideas and thoughts about it. I hope you'll speak up and speak out about what you think education should mean at your school. You also have great ideas about how every kid around the world should have a chance to learn and discover, and I hope you'll share those too.

This chapter focuses on education outside the U.S. and other wealthy countries. Why? Well, because in the U.S., every kid has a guaranteed right to a free, public education from kindergarten through high school. That's pretty standard in wealthier countries, but it's still not common in developing countries.

A quick note on what can be confusing language. Elementary school is usually called primary school outside the U.S., so that's the language I'll use. Around the world, many different words are used to describe the type of school that kids go to after primary school, or once they're around twelve years old. Middle school, high school and junior high school are just a few such names we use in the U.S., and it can be confusing, even in our own lives. For eighth grade, I started off at Horace Mann Junior High School in Little Rock and finished at Sidwell Friends Middle School in Washington, D.C. Around the world, secondary school is the most common name for what comes after primary school, so that's what you'll see throughout this chapter. I'll try to avoid confusion, because the crisis could not be more clear: millions of children are still not in school and millions more do not receive a quality education.

Why is it so important that everyone everywhere can go to school? You may think it's obvious why, but for lots of people around the world, it's not so obvious. Education helps each of us define and then pursue our dreams, whether we want to be doctors or teachers, architects or activists, whether we want to work on a farm, in a store, in an office, whether we want to help invent the next cool technology or drive a race car. It's hard to imagine what we want to be when we grow up if we don't even know what exists. It's also hard to imagine ourselves as being astronauts or running businesses if we don't know what skills we'll need to do those jobs or can't go to school to learn them. School fills us with the knowledge to help us dream big and then to follow those dreams throughout our lives.

Education also helps fight poverty in very real ways. According to the United Nations (UN), an organization that includes representatives from nearly every country in the world, if every child in low-income countries learned to read—just learned to read—more than 170 million people would be better able to support themselves as adults and move out of poverty. In low-income developing countries, every additional year of school young people receive increases their future income by a lot. So if many more kids go to even one more year of school, that's good for them and their countries. When they grow up, those kids will earn more money, helping them move out of poverty. They'll also have more money to spend and invest, which over time will help their countries do the same.

Better education helps people lead healthier, longer lives— if people know more about what keeps them healthy, they're more likely to do those things. A daughter (or son) born in the developing world to a mother who knows how to read is significantly more likely to live past five years old, partly because her mother knows more about how to keep her healthy and partly because her mother is more likely to work and then have more resources to be able to take care of her. Civic education—or learning how government works, what it does, how voting works—helps kids be involved citizens now (through writing to, calling or emailing their mayors or members of Congress) and later in life (by voting, possibly even running for office . . . and still writing to their mayors or members of Congress). Learning how to think about an issue—like education or climate change—also helps each of us make arguments about what we think the right answers are to big questions and articulate why we believe what we do.

The best education also makes life more interesting as we learn about music, the arts and cultures different from our own. Imagine if you had to rely on someone else to always tell you what was happening in your school or your community and you couldn't make up your own mind about how your teachers, your mayor or our president and congress are doing their jobs? Imagine if you never heard music or never had a chance to draw or paint? It's hard to imagine that Mark Zuckerberg could have created Facebook without a computer science class—just think about what would be possible if all kids everywhere who were interested in technology had the chance to explore their passions and could invent whatever they dreamed up? We'll all be better off when any kid anywhere can imagine the unimaginable—it's how we'll solve climate change, cancer, homelessness and hunger, all the things I talk about in this book and more. It's how we'll have the best music to listen to, movies to watch and art to appreciate, whether it's outdoors, online or in a museum. But for all that to happen, we need to get kids in school.

## SHOW OF HANDS

In 2012, 58 million kids of primary-school age (between six and eleven years old) were not in school. That's almost one out of every ten kids in that age group around the world. Fifty-eight million is a lot less than the 100 million primary-school age kids who weren't in school in 2000, but it's still a big number—it's a little less than the population of Italy. Fifty-eight million tragedies of lost potential. How many of those kids might have helped discover a cure for HIV/AIDS or invent a new rocket to Mars? Or simply found a path to a happier, healthier life? Even more twelve- to fifteen-year-olds are not in school. In 2012, 63 million twelve- to fifteen-year-olds were not in school, down from 97 million in 2000. Again, another huge drop, but still a shocking amount of lost potential. Wealthier countries, the World Bank and many

### PRIMARY SCHOOL–AGE CHILDREN: WHO'S IN AND OUT OF SCHOOL?

34 million out of primary school

649 million in primary school

1999

58 million out of primary school

705 million in primary school

2012

Information source: UNESCO

= 10 million children

Please note I am using boy icons only for convenience—not implying only boys are in primary school (even if more still are around the world!).

NGOs and charities (some of which we'll talk about later in this chapter) have helped build lots of schools, train teachers and get more kids in school since 2000—that's why the numbers have dropped by millions. But why are there still so many kids not in school? We'll turn to that question after we talk a bit more about the kids who aren't in school and where they live around the world.

A little less than half of the 58 million kids not in school have never and likely will never go to primary school. Imagine a six-year-old girl living in a country where girls historically haven't gone to school. She knows she'll probably never walk into a school, whether it's a formal classroom or a thatched roof with open air on all sides instead of walls. Instead, she knows she'll either get married when other kids will be in secondary school, or she'll be working. Likely she'll be both married and working, even if she's working only in her husband's home. That's a pretty limited image of your future when you're six.

Now imagine her brother. Maybe it took a while for him to persuade his parents to send him to school or maybe it took a while for his family to find the money to pay for school. Because of that, he's starting late, as almost one in three of the kids worldwide who currently aren't in school will at some point. He worries he won't catch up—and many who start late never do. Imagine if you had to start in second grade, having missed kindergarten and first grade. That's the reality for many kids around the world. And because it's frustrating to always be behind, it's likely the boy will drop out, as many of the students who start school late do. Some will leave because they're frustrated, and many more won't finish primary school because education is not a priority for their families. Or, even if it's a priority, kids are needed to help around the house, help farm the family's fields or otherwise support their parents and family by working outside the home or begging on the streets. So even some of those who start on time will also drop out. Sadly, it's likely the boy will join the girl at work—though he won't be expected to marry as young as she probably will be (more on that in a bit).

Certain countries have gotten more kids in school than others because they've made education a priority and had the money to do something about it. They've become wealthier and had more of their own money to invest in education, or they've attracted aid from wealthier donor countries, foundations and charities focused on getting kids into school (and for some countries, both are true). Parts of Asia have seen the most dramatic declines in the number of kids who aren't in school; parts of sub-Saharan Africa the least.

In sub-Saharan Africa, one in five kids—or 30 million kids in total—of primary-school age aren't in school. In Nigeria alone, more than 10 million young Nigerians aren't in school. But this isn't just a problem in Nigeria, or in sub-Saharan Africa. It's a problem all over the world. In Pakistan there are 5.4 million kids not in school, and India, Indonesia, Niger

### SECONDARY SCHOOL–AGE CHILDREN: WHO'S IN AND OUT OF SCHOOL?

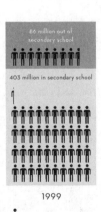

1999

2012

Information source: UNESCO

👤 = 10 million children

Again, only boy icons doesn't mean only boys are in secondary school (though more boys are around the world and lots more are in parts of Asia and Africa).

and Sudan each have at least 1 million children who are not in primary school.

## WHY AREN'T KIDS IN SCHOOL?

Why do you think kids aren't in school around the world? Poverty. Geography. War. Being a girl. Getting married. Being disabled. Having to work. No schools to go to. No teachers to teach classes. Some of those reasons may sound more obvious than others. They are all major barriers kids face in going to, staying in and finishing school. Some days you may not want to go to school, but could you imagine if you couldn't go to school at all?

### *Schools Are Really Far Away . . . and There Aren't Enough of Them*

In Africa and Asia in particular, fewer children are dying from the scary diseases we'll talk about in the next part of this book. That's a very good thing. It also means that more schools are needed, for kids today and the additional kids who are going to be alive and healthy in the future, as health systems get stronger and stronger. And those schools need to be near where kids live. Today, many kids around the world trek two or three hours to get to the closest school. There are no buses to take them—if they want to go to school, they have to walk. Far. You may have heard your parents or grandparents talk about having to walk miles to school (my grandmother Dorothy had to walk or run five miles each way to high school). In most places across the U.S. today, public school buses mean kids no longer have to walk long distances to school, but millions of kids around the world today still do. And sometimes it's a lot farther than five miles. The world needs as many as 4 million more classrooms to ensure every kid can go to school, get to school in a reasonable amount of time (meaning not in two to three hours by foot) and be in a classroom that's not overcrowded (meaning not with 100 kids but closer to twenty or thirty). It's far from a perfect analogy, but here's one way to think about what that means. There are more than 54 million kids in kindergarten through twelfth grade in the United States, attending more than 132,000 schools. To accommodate all the kids who aren't in school in the world, the world would need to add more than twice as many schools as we currently have in the U.S.

## A LONG WALK TO SCHOOL

### DID YOU KNOW?
Children in rural areas around the world sometimes walk two to three hours to attend school.

Information source: Global Education First Initiatve

There are ways you can help build desperately needed classrooms and schools around the world, largely by helping raise awareness and money for programs like Pencils of Promise and Building Tomorrow. Pencils of Promise works in Ghana, Guatemala and Laos to build schools that make sense for the local communities, including teachers. All the schools are safe, supported by the local education ministry and have enough supplies for every student. They also have enough teachers for all the students. Adam Braun got the idea for Pencils of Promise after he asked a boy begging in India what he wanted most in the world and the boy replied "a pencil." Adam then spent years handing out thousands of pencils and pens across fifty countries.

Pretty quickly, Adam realized kids needed more than pencils (though he still gives pencils too). Since Pencils of Promise started, it has built more than 300 schools and helped more than 30,000 kids go to and stay in school. That's a big, life-altering deal for those students and their families. You can learn how to start a Pencils of Promise club in your school to sponsor a school or group of students by visiting their website, pencilsofpromise.org.

Building Tomorrow works along a similar model, focusing on building schools in Uganda. Since it began, Building Tomorrow has built more than thirty schools, often more quickly and for less money than the government had been building them for. Building Tomorrow does this partly by engaging the local community to physically help build the school, and on land that the community donated, a clear sign of how much the adults want their children to learn. The money the government doesn't spend on building a school can then be spent on more supplies for the students and in training and hiring teachers.

In 2012, I visited the Building Tomorrow Academy of Gita, located in Wakiso, Uganda, about an hour from the capital, Kampala. Gita was the first Building Tomorrow academy constructed of special environmentally friendly bricks made out of soil dug out from the building's foundation and dried in the sun. The school—the eighth Building Tomorrow academy in Uganda—was just starting classes when I vis-

*Here I am listening to students in a Building Tomorrow school.*

ited. But the kids and parents I met were thrilled, because previously, students had to walk at least five kilometers (more than three miles) to the nearest primary school and many parents didn't feel comfortable sending their girls to school. There were so many girls—and boys—at the Building Tomorrow Academy of Gita, some in school for the first time, and all excited to learn. Every child deserves that same enthusiasm. To learn more about starting a Building Tomorrow chapter or club to help build their next school, you can visit buildingtomorrow.org.

## Schools Don't Have Lights or Clean Water

Even in places with schools, often the buildings don't have electricity, sanitation and clean water. Can you imagine being in a school with no working water fountain? Or no clean water at all? No toilets that flush? Or just no toilet? How about with no lights? In Chad, three out of every four schools are missing all of the above. I don't remember my school bathrooms being anything special, and certainly there was lots of graffiti on the bathroom walls at my junior high in Little Rock, but I never had to worry about whether there would be a place to wash my hands, a working toilet or toilet paper to use—or lights on in the classroom. But many kids in the developing world do. And even more kids across the world have to worry about whether there will be enough textbooks, workbooks, paper, pencils or pens, and whether they'll have any of those at all.

There aren't good numbers on how many toilets and clean water systems the world needs for every school, but it's likely in the millions. Yes, we need millions of toilets, millions of sinks (or another way to wash hands) and millions of bars of soap so every student can go to the bathroom safely and with dignity.

Building improved sanitation and water systems (think no mixing of poop and drinking water and no icky smells) alongside more classrooms is part of what makes the schools Pencils of Promise, Building Tomorrow and others build so important. But we know buildings and clean water aren't all a school needs . . .

## *There Aren't Enough Teachers*

Have you ever thought about whether or not there would be a teacher when you walked into a classroom? I don't even think I ever did when I was younger because there was always a teacher. I suspect you don't think much about it either—if your regular teacher can't make it one day, you know you'll have a substitute. That's not the reality for many kids in the developing world. There are simply not enough teachers to teach all school-age kids around the world, meaning there is a worldwide teacher shortage. How many additional teachers does the world need to get all kids into primary school? Well, in 2012, the UN estimated that number to be 6.8 million new primary school teachers by 2015 (we didn't make that goal—not by a long shot). Around 100 countries need extra teachers. And the number of teachers we need will continue to grow as there are more and more healthy children to go to school. It's not just about more teachers, it's also about ensuring those teachers are well trained, well supported and well paid for the work they're doing. It's a challenge that extends beyond primary school too.

For secondary schools, some countries have less than one teacher per 100 students; in Niger, if every kid who's old enough were in what's known as lower secondary school or middle school (which we know they're not, but if they were), there would be only one secondary school teacher for more than 1,300 kids! That partly helps explain why so few kids are sitting in classrooms in Niger—if you can't hear or even see a teacher, it's not crazy to think it may not be worth going to school. Niger is an extreme case, but there are also serious teacher shortages in many other countries. In the Central African Republic, for kids who are in primary school, there are more than eighty students for every one teacher.

AVERAGE NUMBER OF STUDENTS PER TEACHER AROUND THE WORLD, 2012–2013

Information source: World Bank

There are people working on getting more teaching assistants into schools while countries are working to train more teachers. Someone who is doing just that is Peggy Mativo. I first met Peggy through the Clinton Global Initiative University (CGIU), a program that the Clinton Foundation runs to assist college and graduate student activists and change-makers turn their world-changing ideas into NGOs or to help them think about strengthening the work they're already doing. Peggy's working to close what's known as the "teacher gap"—the difference between how many teachers there are and how many teachers are needed—in her home country of Kenya. She created PACE (which stands for Promoting Access to Community Education), a program that works to provide qualified teaching assistants to schools in poorer communities in Nairobi, Kenya, where there are often more than fifty-seven students in a classroom with just one teacher. Do you think it would be really hard to concentrate in a class with more than fifty other students? I do. And it's also probably really hard for the teacher.

Through early 2015, PACE teaching assistants have volunteered more than 28,000 total hours in eight public schools in Nairobi, resulting in better grades for students and happier teachers. Scores went up so much at one PACE school that education officials called to make sure the scores had been reported appropriately! To find out more about Peggy's program and how to support more teaching assistants in more classrooms, visit PACE's website, pacemakerinternational.org. You can also encourage teachers you know to mentor PACE volunteers and team members (in person if they're in Nairobi, or remotely through Skype).

## Sometimes School Costs Money!

Until recently in much of the developing world, even if there were schools to go to and teachers to teach classes, parents had to pay a fee for their kids to go to any school, including primary school. There were no free public schools; in some places, there still aren't, though over the past fifteen years almost all countries have eliminated school fees, at least for primary school. This is very different from families in relatively wealthier countries like the U.S. who decide to pay for their sons and daughters to go to private school (because they could go to public school for free). In some countries, even if there aren't school fees, parents have had to pay for uniforms or school supplies before their kids are allowed to step foot inside a classroom, meaning school remains too expensive for many families. And, knowing parents couldn't afford to send their kids to school, some developing-country governments have built fewer or no schools in poorer areas, which helps explain why poor kids often have to walk the farthest to school.

Not surprisingly, in countries where school fees and other fees have been eliminated, more kids are going to school. In Burundi, after school fees were abolished, primary school attendance almost doubled in less than ten years. That's a lot more kids in school! When the Nicaraguan government eliminated school fees and started helping poor families purchase the uniforms and school supplies their kids required, more than half of all kids in Nicaragua who had never been to school quickly enrolled. Imagine if you had to buy your own books, supplies and uniform, and pay for the right to go to school on top of all that. Only in your lifetime have things really started to change for primary school kids and families around the world.

## COUNTRIES WHERE PRIMARY SCHOOL COSTS MONEY*

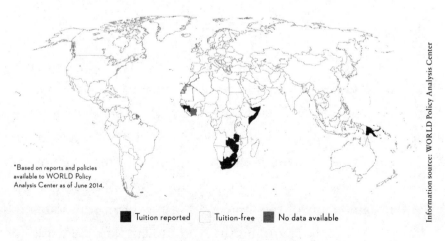

*Based on reports and policies available to WORLD Policy Analysis Center as of June 2014.

Information source: WORLD Policy Analysis Center

■ Tuition reported ☐ Tuition-free ■ No data available

While it's free almost everywhere for kids to go to primary school, in many places, particularly in sub-Saharan Africa and South Asia, families still have to pay for their children to go to secondary school (remember that's the equivalent of middle school and high school in the U.S.). Not surprisingly, in places where people still have to pay to send their kids to school, any type of school, kids are less likely to be in (or stay in) school.

COUNTRIES WHERE COMPLETING SECONDARY SCHOOL COSTS MONEY*

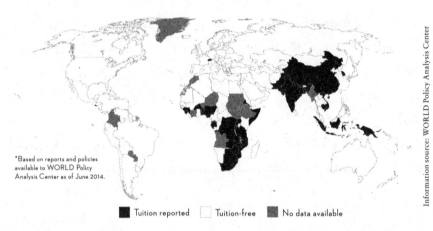

*Based on reports and policies available to WORLD Policy Analysis Center as of June 2014.

■ Tuition reported    □ Tuition-free    ■ No data available

Information source: WORLD Policy Analysis Center

## Some Kids Have to Work

It wasn't until 1918 that every state in the U.S. had laws requiring kids to go to and finish elementary school. One of the reasons states passed those laws was to make sure families chose school for their kids, not work. Even 100 years ago in the U.S., many kids were expected to work—on farms, as chimney sweeps, as maids or as weavers. Similar mind-sets and expectations (and many of the same jobs) help explain why so many kids aren't in school around the world today. They're working instead of attending school, because they have to support their families, or because they have to support themselves, and sometimes because they're not given a choice. This is what's known as "child labor." Out of more than 2 billion kids around the world, an estimated 168 million work, including in the most violent type of work.

There are approximately 250,000 child soldiers around the world, many of whom are kidnapped, and others who join militaries or armed groups for protection during horrible wars. They're from already-dangerous places like Syria and Sudan, Yemen and Afghanistan, the Central African Republic and Somalia, where they are robbed of their youth and forced or tricked into a soldier's life. Child soldiers rarely receive any type of education, other than on who their enemies are and how to kill them. Otherwise, they're too focused on staying alive.

Courtesy of Anadolu Agency/Getty

*Child soldiers aren't in school—instead they learn who
their enemies are and how to fight them.*

I had the great fortune of meeting one extraordinary former child soldier from South Sudan, Bishop Elias Taban, who has devoted his life to helping his country heal after decades of war and strife. Bishop Taban was born on May 10th, 1955, in Yei, South Sudan, the very day fighting broke out. As the fighting got closer to the

*Bishop Taban training former soldiers how to make bricks so they can earn a living beyond war.*

hospital, the nurses and doctors fled, abandoning baby Elias and his mother. Elias's mother took him and ran too, hiding in the jungle for three days until they could safely emerge.

Sadly, safety was not the norm in his life and when he was thirteen, Bishop Taban was kidnapped and forced to be a child soldier. His father begged the commander whose troops had captured Bishop Taban to release him, promising to devote himself to the armed struggle in exchange for his son's freedom. Eventually, the commander agreed and young Elias was brought to the Sudan-Uganda border. He walked alone into Uganda where he was found and rescued by UN staff.

Bishop Taban considers his survival an act of God's grace and has pledged his life to helping others, particularly those who find themselves in similar settings—sometimes literally. He lives in South Sudan and, as a religious and community leader, he works to build a stronger, healthier and safer community. He helps drill wells, build roads and care for orphans, war widows and children who, like him, were child soldiers or had to flee violence. One of the orphans he and his wife are raising was also found in the woods as a newborn. He works tirelessly against child labor, something that is still too common in his country and in much of the world, and works equally tirelessly for the rights of all children to go to school.

For much of human history, children worked and no one questioned it. Particularly children from poor families were expected to work, even in dangerous jobs. Sometimes especially in dangerous jobs, like in parts of factories, in underground mine shafts or up in chimneys that were too small for adults. In much of the developing world, children are still expected to work, because their families need the money or because they do. In rural areas, kids are most likely to work on their family farms. In cities, kids are more likely to work as beggars. And children are still doing dangerous jobs, even beyond soldiering.

In Somalia, an estimated two out of five children work, mainly as farmers, but also as soldiers and miners. Mining is notoriously dangerous work, more so in much of the developing world where there aren't yet the same laws to protect workers that we have in the U.S. There's a good chance a lot of these kids will be injured or even killed doing this dangerous work, in part because their lives are not considered as valuable as adults' lives, which is heartbreaking. I can't imagine anything *more* valuable, with more potential and promise, than the life of a child.

In Pakistan, children are often weavers (because smaller fingers can make smaller knots, which make for more valuable carpets). In many countries, children work in factories that manufacture clothing and shoes. American kids under fourteen are allowed to work in limited settings, like babysitting, in agriculture or for a parent (but not in dangerous places like factories). If you want to learn more about what work young people are allowed to do in the U.S., the website youthrules.dol.gov is a good resource.

*An early petition campaign from Free The Children. Twenty years later, they're still working to support communities all over the world.*

Making sure that more kids around the world get to go to school is hard, partly because eliminating child labor in much of the world is hard. Parents need better-paying jobs and more work so that they can afford to lose the income their kids bring home, and kids' lives need to be considered valuable, which would make child labor unacceptable and schooling the obvious alternative. Until around 1940, child labor (not just babysitting or minding the counter at your parents' store) was a part of American life. In the time of my grandparents and your great-grandparents, that changed. And while more than 500,000 kids still regularly do farm work and thousands more do other work (I had my first paid babysitting job at eleven), unlike in much of the world, kids in the U.S. have to go to school even if they work. If we could change mind-sets about school and child labor in the U.S. in the 20th century, surely we can do the same around the world in the 21st century.

Someone who's worked hard to do that is Canadian Craig Kielburger. One morning in 1995, when Craig was twelve years old, he read a story in the newspaper that would change his life. It was the story of the far-too-short life of Iqbal Masih. The son of a poor single mother from rural Pakistan, Iqbal was sold into bonded labor (basically slavery) when he was just four years old. For the next six years, he worked—and was abused—for twelve hours a day in a carpet factory. When Iqbal was ten, he was rescued by child labor activists and started speaking out about the cruelties of child labor and even traveled to the U.S. and Sweden to share his story. A few months later, back in Pakistan, he was shot and killed. He was only twelve when he died, the same age Craig was when he read Iqbal's story for the first time. Reading Iqbal's tragic story inspired Craig to create Free The Children with his brother and some friends.

What started as a small group of kids petitioning and writing letters (because email wasn't widespread yet and there was no change.org) to raise awareness about child labor has grown into an international movement. Still led by young people, Free The Children aims to support the needs of communities all over the world in a sustainable way so that children can get an education instead of having—or being forced—to work. They do this by building schools, health clinics and clean water systems and supporting family farms and small businesses so kids can go to school and hopefully not to work. There are lots of ways to be involved, particularly because Free The Children empowers young people to run campaigns close to home and around the world. To learn more about Free The Children's work and how you can engage, visit freethechildren.com.

## Some People Think Boys Are More Important Than Girls

Another big reason why there aren't more kids in school is that in many places, girls are valued less than boys, an outrage

I explore more in We're Not There Yet, which is focused on the global status of girls and women. Since girls are often valued less, it's not surprising that across the world, more girls than boys miss out on school. The gap between boys and girls in primary school has shrunk over the last twenty years. There are now ninety-six girls in school for every 100 boys, but in too many poor countries, the poorest girls often never go to primary school at all. In Somalia, very few poor girls go to primary school (95 percent don't). The effects of shutting girls out of primary school last their whole lives. Women are the vast majority of the world's illiterate adults—people who can't read or write—a crippling injustice that thwarts all sorts of progress. It's a lot of wasted potential. And we have a long way to go to fix this.

Globally, many more boys attend secondary school than girls. In many countries and communities, girls never go to secondary school and many more don't finish even if they start. In some countries, the rate of girls in secondary school is very low, in part because of long-held beliefs that girls shouldn't be allowed to go to school, that they'll take opportunities away from boys, that they couldn't possibly make as much money later in life as a boy could—so why bother? These beliefs still hold despite all sorts of evidence from economists that having more girls in school and women in the workforce is crucial to helping economies grow (creating more jobs for men too) and to moving families and countries out of poverty.

In many cultures, the math many parents do in their heads is that a son is worth the cost of secondary school fees but a daughter isn't. That type of thinking helps explain why in Niger, Burkina Faso and Mozambique, less than one out of every ten girls finishes secondary school. And yet the actual math shows the opposite: for every additional year of secondary school a girl (or a boy) gets, she earns 10 percent more money when she's later working—that's good for her, her family and her country. But math alone is rarely persuasive in changing thinking that's lasted hundreds or thousands of years.

It's not only mind-sets that are barriers to girls in school. Other challenges that affect girls more than boys are that the walk to school is often dangerous and sometimes schools themselves are not safe. According to a UN report, in recent years there were more than 9,600 violent attacks on schools, teachers and students across seventy countries. Every day in 2012, there was an average of ten attacks on schools, teachers and students around the world. In the U.S., we have had tragic school shootings, with the shooters motivated by their own twisted reasons. In much of the world, a specific warped reason motivates many of the attacks: violently singling out those who are standing up for the rights of girls to go to school. In 2012, a brave young Pakistani woman named Malala Yousafzai, whose picture is at the start of this section, was one such target.

Malala started blogging for the BBC World Service (a global news organization) when she was eleven, writing about the rights of all kids to go school, her fears of the Taliban and her determination to not allow the Taliban—or her fear—to stop her from getting the education she needed to make her dreams come true. One day, a group of Taliban militants boarded Malala's school bus and shot her in the head; they also shot two of her classmates. Miraculously, Malala and her friends survived. The Taliban tried to silence Malala's voice; they succeeded in helping her become a global and powerful advocate. Today, Malala is an international hero, and in 2014, Malala became the youngest person ever to win the Nobel Peace Prize. Sadly, Malala's situation is not unique. In far too many places, students and schools continue to be attacked by those who don't believe girls have a right to be educated. Through the Malala Fund, Malala continues to advocate for the right of everyone—boy and girl—to go to school and she's specifically working on helping more girls start and finish secondary school, while she herself is working toward her own secondary school graduation in the U.K. To learn more about Malala's efforts today and what you can do to help, read her powerful book *I Am Malala* and visit malala.org.

Another challenge that affects girls much more than boys is child marriage. Around the time of secondary school at twelve years old, and sometimes even earlier, many parents around the world expect their daughters to marry. Every day across the

## FACTS ABOUT CHILD BRIDES

One-third of girls in the developing world are married before the age of eighteen and one in nine are married before the age of fifteen.

Girls living in poor households are almost twice as likely to marry before eighteen than girls in higher-income households.

Girls with higher levels of schooling are less likely to marry as children.

Girls younger than fifteen are five times more likely to die in childbirth than women in their twenties. Pregnancy is consistently among the leading causes of death for girls ages fifteen to nineteen worldwide.

Girls who marry before eighteen are more likely than their peers who marry later to be hurt by their husbands.

Information source: International Center for Research on Women world, 41,000 girls are married before their eighteenth birthday. Many young brides quickly become mothers, making it difficult, if not impossible, for them to also continue going to school. Even if young women don't become mothers quickly, their husbands, their husbands' families and even their own families generally expect them to take care of their husbands and drop out of school. We will talk more about child marriage in the next chapter, We're Not There Yet. Thankfully, child marriage is becoming less common, albeit slowly, as countries make it illegal and families come to value girls more.

## Many Schools Aren't Prepared for Kids with Disabilities

Kids with disabilities have more often than not been excluded from school. They may have a hard time seeing, talking or walking, or not be able to see, talk or walk at all. They may face other difficulties that make it extra hard for them to get to school or learn in conventional classroom settings. In many places, schools don't have the resources or the teachers to help children with disabilities learn in a meaningful, dignified way. Across the world, as many as 150 million kids live with some form of physical or mental disability, some who have been disabled from birth and others who were injured permanently due to violence or accidents. In 1975, the U.S. Congress passed a law to ensure that all children who were able to go to school finally could, even if a child couldn't see or couldn't hear or couldn't walk like most of the kids who were already in school.

Most developing countries are where the U.S. was before 1975. And even in the U.S., our schools don't meet the needs of every student who has a physical or mental limitation. We need to do a better job in our own country of helping every student reach her or his potential, and to encourage other countries with the resources to do the same. And we need to help countries that don't have the resources we do find strategies to use technology and other tools to help kids who aren't in school because of disabilities (or other reasons) still get a quality education. We can't—and shouldn't—assume that countries with fewer resources to invest in education are insensitive to the right of disabled children to go to school (though some places may be). In many countries, the first priority is to get as many kids as possible into schools—by building schools, training teachers, acquiring textbooks and other supplies—rather than getting every kid into school, regardless of his or her abilities and limitations. Hopefully once countries have gotten most kids into school, they'll be able to focus on making sure every child, whatever his or her abilities and limitations may be, has a chance to learn.

Some kids with disabilities in the developing world could go to school if they had access to things like glasses, hearing aids and wheelchairs. One organization dedicated to helping kids in the developing world get wheelchairs, to go to school and generally to be able to get around, is the Walkabout Foundation. My friends Luis and Carolina Gonzalez-Bunster started Walkabout after realizing there were places in the U.S. that Luis, who is in wheelchair, couldn't go. That got them thinking about wheelchair accessibility around the world. When they learned that as many as 59 million people worldwide, including kids, need wheelchairs but have no means of obtaining them, they knew they had to do something. So they created Walkabout to donate wheelchairs to people, particularly kids, in the developing world who need them but can't afford them. The wheelchairs Walkabout donates are light, durable and rely on wheels made out of bicycle tubing, which are easy to repair virtually anywhere in the world. They've donated nearly 7,000 so far and they're working to raise awareness and more funds to help even more kids get to school, adults to work and everyone to have the essential freedom of movement. To learn more about what you can do to raise awareness about kids with disabilities or how you can raise funds to help a kid—maybe even someone your own age—get a wheelchair in the developing world, visit the website walkaboutfoundation.org.

Starkey Hearing Foundation works around the world to identify people who could hear if only they had the right hearing aids, or hearing aids at all. Starkey workers then fit people they think they can help with hearing aids, giving the gift of hearing. I've seen Starkey's work in action and it's amazing watching kids hear their mother's voice for the first time or watching people who lost their hearing in an accident be able to hear again after years of silence.

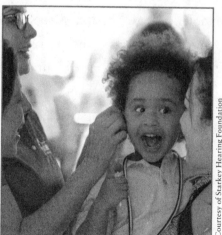

In many ways, those moments are only the beginning of Starkey's work. The foundation teaches everyone who receives a hearing aid how to care for and operate it and gives a year's worth of batteries to every person

*A hearing aid from Starkey Hearing Foundation opened up the world for this three-year-old girl from the Dominican Republic.*

Courtesy of Starkey Hearing Foundation

for their new hearing aids. It also trains local health-care workers, teachers and others to be able to identify hearing loss that can be compensated for with hearing aids so that more people can get help even after Starkey has left. Starkey has given away more than 1.6 million hearing aids to people across the world. There are now tens of thousands of kids in school because they can hear the teacher. To learn more and to see how you can get involved, please visit starkeyhearingfoundation.org.

## *It's Hard to Go to School in the Middle of a War*

In the midst of fighting or fear of violence, whether from a civil war as in Syria or the persistent threat of terrorism as in northern Nigeria because of a group called Boko Haram, life changes. What was normal largely disappears. Schools often are among the first affected. When teachers and students flee from violence and war, they leave their schools too. Sometimes, violence and war comes to schools. Armies or rebel groups frequently take over schools for their own violent purposes (such as for storing weapons or using as prisons). The threat of violence sometimes stops governments and communities from building schools in the first place because they think that the schools might be taken over or will have to be abandoned when fighting starts. Sometimes teachers refuse to work in conflict areas because they're understandably afraid they might get killed or lose their jobs if they have to flee. As many as half of all kids who aren't in school worldwide live in war-torn countries. War is a major reason why kids aren't in school.

War continues to affect kids' ability to go to school even after the fighting has stopped. It's hard to imagine being in school after your home was burned down or a parent or sibling was killed or you're living in constant fear that violence will start again. It's hard to stay in a school if you and your family are constantly running from outbreaks of fighting. Many refugee camps (the places many people live after they've fled their homes and sometimes even their countries) either don't have schools at all or have schools that are bursting with students and short on teachers.

Helping kids who are forced out of their communities by war or natural disasters stay in school is an area where we haven't made a lot of progress. The world needs to do more to figure out how best to help children who are victims of wars or natural disasters get an education, feel safe and recover so that they can lead normal, healthy lives after horrifying experiences. In 2015, there are more refugees than at any point since World War II, because there are more violent conflicts in more places. Although it's not clear what the best answers are to support people, especially kids, who will likely go home when the fighting stops (or to support people who stay in refugee camps or the countries they fled to), there are lots of people and organizations thinking about these questions and working to help families and children in refugee camps around the world today.

Someone on the front lines of such work is Joseph Munyambanza, originally from the Democratic Republic of Congo. He's motivated by his own story to help kids feel safe and get educated, even in dangerous situations. When Joseph was six, violent conflict forced his family to flee across the border to a refugee camp in Uganda. When he finished the camp's primary school, he received a scholarship to go to a secondary school in Uganda, outside of the camp (there were no great options in the camp). Unfortunately, the secondary school didn't go past grade ten. So, in 2005, when Joseph was fourteen and wanted to keep going to school, he and a group of friends started an organization called COBURWAS to educate themselves and other young refugees from the Democratic Republic of Congo, Burundi, Uganda, Rwanda and Sudan who at the time were living in Uganda (that's where COBURWAS comes from—it's a mash-up of all those countries' names). Joseph believed that with tutoring and support, more refugee kids would go to and stay in school (if there were schools to go to) or even go back to school if they'd dropped out.

That faith was clearly well founded. COBURWAS started by supporting dozens of refugee kids in pursuing their education, particularly at the secondary level, and has gone on to support hundreds more. Joseph also expanded COBURWAS's mission to help in the recovery of girls and young women who had been victims of violence, during war or tragically even while living in the refugee camp. Like Peggy's story, I first heard Joseph's at CGIU, in 2013. Joseph talked then about his plans to return to Uganda to get more kids in school and to change farming for refugees in the same way he's changing education. Today, Joseph, a new college grad-

Courtesy of Barbara Kinney/Clinton Foundation

*Joseph sharing the story of why he started COBURWAS to help refugees gain access to education.*

uate, is back in Uganda and hard at work. To learn more about COBURWAS and how you can get involved, please visit the website coburwas.org.

## *Some Schools Just Aren't Doing a Good Job*

Even in places where there are schools and teachers, the quality of education can be lacking (and that is a massive understatement). An estimated 250 million kids who are in school around the world reach fourth grade (or whatever fourth grade is called in their country) without being able to read or write. With so many kids packed into a classroom that may not have electricity or enough pencils and books, it's hard to imagine that much learning can take place, even with an amazing teacher. For other kids, school may only be available in one language and it's not the language they speak at home with their families. This is a big problem. More than 220 million kids are estimated to have to go to school in a language they don't speak, at least when they walk in for their first day of class.

Then there's a broader question that every country confronts, including the U.S., which is how well does school prepare students for the lives they want to lead and the careers they want to have when they graduate? Many of the most exciting fields in the U.S. and around the world—technology, computer science, engineering—are where new jobs are being created. Yet even in the U.S., very few high schools (2,100 out of 42,000!) and even fewer elementary or middle schools teach either computer science or coding. The same questions apply in the developing world, so if parents don't feel like there's a point to all that schooling—that it won't translate to a better job in the future—it may be harder to persuade them to make the sacrifices now to help get their kids safely to school or to forgo the income their kids are earning from working or begging. That's why it's so important for students and families to help decide what schools teach and how it's taught, in every community, in every country across the world.

If you want to know more than what is discussed in this chapter, there are lots of good sources. As was true in the previous chapter, most are written more for grown-ups and for experts than they are for kids, but you might find them helpful anyway. One such example is from the UN, which you can find at en.unesco.org. It has more information about the challenges I talked about in this chapter and on what's helping get more kids into school across the world. Fair warning—it's a great resource, but it's filled with lots of statistics and not as many stories (in other words, if you don't really love statistics like I do, you might find it important but also a little boring).

If you want to help others get more informed about global education, think about how you can encourage people you know who build and design websites to help make kid-friendly sites describing the challenges of getting every child into a good school. Or maybe that's something you could work on with your friends (you'll probably design something better for kids than a bunch of adults would!).

You can also focus on helping solve any of the specific challenges discussed in this chapter. If you're focused on helping kids who are refugees, you can support Joseph's organization, or Save the Children, an organization that works with UNICEF (the United Nations agency focused on kids), to protect kids around the world after natural disasters or conflicts. You can learn more about this shared work or the other work UNICEF and Save the Children do to support kids around the world by visiting their websites at unicef.org and savethechildren.org.

## Help Build Libraries and Fill Their Shelves

If you love reading and going to your local library, maybe you want to help kids learn to read and help them have more to read. Room to Read builds libraries as well as schools and classrooms. They fill the libraries and classrooms they build with books in kids' local languages (this is particularly important for the more than 200 million kids mentioned earlier who start school not in their first language). Room to Read has helped build more than 17,000 libraries around the world, published more than 1,000 books across many local languages and distributed more than 14 million books!

In 2012, almost 10 million books were checked out of Room to Read libraries throughout Tanzania, Zambia, South Africa, Cambodia, Laos, Sri Lanka, Bangladesh, Nepal and India. You can organize a read-a-thon with your friends or classmates in which adults or local businesses pledge a certain amount of money for each book you read. You can find Room to Read's kid-specific site at roomtoread.org/students.

## Help with Math

Just like there are programs aiming to increase traditional literacy and access to books, there are programs to increase math literacy around the world. In 2013, while he was still a graduate student at Santa Clara University, Alejandro Garcia started Math Multipliers, an after-school mentoring program to help kids in the Dominican Republic learn and improve their math skills. After only a few months, Alejandro had recruited so many students and math mentors, he took a leave of absence from his new job at Google to build the program even further. A while later, Alejandro left his job at Google to work on Math Multipliers full-time. His long-term vision is to incorporate computer programming, robotics and physics, expanding to other Latin American countries and to the U.S. To learn how to get involved or how you might start a similar program helping kids with math in another country or even in your own community, visit multiplicadores.do.

There've been lots of innovative attempts to use technology to improve access to quality education around the world—whether linking up students with mentors or giving a laptop to every kid or providing devices with books and learning materials preloaded onto them. These have had mixed success, because many places don't have reliable electricity to charge the devices or wireless service to download educational materials. Thankfully, NGOs, charities and even businesses working in this space are learning and adapting. The potential of technology to help improve education, whether basic literacy or learning how to code, regardless of whether you're at school in the U.S. or a village in Haiti, is immense.

One technological innovation that is helping spread literacy far and wide is Worldreader, which makes more than 20,000 books available for free on basic phones (in other words, phones many technological generations older than the smartphones you're likely used to seeing). This is great because it means kids can get books faster than it takes to build a library or school, and they can get books they want to read—not just ones that were preloaded onto a device.

Millions of people, including lots of kids, have downloaded the Worldreader app and more than 1 million people are reading their free books every month across fifty-four developing countries. Kids are now able to read—if they or their family has a pretty simple

*A kid reading one of Worldreader's books!*

phone—books like the Nancy Drew series in English (which I loved as a kid), plus many books in their own languages. You can support Worldreader by making a donation—or suggesting your favorite book that you think any kid anywhere should be able to read! You can learn more at worldreader.org. Think how cool it would be to know a kid in Rwanda read a book because you recommended it.

## BABY TALK

Education starts well before any kid walks into a classroom. More than 80 percent of our brains are built by the time we are three years old. Wow. Even before babies can talk at all, hearing words—whether through talking, singing or reading—is important to brain development. Parents, older siblings, friends, everyone around kids of any age are now encouraged to talk, read and sing. A lot.

This is something kids of all ages can do to help young children, whether your little brothers and sisters or other kids you know, even babies. You can talk about anything—how you're feeling, what you're learning in school, the football game you watched, the movie you saw. Truly anything. In any language. In any country. What's important for brain development is that kids hear words. Lots of words. It's a simple way we can all make a difference. Older kids can help younger kids' brains grow and literally become smarter while parents or caregivers are at work. For suggestions on how to talk to babies and little kids, one helpful site is talkreadsing.org, a partnership between Sesame Street and Too Small to Fail, an initiative of the Clinton Foundation, and one I am particularly grateful as a new mom myself to be part of.

## PUNISHMENTS

As mentioned at the beginning of the chapter, I believe you and your parents know the most about what your school needs to give you the best education possible. All across America—in government offices, around kitchen tables and in schools—we're having conversations about what education should look and feel like and be in the 21st century. Most of the conversation focuses on what we want kids to learn and how we want kids to learn. Some focuses on the environment we want kids to learn in. One area that is fairly unique to the United States, particularly among other wealthy countries, is corporal, or physical, punishment in schools. More than 100 countries ban corporal punishment in schools. When I was in elementary school in Little Rock, corporal punishment, specifically paddling or spanking with a wooden board, was still legal and even encouraged when students misbehaved or stepped out of line in certain defined ways. As I learned while researching this book, corporal punishment is still legal in Arkansas if the school district approves it. In total, nineteen states still allow corporal punishment.

I was paddled in first grade. A boy in my class told me a certain bad word was the highest compliment anyone could ever give a teacher. I foolishly believed him and promptly walked up to my extraordinary first grade teacher, Mrs. Mitchell, and repeated the bad word with a massive grin. Mrs. Mitchell was appropriately and immediately horrified. I realized something had gone very, very wrong and frantically started apologizing. Mrs. Mitchell brought me out in to the hallway and consulted with Mrs. Phillips from across the hall, another first grade teacher at Forest Park Elementary. Mrs. Mitchell then asked me why I'd said what I said and I explained I thought it meant that she was wonderful (but I didn't tell on the little boy—I didn't want to be a tattletale). Mrs. Mitchell said she believed me because she'd

## STATES IN WHICH CORPORAL PUNISHMENT IS STILL LEGAL, 2014

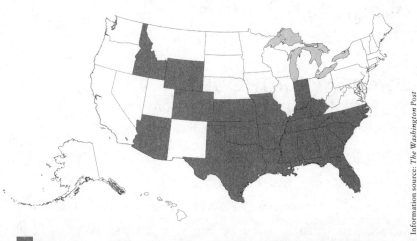

Information source: *The Washington Post*

States that allow corporal punishment: Alabama, Arizona, Arkansas, Colorado, Florida, Georgia, Idaho, Indiana, Kansas, Kentucky, Louisiana, Mississippi, Missouri, North Carolina, Oklahoma, South Carolina, Tennessee, Texas, Wyoming never heard me say anything bad or mean before but that she also expected me to know better than to believe everything I was told. And, even though she believed me, Mrs. Mitchell told me she had to paddle me. Afterwards, I promised that next time, I would ask her what a new word meant before I used it.

I felt awful that day almost thirty years ago—Mrs. Mitchell was more than just a teacher I revered, she was one of my favorite people. Today, Mrs. Mitchell is Dr. Mitchell and the Associate Superintendent of Elementary Education in Little Rock and I still see her sometimes when I'm in Little Rock. I will always be grateful for the valuable lessons she taught me that day, including that not everyone always tells the truth (and sometimes people even outright lie!) and that the best teachers teach us far more than just how to read, add and subtract (though those are all important too).

As is true with all aspects of this chapter and your own school, you have to decide if corporal punishment is an issue you care about, and whether or not you think it's always okay, sometimes okay or, as I do today, never okay for schools and teachers to punish kids by paddling.

## SHARE YOUR THOUGHTS, RAISE YOUR VOICE

Ultimately, education is about you and your future. It's about what you're learning and it's also about what kids around the world are learning—or not, partly because their future will affect your future, just like yours will affect theirs. It's okay if you don't want to help build schools or libraries around the world (though I hope you do!). You can have a real impact by sharing your thoughts and ideas about your local school and what you think every kid everywhere should know, with your parents, your teachers, online through platforms like change .org and anywhere else you can find an audience. You could also start a group in your school or community to bring kids together around an issue you care about. As I said at the beginning, adults should listen to you, particularly about your school. To have us listen, you need to raise your voice and I hope you will!

# Get Going!

- Share some facts from this chapter with your family and at least three people you know, raising awareness about major barriers to school attendance, like child marriage
- Join a campaign with Free The Children to support kids and their communities all over the world
- Join organizations like Girls Not Brides that are working to eliminate child marriage
- Share stories like Joseph's to convey how much kids will do to go to school, including helping start a school, even in a refugee camp
- Support organizations like Save the Children or COBURWAS helping kids go to schools in refugee camps or after disasters
- Encourage people who build or design websites to make one just for kids about education around the world
- Or if you and your friends like making websites, you can create one yourself

- Support Walkabout Foundation's efforts to get more wheelchairs to more kids so they can get to school
- Support Starkey Hearing Foundation's work to get more kids the hearing aids they need to be able to learn at school
- Start a Pencils of Promise club in your school
- Start a Building Tomorrow club in your school
- Organize a read-a-thon to raise money for Room to Read
- Suggest a book you think kids everywhere should read to Worldreader
- Support PACE or other teacher/teaching-assistant programs around the world
- Talk (or sing or read) to any kids you know who are under age three to help their minds grow
- Start a program in your community to help everyone work together to make your schools the best they can be
- If you're thirteen or older, use social media to follow any of the organizations above or celebrities (like John Legend) who are champions of getting more kids into school around the world
- Sign a petition—or start one!—on change.org to raise awareness about something you want to change in your own school or school district

Courtesy of Girl Effect

CHAPTER FOUR

# WE'RE NOT THERE YET
## GENDER EQUALITY

Have you ever noticed that sometimes girls are talked about differently or even treated differently from boys? The first time I realized girls and boys were sometimes (or even often) treated differently was one night when I was in first grade. My mom was at the Parent Teachers Association (PTA) meeting in the Forest Park Elementary School cafeteria. I was in the playroom with the other kids; we we were all waiting for the meeting to end and our parents to come pick us up. John (I've changed his name) kept teasing me and I kept ignoring him. Until he pushed me down and sat on me. He said it was the only way to deal with an annoying girl, he taunted me, called me ugly and said other nasty things. After the "annoying girl" and "ugly" bit, the other specific things he said are admittedly a bit hazy. What is definitely clear (in addition to the first insults) is my memory of being shocked, hurt and surprised.

Once I got over the disbelief of John sitting on me, I asked him repeatedly to please get off (though I might have started demanding it after a while). When he refused to move (after I'd asked nicely), I shoved him off me. The teacher who was supervising walked over then, chastised me and told me that was very unladylike behavior. I apologized and explained that he'd sat on me! And wouldn't move even after I had asked nicely (and said please)! She seemed not to care very much and gave me a warning, saying as a girl, I should have known better, behaved more like a lady and needed to accept that boys will be boys. I remember being very confused. I knew I wanted to always be polite and courteous, but I also knew I wanted to be able to defend myself.

I had a similar experience in eighth grade with an even more aggressive boy. It was much scarier and much more unpleasant. I was again chastised by the teacher while he got a similar "boys will be boys" reaction. That experience more than twenty years ago was far from the last time I've been called ugly, been bullied or otherwise been put down at least in part for being a girl. I've been criticized for speaking up too much or, more often when I was younger, not speaking up enough. I've been blamed for being too tough when men in similar situations have been applauded for their strength of character or integrity. And I've definitely had men try to intimidate me by using their size. But even so, I've always known I was very lucky on many fronts.

For every mean boy or aggressive man, for every teacher who wanted to put me and other girls in a box, I've had more friends, teachers and mentors who have supported me. My parents and husband have always encouraged me to find my own path, and for the most part, my friends were also lucky enough to have parents who supported their dreams. I believe that every girl and woman should have the chance and the choice to be who and what she wants to be, whether it's a wife, a mother, a professional or all of the above. We have so much data now that says when girls and women can make choices for themselves personally and professionally, that's good for their health, their families' health and their countries' economies. Increasingly, in the U.S. and across the world, more and more people recognize this and more and more countries are making discrimination and violence against women illegal. But there are still places where these things remain legal and we have work to do to ensure any girl, anywhere, can have any dream she wants and the opportunity to pursue that dream throughout her life.

In some parts of the world, the worst thing that can happen to a family—as they see it—is to have a daughter instead of a son. Even today, some communities and families continue to favor boys. Yet more so than at any point in human history, girls and women have a greater chance to lead lives of our own charting, to go to school and hold jobs that would have been inconceivable in the past. In much of the world, girls today can dream of being scientists, doctors, race car drivers, entrepreneurs, presidents, prime ministers or teachers—and more boys can see their mothers, sisters and female friends in all those roles. But that's not true everywhere. We're still not there yet on girls and women having equal rights and equal opportunities to those of boys and men.

Everywhere a girl is born, her race, ethnicity, religion and how much money her family has all influence whether she has a better chance and more choices than her mother did to follow her dreams. Sometimes, her choices are limited by customs as well as by laws. Sometimes, she has no choices at all as to whether or not she goes to school, gets married or works. A lot of the information in this chapter is from a report Melinda Gates (an activist and all-around inspiring woman), my mom and I launched early in 2015 called No Ceilings: The Full Participation Report. If you like data, I hope you'll check it out at noceilings.org.

## WHAT GIRLS CAN AND CAN'T DO LEGALLY

Legal rights are all the things that women and girls are guaranteed by law to be able to do. Legal prohibitions are all the things that women and girls are legally not allowed to do, sometimes these are things men and boys are allowed to do (meaning if a boy does it, he's not breaking the law, but if a girl does it, she is). For thousands of years, basically for all of human history, in almost every society, men controlled their countries, their communities and their families, including their wives and daughters. For most of that time, this went unquestioned by most people—men were supposed to rule, protect and provide for their families, while women raised children, tended to their homes and took care of their husbands. Often, this included lots of hard work such as farming, hauling and chopping firewood, tending to animals, cooking and cleaning, in addition to having and raising children (which is arguably the hardest—and definitely the most important work of all!).

Over the past few decades, women around the world increasingly have gained the legal right to work and to vote, while girls increasingly have received the right to go to school. But there are still many places where girls and women do not legally have the same rights that men and boys have. This is part of what I mean when I say "we're not there yet" on gender equality. Laws and how societies treat girls and women both need to change. Sometimes, people in power change laws first and then social practices and customs catch up. Other times, it's the opposite; groups of people organize, raise their voices and demand a change and then people in power change laws. Regardless of how it happens, equal legal rights—and a right to equality—are important.

Nine countries in the world still legally restrict women's movement. What this means is that in some countries, women can't walk, drive, bike or otherwise get from home to work or to see friends or even go to their neighbor's house down the street without a male family member saying it's okay and then going with them or taking them. In Yemen, except in emergencies, women can't even step outside their own front doors without the permission of their husbands. Can you imagine if every woman you knew, whether your mom or grandmother or a teacher, had to get permission first from a father, husband or brother before

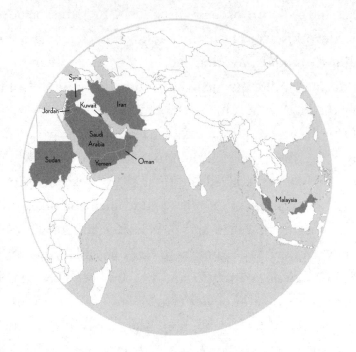

Information source: WORLD Policy Analysis Center

going outside? In Saudi Arabia, even if you have your husband's permission to go, for example, from home to work, you can't drive yourself. You need your husband or another man to drive you, because women aren't allowed to drive, anything, anytime. No cars, trucks or buses. Can you imagine driving down the street and seeing only men behind the wheel? It would probably look pretty odd, because you're used to seeing women driving alongside men.

There are places where women are literally valued less in the eyes of the law. In Yemen, women are considered only half as valuable as men when they're witnesses in a trial. Two women have to testify to equal the testimony of one man. There are also a number of cases in which women are not allowed to testify as witnesses, including theft. Can you imagine if your bag was stolen and the only witness was a woman, but because she couldn't testify to what she saw, the criminal would get away?

## *She Voted!*

Women won the right to vote around the world in most places in the 20th century and in a few others early in the 21st century. In the United States, women got the right to vote in 1919, and voted for the first time in 1920, when my grandmother Dorothy was a year old. Nowhere—in no country, in no state, in no territory—did women automatically get the right to vote. Wherever women have the right to vote today, it's been because of hard work by women and men, often over decades, convincing people in power and society at large that letting women vote is the fair and right thing to do. In many countries, women were bullied,

*A group of suffragettes in New York in the 1910s who fought to win the right to vote.*

*Women going to vote in Pakistan in 2010.*

beaten, imprisoned, tortured and even killed while working for the right to vote. But now, in 2015, women have the right to vote in every country in the world where all men have the right to vote too.

In my lifetime, a number of countries across the world granted women the right to vote for the first time. Having the right to vote is often only a first step. Being able to safely exercise that right is often harder, even dangerous for some women, and sometimes dangerous for women and men alike. In many countries where women are denied a meaningful right to vote, men are too. To be clear, that shared inequality and lack of rights is nothing to celebrate. And, in some countries and communities, women have the right to vote but are still expected to vote however their fathers or husbands tell them to. That's not real equality.

WHERE ALL WOMEN HAVE GOTTEN THE RIGHT TO VOTE, 1980-2015

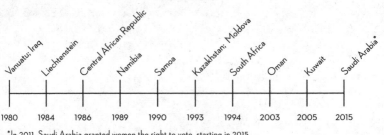

*In 2011, Saudi Arabia granted women the right to vote, starting in 2015.

Information source: No Ceilings Database

## Women Who Work

In many countries, there is at least one legal barrier to women's ability to work in the jobs they want or to start their own businesses. There are rules about what work women can or can't do. There are rules limiting women's rights to own their own businesses or to take out a loan. There are rules restricting when women can open a bank account (if at all), often an important first step to starting a business or even having a job. Imagine if you had a great idea for a business, but weren't allowed to start one, or if you wanted to be a scientist, but were barred from the lab—just because you were a woman. In most countries, it's still legal for employers to decide not to hire women, or to pay them less if they do, just because they're women. In some countries it's still legal to not hire pregnant women just because they're pregnant. Imagine how you would feel if you were more qualified than the other people applying for a job and you didn't get it just because you were a woman—or just because you were a woman who was about to have a baby.

Those are the realities for many women across the world. In a recent global survey, close to four out of ten adults—men and even women (can you believe that?!)—agreed that men should have first dibs on an open job, rather than the more qualified person, regardless of gender. And even if they can get jobs, women are sometimes not allowed to sign any type of contract, which means they're much easier to fire (regardless of whether there was a reason to fire them). In some countries women are forced to retire earlier than men, so they can't work as long as they'd like to. Can you imagine if you (or your mom or your grandma) wanted to keep working, and the boss said you weren't allowed to? Not fair. At all.

## What Women Can Own

In at least twenty countries, women do not have the same inheritance rights as their brothers. In the most severe instances, this means that when their parents die, a brother will get all of the family's money, land and businesses . . . and his sister will get nothing. In some countries, what women own legally becomes their husband's when they get married. Can you imagine if you worked hard, but your husband had the right to tell you what to do with all the money you earned? Or if your parents died and your brother could then kick you out of the house? This is the reality for many women in the world today. Not too long ago— until around 1900—this was also the reality for many women in the United States. It took even longer for unmarried women in the U.S. to have the right to own property and keep all of the money they make at work.

*Women farmers produce 60–80 percent of all the food in the developing world. These women are part of the Clinton Development Initiative's program in Malawi to help increase their crop yields, income and ownership of the land, which is good for them and their families.*

Courtesy of Peter Kasengwa/Clinton Foundation

Yet, even in many countries where women can own property, they rarely do. This is because they're not expected to, they're not encouraged to, and because trying to do so might mean that their husbands, fathers or brothers would hurt them. Women farmers produce a majority of the developing world's food. It's impossible to imagine the diet in sub-Saharan Africa and Asia without women farmers. There are lots of different estimates on how much of that land women actually own but no one thinks it's close to 50 percent. In many places, women's work largely benefits men.

## *Marrying Far Too Young*

In the developing world, one out of every three girls gets married before she turns eighteen and one in nine gets married before she turns fifteen. That works out to more than 15 million girls getting married every year. In all, more than 720 million women around the world today were married before their eighteenth birthday. Can you imagine getting married so young? To someone your parents likely chose for you? To someone you've probably never even met? To someone who's likely (much) older than you are? Maybe a lot older than you are? In many countries, girls aren't given a real choice. It's what's expected.

In Niger, which has the highest percentage in the world of women who were married as girls, more than three out of four women were married before they turned eighteen and close to one out of four before their fifteenth birthdays. Niger isn't alone in allowing girls under fifteen to marry. More than one out of

HOW OLD GIRLS HAVE TO BE TO GET MARRIED
AROUND THE WORLD, 2013

Information source: No Ceilings Report

Countries where marriage at 15 is not legal

Countries with no data

Countries where marriage at 15 is legal in certain circumstances

every three girls in the world who married before eighteen lives in India. In the U.S., Canada, most of Latin America and much of sub-Saharan Africa, girls under fifteen can marry if their parents say it's okay. In certain U.S. states, there are still laws on the books saying girls can marry, if their parents and a court approve, as young as thirteen or even twelve (Massachusetts)! Even though parental consent is required, it's not a healthy message to send that girls are ready to get married at twelve or thirteen. That's when girls should be in seventh or eighth grade learning algebra or thinking about how to set up an Instagram account when they turn thirteen.

One amazing young leader working to help more girls be girls, not brides, is Memory from Malawi. Memory's sister Mercy was forced into marriage at only eleven and by sixteen had three children and was no longer in school. Memory became

### HOW OLD YOU HAVE TO BE TO GET MARRIED IN THE U.S.*

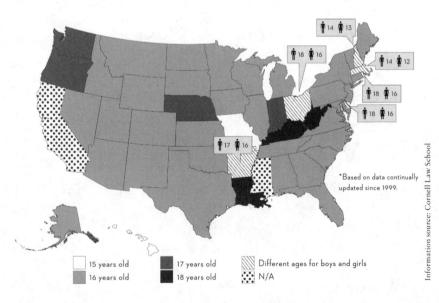

*Based on data continually updated since 1999.

Information source: Cornell Law School

15 years old   17 years old   Different ages for boys and girls
16 years old   18 years old   N/A

an advocate to end child marriage, bringing voices like her sister's into the conversation in her community and her country so that people understood child marriage not just as a concept, but in the very real ways it denies girls the right to make choices for themselves (like whether to go to secondary school). Memory and other advo-

Memory's sister Mercy was forced to get married at eleven years old. Here Memory is talking to a member of Malawi's parliament about why no girl should ever have to get married.

cates against child marriage have clearly made an impact—in early 2015, Malawi passed a law banning child marriage. To learn more about how to end child marriage and join the global movement to do just that, you can visit girlsnotbrides.org. And to find out more about young women all over the world who are raising their voices to make change in their communities around child marriage and more, visit letgirlslead.org.

# HEALTH

## *Pregnancy and Babies*

One thing everyone in the world has in common is we all have belly buttons. One area where the world has made progress is helping mothers stay alive while they're pregnant (why we have belly buttons) or while they're having children. There are more doctors, nurses and particularly more midwives and skilled birth attendants in the developing world who've been trained specifically to help support pregnant women and safely deliver their babies. They play a key role in making sure every mother can stay healthy and deliver a healthy baby. Improved sanitation (remember—no mixing of poop and water) and hygiene (lots of hand-washing and keeping medical tools safe and sterile) for midwives, family members and anyone around pregnant women have also been important. Still, around 800 women die every day due to preventable complications while pregnant or giving birth.

One death is too many. The majority of women around the world who die while pregnant or giving birth are poor. Most die in sub-Saharan Africa and parts of Asia, but poor women are vulnerable everywhere, including in the United States. In fact, in the last twenty years, the U.S. is the wealthy country that has seen the biggest rise by far in the percentage of moms who die while they're pregnant or giving birth. In 2013, the U.S. ranked sixtieth in the world on maternal mortality (meaning fifty-nine countries did a better job keeping pregnant women and new moms alive and healthy).

Why? Many American women are obese, have high blood pressure or have diabetes when they get pregnant, and even though those are health risks in general (as we'll talk about in Staying Healthy), they're especially dangerous for pregnant women. In the U.S., women living in poverty—particularly immigrant women—who are obese are most at risk, both because they're overweight and because they're less likely to see a doctor, nurse or midwife regularly (and so they're not getting the care and advice all pregnant women need). Going to a doctor can reduce these risks. You can help educate people in your life who are pregnant or thinking of starting a family about how important it is to try and eat healthy, keep their blood pressure low and to go to the doctor as soon as they find out they're pregnant, if not even earlier.

Every Mother Counts is a great place to start to learn more about what you can do to help mothers in the U.S. and around the world get the care they need for themselves and their babies. Started by the courageous Christy Turlington Burns after she had a very scary experience with the birth of her first child, Every Mother Counts helps raise awareness about what's needed to ensure every mother can have a safe, healthy pregnancy and delivery. If you want to know even more about the work they and other organizations are doing to save mothers' lives around the world, you can visit everymothercounts.org.

## Making Dinner (and Breakfast and Lunch)

Another health risk billions of women every day confront relates to cooking. Nearly 3 billion people in the developing world cook or are dependent upon food cooked on open fires or using simple, often hand-made stoves. Instead of using electricity (because there isn't any) or gas (because there isn't any), women (who do most of the cooking) rely on a mix of more basic fuels like wood, animal dung and coal. Breathing in the wood or coal fumes weakens and damages people's lungs and also increases the risk for various cancers, heart disease, pneumonia and cooking-related injuries like burns or blindness. The women who are generally doing the cooking and the children who are frequently nearby are the most likely to be burned or get sick over time from the smoke. More than 4 million deaths every year are linked to exposure to smoke and fire from unsafe cooking. We don't often think of cooking as dangerous, but clearly it is for so many around the world.

One way to make cooking safer is to spread the word about the need for what are called clean cookstoves and fuels, something my mom has long championed. Clean cookstoves are still simple and can use local fuel sources (like wood or charcoal) or cleaner options like solar energy. They're safer for women to use, in part because they emit less dangerous smoke and burn fuel more efficiently. They're

*Example of an unsafe cookstove and a safe, clean cookstove.*

also generally better for the environment. To learn more about different types of clean cookstoves (like what works best in China versus what works best in Guatemala) and what you can do to help, check out cleancookstoves.org.

## *Violence Against Women*

Probably the biggest health problem facing women today is violence. Health experts estimate one in three girls and women have suffered some form of physical violence or abuse in their lives, most at the hands of someone in their family—a husband or partner, a father, a cousin, an uncle, a brother or a grandfather. This violence knows no boundaries. It affects girls and women of all nationalities, races, ethnicities, religions and income groups. Violence also comes in many forms and we need everyone to combat it, including men, like Jimmie Briggs and Brian O'Connor. Through the Man Up Campaign, an organization he founded, Jimmie works to educate people, particularly young men, about why violence against girls and women is never okay—and not good for men either in their own families or communities. Man Up has helped men like Thierry Kajeneza, an activist from Burundi, become more vocal on women's rights and more effective in protecting and supporting women in their own communities across his country.

Brian O'Connor runs a program called Coaching Boys Into Men, part of Futures Without Violence, an organization that has been working to prevent violence for more than thirty years. Coaching Boys Into Men works with high school athletic coaches across the U.S. and around the world to give them the tools and training they need to promote respect among their athletes for one another and for the people in their lives, along with what they learn on the field or turf. Coaches learn how to help their teams understand that violence is never okay. In southwestern Pennsylvania, Woodland Hills High School football player Jo-El grew up seeing his father abuse his mother. Coaching Boys Into Men helped him understand how important it is that he and his teammates respect and stand up for their mothers and all the girls and women in their lives.

Work like Jimmie's and Brian's is so important because violence against women sadly is common everywhere. This is partly because in many countries it is legal for a husband to hurt his wife if he wants to, without any fear of consequences (in other words, the police won't come because he hasn't broken the law). Even in places with laws that say men can't do that, many women do not report violence for fear of punishment. Even when women do report violence, the men who abused them are not usually charged with a crime or punished. That's sadly true in the U.S. as in so many countries.

In some countries, many people—even women—think it's okay for husbands to use violence to make a point or "win" an argument with their wives. In Ethiopia almost one out of two women think it's okay for a husband to beat his wife. This has an impact long after a wife or mother has recovered. Witnessing violence as a child is a risk factor for experiencing violence later in life—girls watch their mothers or sisters being abused and do not know that it's never okay for someone to hit or beat them or anyone. They grow up expecting violence and are often hurt later in life by their boyfriends and husbands.

Courtesy of Girl Up

*It's not just girls supporting each other—boys are supporting girls too (like here after a race this Girl Up club ran together as a community service project).*

It's not only family members who pose risks to girls and women. Human traffickers are criminals who take people, generally women and even young girls, from their homes by force or by tricking them—promising good jobs or education while all along planning to sell their victims into slave-like conditions or outright slavery. Because girls are generally perceived as less valuable to their families than their brothers, they are especially vulnerable to being turned into slaves. At any point, there are approximately 2.4 million people who have been trafficked from one country to another and as many as 30 million people living and working in slavery. Yes, slavery—in our world today. Most are women and girls who aren't allowed to go to school, to lead their own lives, to make their own decisions and who suffer horrible abuse and violence. Many will die in slavery.

Women and girls are also uniquely vulnerable to violence during conflicts or wars. As you may have read in religious stories or history textbooks, armies and soldiers have used violence on civilians (versus solely on other soldiers) as a tool of war and terror forever. Sadly, this still happens today. While men are more likely to die in an armed conflict—because they're more likely to be soldiers and therefore directly involved in fighting—women are more likely to die from the indirect effects of conflict. That may be from violent abuse or because they can't get the medical care they need when they're pregnant or having babies. Yet women are still only rarely included in the negotiations between leaders that end wars or in the resulting peace agreements that countries and combatants commit to live by. Not surprisingly, in the few peace talks, like in Guatemala or Sudan, where women were meaningfully involved, the resulting agreements included support to help women who were victims of violence and their families heal and move forward. That's good for women and their families—and for their societies. It matters who's in the room.

Someone who takes over every room she's in is Sana (I have changed her name to protect her identity). I had the honor of meeting Sana at an event. She helped create the Girl Declaration, a document shown in the opening photograph of this chapter, with other girls from developing countries that puts girls at the center of every conversation about health, the economy, rights and ending violence (you can find the Girl Declaration on girleffect.org). Sana continues to work to end violence against women in her home country and across the world. And while she's not waiting for the grown-ups, she's also determined that working against violence not be her job alone. In one appearance, Sana said that she is fighting against child marriage and to end violence against women, and asked the audience what they were going to do. It's a question we all should have an answer to, and not just those of us who are (or once were) girls.

## GIRLS IN SCHOOL

As mentioned in Time for School, globally, girls are not in school at levels equal to boys, and there are many reasons why this is true particularly in secondary school (remember that's what middle school and high school are called in much of the world). While progress has been made, it's been uneven around the world. For example, in Niger, there were thirty-seven girls for every 100 boys in secondary school in 1990. In 2012, it was sixty-seven girls for every 100 boys. That's a big increase, but it's also still a lot of girls missing from secondary school—girls who were likely married off or considered less valuable than the school fees their parents would have to pay.

Other countries have made relatively more progress. In some places, like Lesotho, there are a lot more girls in secondary school than boys. While that at first may seem very cool (to a girl), often it's because boys are already working in places like mines or factories. It's not good when boys are missing from school either. The view that girls don't deserve to be educated, aren't worth the schools fees, need to work (child labor), are more fit to be wives (child marriage) and concerns about safety are just a few reasons why girls are not in school.

Safety is a major concern as many girls are hurt or abused on their way to and from (or even in) school. This is partly because

## Numbers of Girls vs. Numbers of Boys in School

### Did you know?

Girls are not in school at equal levels to boys, and while progress has been made, it's been uneven around the world. Here are some examples:

For every 100 boys in secondary school...

Niger had 37 girls in 1990 and 67 girls in 2012

Malawi had 58 girls in 1990 and 90 girls in 2012

Turkey had 59 girls in 1990 and 95 girls in 2012

China had 73 girls in 1990 and 102 girls in 2012

Chile had 106 girls in 1990 and 104 girls in 2012

Lesotho had 157 girls in 1990 and 140 girls in 2012

Information source: UN

girls, like Malala, are targeted for exercising their right to go to school, and partly because, in too many places, men and boys still think it's okay to harass and abuse girls. This may be another thing that sounds obvious, but the best way to help get girls safely into school is to support schools committed to doing just that.

In Kibera, a large slum in Nairobi, Kenya, Kennedy Odede started a free school for girls to provide a high-quality education in an environment where it's safe for girls to learn and play. It's appropriately named Shining Hope for Communities (SHOFCO for short) and today is made up of the girls' school plus a variety of services open to the public, including a health clinic, a clean water facility and a library with Internet access, all sending a signal that SHOFCO is investing in girls and their families, friends and neighbors.

SHOFCO is transforming its Kibera community, and it all started with a focus on girls, like Esther (whose name has been changed for her safety). Esther was an orphan who, after being taken in by an uncle, was overburdened with housework, which she was expected to do before she did anything else (like her homework). She was

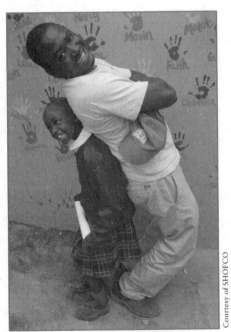

*Kennedy with one of his students. (Notice that she is holding him up!)*

severely beaten by her uncle's wife. Already a student at the Kibera School for Girls, Esther was brought to SHOFCO's safe house, where she was given the time and space to heal. Today, she's thriving personally and academically. Esther dreams of being a teacher when she grows up, and even of starting her own school, just like Kennedy did, where girls can be safe while studying and dreaming.

Getting to know Kennedy and his wife, Jess (his partner in SHOFCO), over the past few years has been inspiring—and a lot of fun. If you look at the picture of Kennedy here and the one of Jess surrounded by their students on the back of this book, I think you'll understand why. I had the chance a couple of years ago to see their work firsthand in Kibera and to meet the remarkable SHOFCO girls. Given all Kennedy's already done in Kibera—and all he hopes to do for girls—I wasn't surprised that most people called him "Mr. Mayor." Any place would be lucky to have a visionary leader like Kennedy. For more about SHOFCO, about how you can get involved, and to learn more inspiring stories like Esther's, visit shofco.org.

## COMPUTERS, CELL PHONES AND ENGINEERS

Santa Claus gave me my first computer in 1987. It was a Commodore and looked nothing like the computers you likely use. It was clunky, weighed a ton and had only one color on its home screen (a weird green). But to me, it unlocked a magical world, populated by Carmen Sandiego (you've probably never heard of her, but she starred in her own pretty awesome game) and pioneers along the Oregon Trail (another game you're probably not familiar with that I bet you could find online if you were curious). I remember when I sent my first email in high school and my first tweet only a few years ago. I remember when I got my first cell phone during my senior year in college. Today, I couldn't imagine my life or our world now without technology, without computers, cell phones, the Internet or social media.

In 2013, approximately 2.7 billion people used the Internet and there were almost 7 billion cell phone numbers. More cell phones have been bought than there are people in the world, and they're almost as common in the developing world as in the developed. Yet in many places women are less likely than men to own a cell phone or have access to the Internet. This may be because their fathers or husbands don't think it's appropriate for girls and women to have the freedom to call who they want or look up what they want online. Or it may be because women are more likely to be poor and then unable to afford a cell phone, computer or trip to an Internet café.

Whatever the individual reasons, an estimated 200 million more men than women have access to the Internet in the developing world. Three hundred million more men than women have cell phones. Can you imagine if you couldn't use Google or Wikipedia for research or couldn't call a friend or your parents, just because you're female?

Across the world, girls and women aren't just less likely to have access to technology, they're also less likely to be involved in the making of new technologies or to be part of the so-called STEM fields: science, technology, engineering and math. This is true in the U.S. and virtually everywhere. In the mid-1980s, around when I got my first computer, women were a little more than one out of every three computer science college graduates in the U.S. When I graduated from Stanford in 2001, women were a little more than one out of every four computer science graduates. In 2012, it was less than one in five.

The decline in women computer science graduates is particularly surprising since women are now the majority of college graduates in the U.S. So why is this happening? Well, here are a few possible explanations. There aren't as many female role models in STEM for girls (or boys) to look up to.

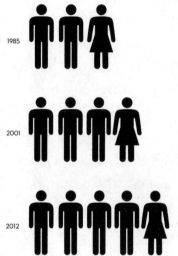

PERCENTAGE OF COMPUTER SCIENCE COLLEGE GRADS IN THE U.S. WHO ARE FEMALE, 1985-2012

Information source: National Center for Education Statistics

In general, girls are called on less in middle school science and math classes, so girls are sent a subtle but persistent message that their answers or opinions are less valued in those subjects. There's also little general awareness of how computer science and coding relate to the future of all kinds of jobs—in fashion, film, even farming (like for knowing when crops should or shouldn't be watered) and more—not just to the newest cell phone or computer.

The absence of young women in computing has attracted a lot of attention recently—because it's so stark and because the U.S. expects to have more than a million new jobs in computing and technology by 2022. Our country needs as many people as possible, including as many women, who are qualified and interested to fill those jobs and help imagine the next Pinterest or the next big animated hit movie like *Frozen*. We need more girls to understand how coding and computer science can help shape a career in almost any field—and schools to help support more girls (and boys) in imagining such careers. And that's not only true in the U.S., it's true everywhere. No country can be as creative or productive as possible if it leaves half its population (girls) behind. Recognizing this, various national, state and local efforts have been created in an attempt to recruit more STEM teachers and engage more girls in STEM subjects.

Technology companies are also on the front lines of these efforts, because they know if they're not getting the best and most creative brains, they're not going to be able to develop the next cool new products. One way Google is trying to attract girls to technology is through the initiative Made with Code, which looks to show girls how, increasingly, everything, including in fields like fashion, is "made with code." If you want to learn more and participate, you can visit madewithcode.com.

Another effort, led by the remarkable Reshma Saujani, is Girls Who Code, a nonprofit program that teaches female high school students how to code and mentors the young women in the program as they create their own innovative apps. Girls who've participated in Girls

*Girls Who Code teaches girls how to code and create very cool apps, many that help people in very real ways.*

Who Code have created apps that help kids with autism learn through music, help users decide what items to recycle, help improve public safety by locking a phone's texting function when a driver is going over fifteen miles per hour and even one to help girls learn self-defense. Alise and Diamond, members of the Chippewa tribe in Minnesota, created "Ojibwe Helper," an app to help preserve their heritage and culture through teaching their traditional Ojibwe language to app users. Very cool. If you're interested in learning more and applying, go to girlswhocode.com.

The Girl Scouts has built an awesome program (that I wish had been around when I was a Brownie) to help Scouts and Brownies build STEM skills. Check it out at girlscouts .org. The Girl Scouts also recently introduced an option for Brownies and Scouts to start online cookie stores, helping girls build e-commerce and entrepreneurship skills. I loved selling (and eating) Girl Scout Cookies when I was a Brownie and wish this had been an option twenty-five years ago! Boys can help too—by encouraging their sisters to get involved in STEM (whether to sell cookies or to create apps), by playing and even designing games together and by talking

*As a Brownie, I loved selling Girl Scout Cookies at my mom's law office and wish I could have learned how to sell online too (though there was no online yet)!*

Courtesy of the Author's Parents

about women pioneers in math and science like the women pictured here.

*Dr. Marie Curie helped invent X-rays; Dr. Mae Jemison was the first African American woman in outer space.*

## WHO'S RUNNING THE COUNTRY?

In many countries, most people (women as well as men!) say they would not support a woman to serve in a legislature or congress or to lead their country as president or prime minister, no matter how well qualified she was. That helps explain why in early 2015 less than one in every four members of parliaments and congresses around the world is a woman. In the U.S., in 2015, it's less than one in five. In early 2015, nineteen countries currently have a woman president or prime minister. That's out of almost 200 countries in the world.

Almost everywhere there are more women in national office today than ten or twenty years ago, but we've got a long way to go to reach equal representation.

In many cities and villages around the world, there's been more progress in terms of women being elected as mayors or to

## COUNTRIES LED BY WOMEN IN EARLY 2015

Information source: Inter-Parliamentary Union and UN Women

## COUNTRIES WITH THE HIGHEST AND LOWEST PERCENTAGES OF FEMALE REPRESENTATION IN NATIONAL PARLIAMENTS OR CONGRESSES IN EARLY 2015

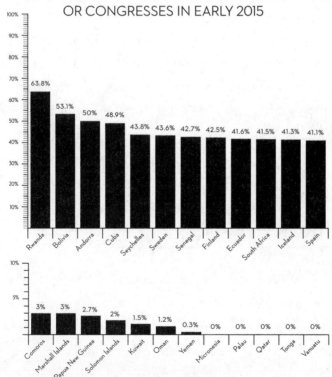

These numbers reflect the representation in single- or lower-house parliaments.

Information source: Inter-Parliamentary Union and UN Women

serve on local councils. In India, village councils generally are required to have 50 percent women, so that the councils look more like the population (equal numbers of women and men). There are lots of different views about the role of such rules, known as quotas, to give more women the chance to participate politically (or in business). Some people think quotas are great because they guarantee that women are included; others think they are terrible because they limit choice (meaning in seats reserved for women, only women candidates can run). You will have to decide whether or not you think quotas should be used to create opportunities for women like in Indian village councils.

Today, more than 1 million women serve on local village councils in India, some through quotas and others who win open seats in general elections. This greater and more visible public service by women has helped change policies and mind-sets. Indian girls now have female village council chiefs and members as role models. That's revolutionary—it transforms immediately what girls think possible for their own lives and what their parents think possible and acceptable for their daughters. More and more Indian girls are not just seen as future brides and mothers, but also as future leaders.

## WORKING HARD

You can't make decisions, or even participate, if you're not allowed in the door, if you're not allowed to apply for the job you want or make the most money you can (and deserve) while in that job. For those reasons and others, millions and millions of women (and also millions of men) work in what's called the shadow economy (because if there were sunlight on it, no one would think it was okay) all over the world. Their work is considered "unofficial"—even though crops wouldn't be picked and houses wouldn't be cleaned without their hard work. They're not counted as "official" because they're not registered with the government and not paying taxes. There are also millions of women, if not billions, who do most of the important work taking care of their children and homes. They're also not counted as part of the labor force, even though without people doing those jobs, the world would stop. Dinners wouldn't be made, laundry wouldn't be done and children wouldn't be cared for.

Looking at the people who in 2015 are running the biggest businesses in the world, there are few women. But, like in politics, there are more than there were twenty years ago. In 1995, there were zero women CEOs among the Fortune 500 companies, a name for the 500 largest companies in the United States. The top ten includes names you're probably familiar with like Walmart, Exxon, Apple and General Motors. In 2015, 5 percent of the Fortune 500 had a female CEO. So yes, there are some women now in the Fortune 500 CEO ranks, just not many.

One such example is Ursula Burns. She's the CEO of Xerox and the first African American woman CEO of a Fortune 500 company. Ursula started off as an intern at the company and rose to the top. I'll never forget Ursula telling me a few years ago how important the support and mentorship she got at home, in school and at Xerox was to her success—it's why she is so committed now to mentoring young people at Xerox, particularly young women.

The people who are ultimately responsible for companies and who hire the CEOs (like Ursula) are groups called boards of directors. Each company has one, and CEOs work for their companies' boards. In 2009, only 10 percent of public company board members in wealthy countries were women. In the U.S., in early 2015, it's less than 20 percent. There are more board directors named John, Robert, James and William than all women combined, of any names (please don't think the moral of the story here is for more babies, including girls, to be named John, Robert, James or William . . .).

BREAKDOWN OF U.S. BOARDS OF DIRECTORS BY GENDER, 2015

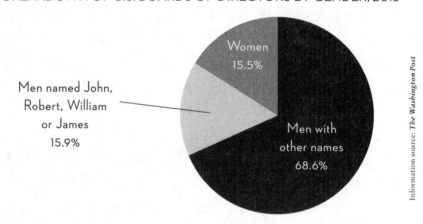

Information source: *The Washington Post*

I think these statistics are particularly surprising because women are more visible in more and different types of professional settings than ever before. Think about who you see as teachers, school principals, doctors, nurses, pharmacists, or people who work in or manage department stores, grocery stores, restaurants, movie theaters and more—probably at least some, maybe even lots, of the professionals you see during a normal school day or weekend are women. But the people we don't see who are managing school districts, hospitals, pharmacies, department stores, restaurant chains, movie theater chains— most, the vast majority, are men. This is what's referred to as a leadership gap for women. Someone who's worked hard to shine a light on the women leadership gap that still exists at the top of almost every industry is one of my heroes and friends, Facebook Chief Operating Officer Sheryl Sandberg.

As Sheryl and others have pointed out, there are many reasons why so few women hold corporate leadership positions. A big one is that many companies lack policies that support women who want to work and be moms—for instance they don't give new mothers (or fathers) paid time off after a new baby is born so they can bond with their children and not worry about losing their jobs. Another is that women don't expect and then don't ask for more career opportunities, for more raises, for more chances to get ahead. Yet another is (again) the absence of positive female role models. We need more people who look like Ursula Burns or Sheryl Sandberg—and more women and men focused on mentoring young women to be the next Ursula or Sheryl, and more women believing they themselves can be the next Ursula or Sheryl.

You may have heard the term "glass ceiling"—those barriers, like the ones listed above, that are invisible but very real in preventing women from advancing to leadership positions. Now used broadly, the term "glass ceiling" originated to describe what happened to many women in the workplace. Women would get hired at a law firm, or at a supermarket, school or hospital, and they would work hard and get good reviews (the equivalent of straight As). But then they wouldn't get the same raises men in the same jobs would receive. They wouldn't get promoted to jobs with more responsibilities at the same rate as men, even relatively less qualified men (think of someone with Bs getting all the awards rather than the person who got As).

Not fair, but still all too common, even in the United States.

There's not just a leadership gap (many more men than women in power) but there's also a pay gap (what it sounds like—men earning more at least in part because they're men!). In the U.S., women earn seventy-eight cents for every one dollar men earn. That compares all women who work full-time with all men who work full-time. Critics of that comparison say it doesn't take into account things like different types of jobs or different levels of education or age. While that's true, it's also true that economists and others who study the pay gap think a significant chunk comes from gender discrimination. That means women are paid less because they're women and for women with the most education, the pay gap is the largest. Although things have gotten better in the past few decades, a recent report said at the current rate of progress, the pay gap wouldn't close until 2058. That's forty-three years away, and literally a lifetime from now—you will be in your fifties before women are earning the same as our husbands, friends and even our sons!

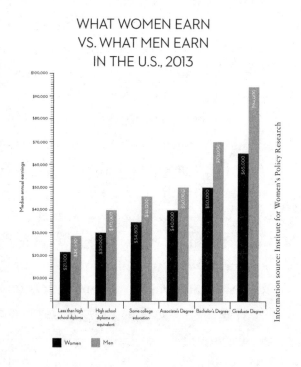

WHAT WOMEN EARN
VS. WHAT MEN EARN
IN THE U.S., 2013

Information source: Institute for Women's Policy Research

# SCREENED OUT . . . WHERE ARE GIRLS AND WOMEN?

It's hard to imagine what we can't see. We all look to news media and the entertainment industry, whether newspapers or magazines, movies or video games, apps or music videos, to help us better understand what's happening around the world (news media) or what's being made possible or imagined (entertainment). One recent study showed that only about one in four news stories worldwide focused on women. In business and political reporting, it's an even lower percentage. While that's somewhat understandable since most leaders in politics and business are men, the news media has an important role to play in highlighting women who are coming up in the ranks in all these fields. Their breaking the glass ceiling should make them worthy of stories, until it's no longer exceptional that a woman is a CEO or prime minister.

Women aren't only missing from the stories being told. They're also missing from telling stories. A recent study in the U.K. showed that men wrote almost four out of every five stories on the front pages of British newspapers. Women are missing from commenting on the news too. You've probably seen lots of "experts" on TV, whatever channel you're watching. Another recent report showed that only about one out of every five TV experts on all major television channels in the U.S. was a woman. This is despite millions of women now holding PhDs, law degrees, medical degrees and having years of experience working in and starting businesses, running for and holding office, treating patients, doing research, teaching at the university level and doing all sorts of other things that generally make one an expert.

*Emma, Sammi and Elena with their petitions asking for a woman to moderate one of the presidential debates.*

Another place where women often were missing was in moderating U.S. presidential debates. In 2012, New Jersey high school students Emma, Sammi and Elena launched an effort on change.org in support of a woman moderator for at least one of the major presidential debates in advance of that year's election. Within a week, they had more than 100,000 signatures on their petition. They reached out to the executive director of the Commission on Presidential Debates (an organization that does exactly what its name implies—oversees presidential debates) to make the case for a woman moderator on behalf of everyone who signed their petitions. They never heard back. So, as you can see in the picture, they went to Washington and delivered a flash drive with all the signatures—and boxes full of printed-out signed petitions. While no one from the Commission ever met with the students or acknowledged that the petitions made a difference, shortly after their trip to D.C., a woman moderator was announced for one of the 2012 presidential debates for the first time in twenty years. It's not hard to think that Emma, Sammi and Elena may have made a real difference.

PERCENTAGE OF FILMS WITH WOMEN LEADS
AROUND THE WORLD, 2012

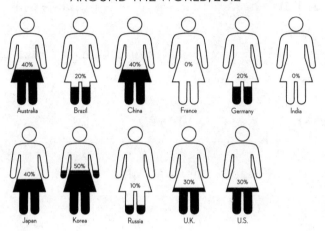

Information source: Geena Davis Institute on Gender in Media

Just as women are often missing from news media, women are often missing from movies too. In 2012, only 10 percent of popular movies across the world had roughly equal speaking parts for women and men in lead parts! It's hard to imagine what you can't see (or can't hear). Some places are better than others. Some places are worse than others. India and France had no female leads in the 2012 movies researchers watched. Not a one. Wow. There are also a lot more male movie directors making big movies—the ones that come to your local theater—than female. In the U.S., less than 10 percent of major movie directors are women, and it's not much better elsewhere. If the graphic here were about directors instead of movie stars, it wouldn't look much different.

It matters who tells our stories. In movies (most of the time made by men), comments about how a character looks—hair, body, eyes, if someone is pretty, if someone is thin—are almost always about a woman or girl. Female characters (even young ones) receive comments about their appearances five times more often than male characters, sending a not-so-subtle message that girls are judged mainly on their appearance. This is reinforced by what women are not doing in movies—often, they're not working. In the real world, women are more likely to work than not. In movies the opposite is true.

## FEMINIST . . . OR NOT?

Words matter—a lot—but we shouldn't get so hung up on them that we worry more about words than actions. You may have heard the terms "feminist" or "feminism." If you look them up in a dictionary, you'll see the actual definition of feminism is the idea and belief that women should have equal rights to men. A feminist is defined as someone who believes the same. When I'm asked, I always say I am a feminist because I absolutely believe women should have equal rights to men, that girls should be able to get an education, that a woman should be able to vote, have any job she wants, own property, travel and make the decisions she thinks are right for herself. And when my husband, Marc, is asked, he answers the same way, for the same reasons.

Both words, feminist and feminism, have become loaded terms in recent years, for women and men. This is partly because there are still people who don't believe women should have equal rights to men and who believe it's okay to insult, criticize and even bully girls and women. For others who absolutely believe women should have equal rights to men, they're terms that feel dated or old. What matters more than any given term is what you believe. If you believe that girls and boys should be given an equal chance to succeed in school and life, we have to work to erase all legal, cultural and social obstacles that still remain across the world for girls and women. And maybe you could come up with terms that capture the same meaning without any of the controversy about the words themselves.

What else can you do in addition to inventing new words? You can watch media—at home, online, in movie theaters—with strong, healthy female characters and avoid media that only focuses on what women look like rather than who we are. Entertainment companies want to make what people want to watch—if we prove we want more strong female characters in movies, shows, apps, games, websites, then more will be made. You can help send the same message to news companies by reading stories about strong women who are moving up the corporate ladder, the political ladder, the entertainment ladder, the fashion ladder . . . you get the picture (no pun intended).

Speaking of pictures, you can also help your friends realize that part of the job of movie stars and models is to look good for the photos and movies they're in, and they spend many hours and lots of money on exercise and healthy food. If you want to help close the imagination gap of what it's okay for girls to look like or what it's okay for women to do, you can create and share your own stories with strong female characters (maybe you or your friends) who are valued for their hearts and brains and not their bodies. That's what's so great about Tumblr and other platforms that didn't exist when I was younger—you can create powerful, amazing stories to share with your friends or the whole world and the only cost is your own time. You can also tell media companies you want more real people (not just fictional characters) who look like . . . real people.

Maine-native Julia did just that. In 2012, when she was in eighth grade, Julia, her friends and fellow activists launched a petition on change.org asking *Seventeen* magazine to start printing unaltered or un-photoshopped images on their covers and in their magazine. More than 85,000 people signed Julia's petition—and *Seventeen* listened. It made a commitment to no longer alter photos and images and to show what real girls and women look like.

You don't have to be on the cover of a magazine to be targeted for what you look like or who you are (or who people think you are). Anyone can be bullied, and too many people of all ages, but particularly kids, are. We can all stand up against bullies, whether they're boys or girls, who say nasty things about people's bodies, whether it's about their weight or type of hair or height or anything. It's also important to ask for help if you're scared or if you don't know how to stop a bully—sometimes standing up to a bully means turning to a parent, teacher, older sibling or trusted adult. There is no shame in asking for help. We all need help sometimes. I wish I had asked for help earlier when the boy sat on me in first grade—the teacher may still have dismissed my concerns, but I'll never know. We'll talk more about bullying in the next chapter.

Girl Up is an organization that helps girls learn about how to speak up for themselves and for girls who are vulnerable in their communities and around the world. It also helps girls learn how to support one another and stand up to bullies. There are more than 850 Girl Up clubs across the world—many started by girls themselves. In 2011, in Belize, Thandiwe started a girls empow-

*Girl Up helps girls become strong and empowered women.*

Courtesy of Girl Up

erment club, which later became the very first Girl Up club in her country. She worked with Girl Up to empower girls in her high school and community through workshops and celebrations on International Day of the Girl and through UN Women's 16 Days of Activism. Thandiwe has Devic's Syndrome, an autoimmune disorder, but she didn't let that stop her from mobilizing girls to stand up for themselves at school, at home and in their communities. To learn more about starting your own Girl Up club, you can visit GirlUp.org. And boys can join and start Girl Up clubs too! You can also think about how to celebrate Women's History Month (March), International Women's Day (March 8th) and International Day of the Girl (October 11th) in your school or anywhere to help make women who inspire you more visible to your friends and community.

A lot of what's discussed in this chapter is serious and can be hard to talk about. If you want to help raise awareness about the challenges girls and women still face but don't want people to tune out because it can be scary or depressing, check out the Half the Sky game on Facebook, either on your own if you're at least thirteen or with your parents if you're younger. It's a great way for anyone to learn about these issues and to learn more about amazing people and organizations working to empower and support girls around the world.

Not every woman or girl who is given an opportunity will succeed—and not every woman or girl given an opportunity will succeed in ways you or I might support. There have been women CEOs and prime ministers whose policies and practices I haven't agreed with, but I'm thrilled they were there to be criticized instead of not there at all. We will never know what we as a world can accomplish unless we allow the half of the world too often ignored, held down, denied and abused—otherwise known as girls and women—to be educated, supported, freed from violence and empowered to dream big and pursue those dreams, whatever their income level or race. We've made progress, but we're still not there yet.

# Get Going!

- Raise awareness about challenges girls and women still face around the world today—because they're girls and women—by sharing some of what you learned in this chapter with your family and at least three friends (CARE has great snapshot statistics you can also post, tweet or pin)
- Go online to join the movement against child marriage at girlsnotbrides.org
- Share inspiring stories of young women leaders around the world, like Malala's and Memory's, and learn about other inspiring girl leaders through Let Girls Lead at letgirlslead.org
- Encourage women who are pregnant to eat healthy and see a doctor
- Support Every Mother Counts to help women in the U.S. and

around the world have safe, healthy pregnancies

- Spread the word about the need for safe, clean cookstoves through the Global Alliance for Clean Cookstoves
- If you're a girl who is interested in science or math, apply to Girls Who Code and check out Made With Code
- Support programs like Shining Hope for Communities (SHOFCO) that are focused on getting more girls into safe and good schools
- Spread the word about the Girl Declaration (found at girleffect.org) and tell everyone—including boys and men— how important it is to value girls
- Go to movies with strong women characters in them (not ones with just men) and to movies directed by women
- Read—and comment on—news stories about girls and women
- Write—and share—your own stories about strong girls and women
- Start a petition to get your favorite magazine to stop photoshopping models
- Stand up for yourself or your friends if they're bullied because they're girls (or for any reason)
- Start your own Girl Up club in your school
- Help organize a celebration of International Day of the Girl
- If you're at least thirteen, use social media to follow organizations (like SHOFCO) and leaders (like Melinda Gates and Christy Turlington Burns) who are working to protect, support and empower women around the world—play the Half the Sky game on Facebook too (and share it with a friend if you like it!)
- If you want to know even more about the rights and opportunities for girls and women around the world, visit noceilings.org

# PART III

# It's Your BODY

Courtesy of Magi Linscott

CHAPTER FIVE

# STAYING HEALTHY

When I was seven, my grandmother Ginger, my dad's mom, asked me what I wanted for my eighth birthday, which was then a couple weeks away. I said I wanted her to quit smoking. I'd recently read every Beverly Cleary book I could find in the two bookstores in Little Rock's Park Plaza Mall and the library near where my mom and I went to church. Ramona Quimby, one of Beverly Cleary's main characters, quickly became one of my heroines. In one book, Ramona launches a campaign to get her dad to quit smoking. I was prepared to launch a similar campaign if Ginger (my grandma preferred "Ginger" to "Grandma") had said she couldn't or wouldn't quit. Thankfully, she said she would try and she more than tried, she succeeded. When she got sick with breast cancer a couple years later, her doctors told her she had a better prognosis because she had already quit smoking before she got sick. I don't know how much longer she lived because she had stopped smoking, but even one extra day made her gift to me on my eighth birthday the best birthday gift ever.

*Here I am with my grandma Ginger in 1988.*

Courtesy of the Author's Parents

If you just looked at news headlines, you might think most people in the United States die of cancer or maybe in horrible car crashes. You might also think most people in the developing world die of HIV/AIDS or, in 2014, maybe of Ebola. And, sadly, people do die in car crashes and of cancer in the U.S. every year and more than 11,000 people have died of Ebola in the most recent outbreak, as of May 2015. As awful as those all are, they are not the main things people die of around the world. The leading causes of death in the United States and in all but the poorest countries on earth are heart-related. In 2012, cardiovascular diseases, or diseases of the heart and circulatory system, took the lives of three out of every ten people who passed away around the world. The same year, more people died from cancer than from HIV/AIDS, TB (tuberculosis) and malaria combined. This is not to trivialize infectious diseases. As we'll see in the next two chapters, if left unaddressed, infectious diseases can kill millions of people very quickly. Rather, recognizing how deadly heart disease is helps us be aware of all the risks we face, wherever we live, so that we can better protect ourselves and our communities.

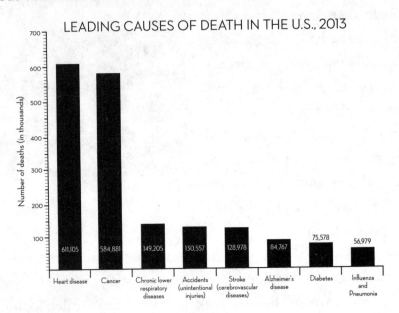

LEADING CAUSES OF DEATH IN THE U.S., 2013

Number of deaths (in thousands)

| Heart disease | Cancer | Chronic lower respiratory diseases | Accidents (unintentional injuries) | Stroke (cerebrovascular diseases) | Alzheimer's disease | Diabetes | Influenza and Pneumonia |
|---|---|---|---|---|---|---|---|
| 611,105 | 584,881 | 149,205 | 130,557 | 128,978 | 84,767 | 75,578 | 56,979 |

Information source: Centers for Disease Control and Prevention (CDC)

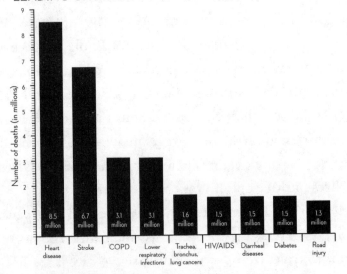

LEADING CAUSES OF DEATH AROUND THE WORLD, 2012*

Number of deaths (in millions)

| Heart disease | Stroke | COPD | Lower respiratory infections | Trachea, bronchus, lung cancers | HIV/AIDS | Diarrheal diseases | Diabetes | Road injury |
|---|---|---|---|---|---|---|---|---|
| 8.5 million | 6.7 million | 3.1 million | 3.1 million | 1.6 million | 1.5 million | 1.5 million | 1.5 million | 1.3 million |

*Heart disease includes ischaemic heart disease and hypertensive heart disease.

Information source: WHO

This chapter focuses on what are known as noncommunicable diseases (sometimes called NCDs for short). These include heart disease, cancer and diabetes, diseases that you don't "catch" from another person the same way you catch a cold or the flu. The term "noncommunicable disease" is a mouthful to say and also not quite accurate. There are some viruses that increase cancer risks. And there are some behaviors or habits that increase the risk of heart disease or cancer that we do arguably "catch" from our family and friends (meaning we're more likely to do things, like smoke cigarettes, if our friends and family already do them).

You may have family members and friends, like I do, who have had heart disease, diabetes or cancer. You may have lost a loved one to one of those diseases as I have. My grandma Ginger died of breast cancer and my mom's dad, who I called Pop-Pop, had diabetes and died after suffering a stroke. I miss them and wish they, as well as my grandma Dorothy and Ginger's husband, Dick, all had lived long enough to meet their great-granddaughter, Charlotte. They tried to make the best decisions they could about being healthy based on what they knew at the time. When Ginger started smoking as a young woman in 1940, she didn't know how bad smoking was for her lungs or her health; nobody really did. When my Pop-Pop was diagnosed with diabetes, he started eating a much healthier diet—but he hadn't known how much of what he ate before was bad for him. What we know now is that staying heart healthy can help us avoid heart disease and minimize our risk for getting cancer or diabetes. Being heart healthy can help us all lead healthier—and longer—lives.

You may have heard the saying: "Knowing is half the battle." It's how G.I. Joe cartoons would end in the 1980s (when I was watching them). It means you have to know what to do, but then you actually have to do it. But "doing it" in heart health is often hard, particularly for people living in or near poverty. Families and communities, schools and charities, the government and private companies all have a role to play in helping heart health be an easy, affordable and even fun choice for everyone, particularly for kids. We'll talk more about what that means later in the chapter.

## HEART DISEASE

### *The Heart of the Matter*

Hearts have fascinated me for as long as I can remember. When I was little, I thought each of us had a mini Thomas Edison inside our body electrifying light bulbs to help our hearts pump. Somewhat silly and wildly inaccurate, but I've long been captivated by the fist-sized muscle that fuels our bodies and beats due to its own electrical system.

Our hearts are amazingly powerful, beating about 100,000 times every day, powering 2,000 gallons of blood throughout our bodies, carried by a series of arteries and veins. We literally feel life through our hearts. They beat faster when we're excited or scared and they beat faster to help us run or jump. This is part of what makes the epidemic of heart disease across the world so tragic. This most essential organ is increasingly tied to rising amounts of sickness and death. In the United States, more than one in three American adults have some variety of heart disease and it's the number one killer of American men and women. It's expensive, too. Heart disease alone cost the U.S. $444 billion in treatments in 2010. That's close to how much money all the Walmart stores in the world earned in 2014.

Heart disease is a wide category. It includes anything that hurts either the heart's ability to do its pumping job, or our arteries' and veins' ability to carry blood throughout the body. These are distinct from congenital heart defects, which include irregular heartbeats, tiny holes in the heart and enlargement of the heart. Congenital heart defects are present from birth, often requiring surgery on tiny infant patients. We don't know a lot about what causes congenital heart defects but we do know they're not triggered by the choices we make about what we eat or whether we smoke—because clearly infants haven't made any such choices for themselves yet. That's very different from what we know about heart disease.

For adults, and also for kids, the choices we make about what we eat, how much we move around and how we deal with stress all influence our heart health and risk for heart disease, partly by affecting things like blood pressure. Hypertension, or high blood pressure, heart attacks, cardiac arrest and strokes are common types of heart disease and ones you've probably heard of, maybe even experienced in your own families. High blood pressure happens when a person's arteries narrow, forcing the heart to work harder to pump blood through them. Untreated or uncontrolled high blood pressure increases the risk that a person could have a heart attack or stroke. Most people with high blood pressure have no symptoms, so it's important to go for your annual checkups and encourage your parents, grandparents and others to go for theirs, since blood pressure will be checked as part of those visits.

Heart attacks occur when blood flow to the heart is blocked, or even prevented, often because something called plaque (think sticky deposits) has accumulated in the arteries. It's a similar process to when plaque builds up on your teeth if you don't brush them. Plaque results from, among other things, too much cholesterol and fat in someone's diet, and

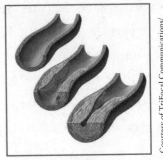

*Increasing plaque buildup in arteries isn't pretty; even more, it's dangerous.*

high blood pressure is generally a warning sign of clogged arteries (another reason to go to the doctor to get it checked). Arteries can become so clogged that very limited or even no blood can get through, including to the brain, which can result in a stroke.

If you see someone who has numbness or drooping on one side of his or her face or arm and who is having difficulty speaking clearly, that person may be having a stroke. If you see someone experiencing chest pain or tightness, shortness of breath or wheezing, particularly if he or she has a history of heart disease, that person may be having a heart attack. And women having a heart attack may have different symptoms than men, including fatigue, back pain or an upset stomach. Strokes and heart attacks in kids are not common but sadly do happen. Anyone of any age can call 911 and should immediately (or ask an adult to) if you think someone is having a heart attack or a stroke. The sooner treatment starts—like providing oxygen and a mix of medicines to prevent heart damage after a heart attack—the better.

When there's an electrical malfunction in the heart and the heart stops, that's called cardiac arrest. It happens very quickly and without warning; adults or kids in cardiac arrest collapse, lose consciousness and stop breathing. They also lose their pulse because their heart has stopped. In addition to calling 911, you can (and should) perform what's commonly known as CPR—shorthand for cardiopulmonary resuscitation—while waiting for emergency help to arrive. Traditional CPR has two main parts: chest compressions (pushing hard and fast on the center of someone's chest) and assisted breathing (blowing air into the patient's mouth). The American Heart Association now recommends that people without advanced training (meaning most of us) perform only chest compressions. This is known as "Hands-Only CPR."

You can perform CPR correctly once you're at least nine years old, provided you're strong enough, which is something a CPR instructor can help you figure out. There are online CPR course options that are available for free and can help you start learning about CPR, but it's not something we can learn through online videos alone. Just like we generally need to be taught how to ride a bicycle or kick a soccer ball (at least that

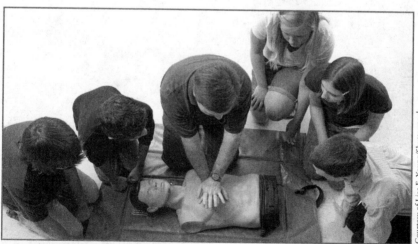

*Kids practicing Hands-Only CPR and learning how to save a life.*

Courtesy of Lisa F. Young/Shutterstock

was true for me), we need to be shown how to perform CPR so we know how to properly administer chest compressions. And then we need to practice. A lot.

Increasingly, states are offering CPR training at the high school level, and some states, including Arkansas, where I'm from originally, have started making CPR training a prerequisite for high school graduation. If you don't want to wait until high school, you can encourage your elementary or middle school to start offering CPR training to students who meet the strength requirements. The American Heart Association's BetheBeat.heart.org is a good place for your school to find CPR lesson plans. It also has free resources for kids on learning CPR basics.

AS OF EARLY 2015, TWENTY-TWO STATES REQUIRE CPR TRAINING FOR HIGH-SCHOOL GRADUATION

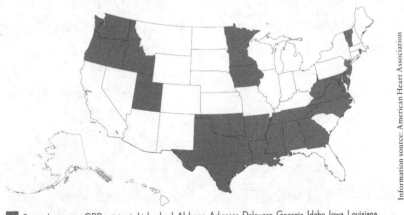

Information source: American Heart Association

States that require CPR training in high school: Alabama, Arkansas, Delaware, Georgia, Idaho, Iowa, Louisiana, Maryland, Minnesota, Mississippi, New Jersey, North Carolina, Oklahoma, Oregon, Rhode Island, Tennessee, Texas, Utah, Vermont, Virginia, Washington, West Virginia

Even knowing a little can save a life. Doctors recommend that it's better to try chest compressions than do nothing if you think someone is in cardiac arrest provided that person is at least eight years old. If you see someone in cardiac arrest, you can perform "Hands-Only CPR" and double or triple the chance of that person's survival. That's incredible and it's something we can all be ready to do (and do even better with training) if we're strong enough.

## How to Help a Heart

What can be done in addition to CPR? Well, sometimes doctors perform minor or major surgeries on the heart to prevent a heart attack as well as to treat one. My father had quadruple bypass surgery in 2004 after experiencing chest pains and shortness of breath. In bypass surgery, doctors build a detour around the part of a blood vessel that's too clogged for blood to flow through. All of that sounds scary, but if it's necessary, it's lifesaving. I am grateful every day that my dad called his doctor quickly after experiencing tightness in his chest and she recommended he come in immediately. He started taking medicine and had his bypass surgery a couple of days later.

After my father got out of the hospital, he thankfully listened to his doctors and followed his prescribed regimen of exercise, healthier eating and limiting stress—well, he's still working on the last one! He completely changed his diet, eating less fat, less cholesterol, less sugar, more vegetables and more whole grains. He started walking regularly, most weeks walking at least four days and often walking a couple of miles each time. My father's doctors' recommendations are fairly standard. My mom and I strongly supported my father's healthier eating choices and walking routine because we wanted him to feel better and lead a (much) longer, healthier life.

One way you can help a heart disease patient in your life is to encourage them to make healthier and often different choices after a heart attack, stroke or a serious heart scare like my dad's. Actually, this is all good stuff to do to prevent heart disease too. You can learn how to cook healthy and tasty meals as a family and even exercise together. My dad walks with my mom, with their dogs, with friends—and yes, sometimes alone—but what's important is that he keeps walking. This is easier for some people than others. Some heart patients don't live in safe neighborhoods, and some live in places where winters are long and it's hard to walk outside in freezing temperatures. In many places—though not all—there are high school tracks, community centers, shopping malls and other places indoors or outdoors where it's safe and free to walk. And little things—like taking the stairs, parking farther from the mall—all add up. So encourage your family and friends to think about where best to walk and set a routine that fits their needs.

*This picture was taken in 2004, a month and a half after my dad had emergency bypass surgery. He looks far healthier here than he did right after— or right before—his surgery.*

Courtesy of David Scull/Clinton Foundation

Heart disease, like any disease, can be scary. In an effort to learn more about what I could do to support my dad after his surgery, instead of being scared about what might happen to him, I asked his doctors lots of questions. In fact, I still ask my dad's doctors questions. I don't think anyone is too young—or too old—to ask doctors questions to better understand heart health and to advocate for one's self and family. If you have questions about the heart care (or any care) a family member or friend is receiving, why a doctor is prescribing something or what advice is being given, ask. The worst thing that can happen is you get a highly technical answer only another doctor would understand, or you

*One way to help your whole family stay healthy is by exercising together.*

get brushed off. If that happens (and hopefully it won't), ask another doctor, nurse or care provider, or look at the American Heart Association's website (heart.org) with your parents or grandparents or any adult whose heart you want to help. Knowing more about heart disease and heart care will help ensure your family and friends get the best possible care.

## Who Is at Risk?

Although heart disease is the leading cause of death around the world and in the U.S., it does not strike equally. Genes (what we inherit from our parents, grandparents and all our ancestors) matter in determining who is at risk for heart disease (meaning if there's a family history of heart disease, we're more likely to get heart disease). As discussed above, high blood pressure and high cholesterol, as well as diabetes and obesity, play a role in whether or not someone gets heart disease. Stress, an unhealthy diet and lack of physical activity or exercise all also influence if and when someone gets heart disease. Access to good medical care helps determine if someone with heart disease will be able to get the treatment needed to lead a healthy, long life or not. In the developing world, heart patients on average are much younger than in the United States. For example, the average age of a heart failure patient in Ghana is forty-two. It is seventy-seven in Minnesota. Thirty-five years is a massive difference.

Heart disease also does not equally impact all Americans. In the U.S., African American men are more likely to die from heart disease than white men, in part because they typically have higher average blood pressure. Why? A number of complex, interconnected reasons, including higher poverty rates that correspond to a less healthy diet and more stress, both of which can lead to higher blood pressure. People of any racial background living in poverty are also more likely to not have health insurance, which means they're less likely to see a doctor for early diagnosis and treatment of heart disease, putting them at higher risk for heart attacks. Yes, being poor can be very bad for your heart. Studies have also shown that a history of segregation and doctors favoring some patients over others—without even realizing that they are doing so—means some African Americans still receive lower-quality care. For those patients, high blood pressure may not be diagnosed and treated as quickly as necessary to avoid a heart attack or stroke. It's sadly not surprising then that African American men and women on average are burdened with relatively more of what are called "risk factors," or things that increase the chance of getting diseases like heart disease, many related to history and poverty, and many of which prove to be deadly.

Women in general are also at a greater risk of getting and dying from heart disease than men. Research has shown that, for some reason, smoking, stress and diabetes all increase the risk of heart disease relatively more in women than men. That's deeply unfair (writing as a woman), but it would be worse to pretend women don't need to be extra careful with our hearts (and no, I am not talking about romantically, although that may be true too!).

While fewer Americans are getting and dying from heart disease than even a few years ago thanks to better prevention and treatment, too many still are, particularly African American men, and women of all different racial and ethnic backgrounds. We've made progress but have a long way to go. Part of how we'll defeat heart disease is by making sure that all

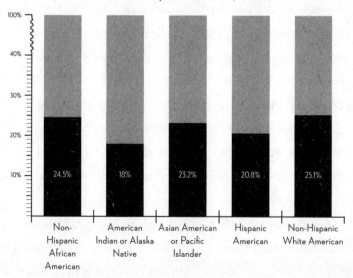

PERCENTAGE OF DEATHS CAUSED BY HEART DISEASE IN THE U.S. BY RACE/ETHNICITY, 2008

Information source: Centers for Disease Control and Prevention (CDC)

Americans have the opportunity to grow up and live in neighborhoods where healthy choices about food and exercise are safe, easy and affordable, which we talked about in $32 a Day and will talk more about later in this chapter. Another part is everyone having a doctor or nurse they can call and ask for advice if they're worried about heart disease or just want to ensure they're keeping their heart healthy. If you want to learn more than what's discussed here about heart health, explore the American Heart Association's various resources through heart.org. The earlier you start taking care of your heart, the longer it will likely last.

## CANCER

### A Cell Invasion

Cells are the microscopic building blocks that form all the parts of our bodies—our hair, heart, muscles and bones are all made of cells. Cancer happens when cells become abnormal and start growing uncontrollably. These out-of-control cells then invade otherwise healthy parts of the body. It's sort of similar to how viruses attack our bodies, as we'll learn in the next chapter (except that cancer doesn't spread from person to person). Cancer is not one disease but many, affecting different organs and making people sick in many different ways. Currently, there are more than 100 known distinct types of cancer, and sometimes their names don't capture how dangerous they can be and how widely they can spread. For example, there are cancers that start in the lung and then move to the liver; they're still lung cancers, even though they're now in the liver too. And in every patient, cancer is different. Thankfully, every year scientists and doctors are learning more and more about what cancer is, how to prevent it and how to beat it back.

Like heart disease, you cannot catch cancer from another person in the same way you can catch a cold, although some viruses and bacteria increase a person's risk for specific types of cancers. Often, cancer cells come together to form masses known as tumors. Sometimes, depending on where the cancer is, tumors can grow so big they're visible as lumps under the skin. If part of a tumor breaks off (wherever it is) and those cancer cells invade another part of the body (like in the lung-to-liver example I just mentioned), that's called "metastasis." If metastasis occurs, it makes eliminating the cancer that much harder.

One in two American men and one in three American women are projected to get cancer at some point in their lives. That adds up to more than 100 million people, or more than the populations of California, Texas, New York and Illinois combined. Not surprisingly then, a lot of Americans get cancer every year. In 2012, more than 1.6 million Americans were diagnosed with cancer (not including certain types of skin cancers that are incredibly common and usually can be treated if caught early enough). As is true in treating heart disease, treating and curing cancer

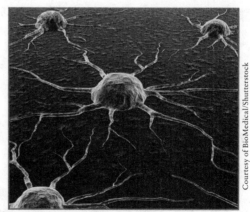

*This is what cancer looks like inside someone's body.*

is expensive. In 2011 alone, the U.S. spent more than $88 billion on cancer treatment (that's more than all the food and drinks McDonald's, Subway, Starbucks, Wendy's, Burger King, Taco Bell and Dunkin' Donuts combined sold that year). Also like heart disease, cancer is a global challenge, and a growing one. In 2012, more than 14 million people were diagnosed with cancer across the world (again not counting relatively minor skin cancers). That number is expected to rise to close to 24 million in the next two decades (in other words, by the time some of you are my age).

After skin cancer, lung and breast cancer are the most common cancers in American women. Prostate and lung cancer are the most common cancers among American men. (The prostate is a body part found only in men.) Prostate cancer is diagnosed in more men than any other cancer, while lung cancer kills more men than any other cancer. That's true across different racial and ethnic groups. Breast cancer is the most common cancer among American women, but lung cancer kills more American

COMMON TYPES OF CANCER IN THE U.S., 2015

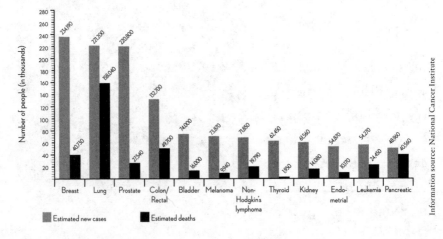

Information source: National Cancer Institute

women. This is also generally true across racial groups with one exception: Breast cancer kills more Hispanic American women than lung cancer. It's important to be aware of which cancers may pose more of a risk to your family.

Different types of cancer generally affect American kids. Leukemia, or cancer of the blood and bone marrow, is the most common, and along with brain and central nervous system tumors, makes up about half of the cancers that affect kids in the U.S. Kids can, but rarely do, develop the cancers most common in adults. Unlike with certain adult cancers, there are no risk factors for kid cancers. If kids get leukemia, they often first feel tired and achy, lose weight and have a fever. These symptoms are similar to what kids often feel with a cold or flu (and are most likely the result of a cold or flu). The American Cancer Society says it's important to let your pediatrician know if you have those symptoms and if they last for longer than your parents think is normal. While very few kids get cancer, making sure that it's caught early is crucial. More than 80 percent of children who get cancer now survive because cancers are caught earlier and treatments are more effective.

## Treatments Can Help

If you have relatives or friends who have had cancer, you may have noticed during their treatment that they were tired and maybe lost their hair. That's because they were receiving chemotherapy as cancer treatment. While new cancer therapies are being actively developed (including personalized cancer drugs), there are three main types of cancer treatments in use today: chemotherapy, radiation therapy and surgery.

Chemotherapy is made up of very strong drugs that kill cancer cells. More than 100 chemotherapy drugs are commonly used today. Different types of chemotherapy are utilized depending on what type of cancer a patient has and how advanced it is. All chemotherapy targets and kills all cells that are fast-growing, even those that are not cancerous—like new hair cells (which is why people in chemotherapy often lose their hair). Hair loss isn't the only side effect, as chemotherapy often makes patients feel awful, but it is the most well-known one. You may have noticed people who've gone bald because of chemotherapy; maybe they decided to wear a bandana or wig. You may have also seen people who've shaved their heads to show support for loved ones and friends getting chemotherapy.

My grandmother Ginger's hair thinned (though never completely fell out) when she was being treated for breast cancer. She had a beautiful wig, but didn't love to wear it. Knowing she could wear it for special occasions (and when she wanted to), I think made her feel better about the days she chose to not wear it. The wig freed her to make her own choices. Every cancer patient should have that same freedom, to choose to wear a beautiful wig or not, whether their hair has thinned or fallen out, whether they've cut their hair short or shaved their head entirely.

There are terrific organizations that provide hairpieces to kids with cancer and other diseases who've lost their hair because of the disease or the treatment, and who are not able to afford them on their own. Locks of Love is probably the biggest. You can nominate anyone under twenty-one who needs a hairpiece and can't afford one to receive a free custom-made one. They receive a new hairpiece every other year until they are twenty-one years old. You can also donate your hair to be used in hairpieces and encourage your family and friends to donate hair—almost any hair ten inches or longer, and almost any color (except gray), whether it's curly or straight, is welcome. To find out more, please visit locksoflove.org.

While writing this book, I read a story that really struck me (in the best, most positive sense). When he was six years old, Christian from Florida decided to grow his hair out to ten inches long and donate it to Children With Hair Loss so they could make wigs for kids who'd lost their hair. He decided to do this after watching a

*Christian holding the forty inches of hair he donated to Children With Hair Loss.*

commercial for St. Jude Children's Research Hospital (a hospital that focuses on researching and treating childhood cancers) and finding out more about its work. Christian was bullied for having long hair because it wasn't considered very boy-ish. He wasn't deterred. After two years, Christian reached his goal of ten inches. He had so much hair, he could donate a total of forty inches (because he was able to put his hair into four ten-inch ponytails before cutting it) to Children With Hair Loss. That's amazing. To find out how you could do the same, please visit childrenwithhairloss.us. I've never donated hair, but it's on my bucket list of things to do.

Radiation therapy is another cancer treatment and it uses super-high-energy particles or particle waves like X-rays to kill cancer cells. If you've had an X-ray, radiation therapy is similar but on a much more massive scale—think a big lake versus a local pool. Unlike chemotherapy, radiation targets only where the cancer lives and not cells throughout the whole body. That's why some people say radiation is a "smarter" treatment for certain cancers than chemotherapy is. There also tend to be fewer side effects associated with radiation than chemotherapy. Radiation may work better against some cancers, like certain lung cancers, but less so against others. Chemotherapy is better at treating and beating other cancers, which is why it's still used. Sometimes, chemotherapy and radiation are used together. These are all decisions that patients, families and doctors make together to find the best treatment for each patient.

The American Cancer Society has a website with ideas and tips on how to support friends or siblings with cancer, whether they're in the hospital getting treatment or going to school while fighting or recovering from cancer. As scary as it might be for you, for me or for anyone to see a family member or friend with cancer, it's much scarier for our family or friends who are cancer patients. We can show our support and love by calling, visiting, helping make the transition back to school easier, bringing Halloween or Valentine's Day or other holidays—and birthdays—into the hospital (provided the doctors and nurses say that's okay) and doing anything else we think might help. You can find out more at cancer.org.

Someone who's thought of a creative way to help support kids with cancer is Indiana-native Kendra. When she was ten years old, Kendra was diagnosed with a childhood cancer called neuroblastoma. She underwent two years of treatment—including chemotherapy, radiation, surgery and other therapies. Thankfully, Kendra's cancer has been beaten back for now, and she decided to do something to help other kids undergoing cancer treatment. So she created Kendra's Call for Komfort, which makes care packages for kids who aren't yet as far along as she is in their fight against cancer. The 200 (and counting) care packages have games, crafts, gift cards and clothes that are customized to each kid who receives one. Kendra's already raised over $50,000 for the project and she's just getting started. To find out

*Kendra with a nurse and social worker delivering one of her care packages to the unit where she used to be a patient.*

Courtesy of Julia Springs

more about Kendra's Call for Komfort, and what you can do to help, please visit kendrascallforkomfort.org.

When I was in college at Stanford, I volunteered for a couple of years at the Lucile Packard Children's Hospital. I worked in the art therapy room with kids who were patients, many who were cancer patients. We drew together, did finger painting, made glitter-paint pictures. I helped organize a couple of birthday parties and sometimes helped kids with their homework. The best moments were when the kids I got to know forgot they were patients and remembered they were kids first—and the hugs I sometimes got. Although you have to be eighteen to volunteer at most hospitals, some hospitals allow people to start at sixteen. But, provided their doctors say it's okay, you can visit your friends or family in the hospital and help brighten their days with art, treats and hugs or one of Kendra's care packages. You can do the same for anyone you know who's in the hospital for whatever reason.

Even with chemotherapy and radiation, most people who have cancer will have surgery at some point, to treat or remove all or part of a tumor. Surgery is also used to diagnose whether someone has cancer, by removing a piece of body tissue suspected to have cancerous cells, a process known as a biopsy. Cells from the removed tissue are examined under a microscope to see whether or not they're cancerous. Scientists are currently working on blood tests that could be used for cancer diagnoses. Diagnosis can be scary too and we can all support family and friends who are worried about whether they have cancer until they know for sure one way or the other.

## RISK FACTORS

Scientists have discovered that some genes can increase the risks for certain cancers and that some infections can do the same. It's important to get vaccinated against those viruses known to increase cancer risk, such as Hepatitis B, which can cause liver cancer, and the human papilloma virus (HPV), which can cause cervical cancer. The Pink Ribbon Red Ribbon partnership spearheaded by the George W. Bush Institute is leading an effort to increase HPV vaccinations in the developing world. If you're interested in knowing more about their work, visit bushcenter.org. Certain bacteria are linked to certain types of stomach cancer—another reason to take all your antibiotics if you're sick with a bacterial infection. Particular parasites can also increase cancer risk, though like the parasites we'll discuss later in Bugs and Bacteria, these are generally found outside the United States.

Every cancer risk factor is important to take seriously, regardless of how frightening. Some risk factors can be lessened or even avoided through choices we each make, while some, like those in our genes, cannot. Other risk factors are difficult to avoid not because they're inside us but because they're all around us, like secondhand smoke—smoke that someone has breathed out when they're smoking a cigarette or cigar, which we then breathe in—or heavy air pollution, both of which are tied to higher lung cancer risk. We should—if we can—move away from secondhand smoke (and encourage the adults in our lives to stop smoking, like my grandmother Ginger, or at least to stop smoking around us). But it's harder, if not impossible, for kids to move away from relatively polluted areas. Since we often can't move away from pollution, we need to urge people in positions of power—like elected officials and business owners—to move the pollution away from us, or even better, to make it disappear, or at least make it less dangerous to our lungs. There are also choices we can make in our own families to lower the pollution we generate. We'll talk more about both in Weather Report and more about smoking later in this chapter.

While there's a lot we know about what causes cancer, there's still a lot we don't know yet. Science has proven the link between tobacco and many types of cancer. We know that exposure to radiation—whether from the powerful rays of the sun or from nuclear weapons or even from lots and lots of X-rays—is a major cancer risk factor. That's why it's important to only get an X-ray when your doctor recommends one to help with a diagnosis (like for an injury) and to get radiation treatment for cancer only when your doctor prescribes it (so that you'll avoid unnecessary exposure). There's no evidence that what's called "non-ionizing radiation" from microwaves, cell phones, iPads or radios has any link to cancer. We know that heavy use of certain pesticides increases the risk of cancer for the farmers who use them on their crops, but science doesn't have a clear answer yet on whether the cancer risk is also increased for people who eat food from those crops. We know an unhealthy diet and obesity increase the risk of cancer and that exercise can lessen the risk of cancer, but more research needs to be done on the ideal balance between diet and exercise to minimize cancer risk. But for all we don't know, it's important to recognize we do know a lot. If you want to do something about lessening the risks we are aware of for yourself, your family or more broadly, the American Institute for Cancer Research has lots of ideas at aicr.org. If you're interested in joining (or starting) a club working on cancer prevention, standup2cancer.org is a good resource.

## DIABETES

### *Sugar Rush*

Remember those sugary cereals I wanted as a kid but my mom wouldn't let me have? And the honey-drenched cereals I secretly ate behind the newspaper? When we eat, our digestive system breaks our food down into the tiny nutrients and sugars our bodies need for fuel—the rest is stored as fat or comes out as waste. Diabetes occurs when a patient's body cannot adequately break down and process sugar (regardless of whether it comes from what's already in a cereal or the added honey). As a result, too much sugar circulates in the bloodstream and not enough gets to cells for fuel. Cells then don't get the sugar they need to do their work—our bodies must have some sugar to function and for us to stay alive. A lot is bad, but at least some is necessary.

There are two types of diabetes. The number of Americans diagnosed with type 2 diabetes is growing very fast. In 1997, the year I graduated from high school, there were less than 10 million Americans with type 2 diabetes. In 2012? More than 29 million. In the U.S., more than one in three American adults have pre-diabetes, meaning they're at risk of developing type 2 diabetes. The good news is that with different choices (like what we eat), many pre-diabetics can avoid developing type 2 diabetes. Type 1 diabetes affects as many as 1.25 million Americans and although they share a name and are somewhat similar, type 1 and type 2 diabetes are distinct challenges.

In people with type 1 diabetes, their body's immune system attacks the insulin-producing cells within the pancreas; insulin is necessary to our bodies' ability to transfer sugar, or glucose, from the bloodstream into the billions (or, as adults, trillions) of cells that need it to function and keep us healthy. Over time, type 1 diabetes, if not treated, can lead to heart disease, kidney damage, eye damage, nerve damage and foot damage—sometimes so severe, the foot needs to be amputated.

One symptom of type 1 diabetes is being constantly thirsty (and having to pee all the time)—this is because the body is trying to rid itself of extra sugar however possible. Additionally, people with undiagnosed type 1 diabetes are often really hungry because their cells are struggling to get the sugar their bodies cannot process due to lack of insulin. Their bodies are telling them to eat more in the hope of getting more sugar. But it doesn't work. And even with eating more, type 1 diabetics who don't know that they are diabetic often lose weight and feel exhausted because of a lack of sugar as cellular fuel. I imagine it can be very frustrating to eat a lot, lose weight and still be hungry and tired.

We don't yet know what causes type 1 diabetes. It could be genetic or a result of a mysterious infection, but since we don't know for sure, it's impossible to know how to prevent it. You may have a friend with type 1 diabetes. Most people with type 1 diabetes are diagnosed before they turn fourteen, though adults can get type 1 diabetes too. Once someone develops type 1 diabetes, it lasts forever, because there is no cure, at least not yet, and people with type 1 diabetes must inject or pump insulin into their bodies every day. The good news is this type of treatment means they likely can lead a full life and avoid the scary complications listed above.

Type 2 diabetes occurs when the pancreas makes *some* insulin, but not enough for the body to function well. Or when there is enough insulin, but the body cannot use it effectively to process sugar. People with type 2 diabetes feel tired, feel the need to drink a lot of water and other fluids and also need to go to the bathroom often. Historically, type 2 diabetes was known as adult-onset diabetes as it occurred mainly in adults who were overweight. It almost always was diagnosed in adults over forty-five, mainly those over sixty-five.

But this has been changing. As more children are overweight, more kids are at risk for and are getting type 2 diabetes. High blood pressure and having family members with type 2 diabetes also increases the risk someone will get the disease. African Americans, Hispanic Americans, Native Americans and Asian Americans face a relatively higher risk of type 2 diabetes for reasons that nobody really understands yet.

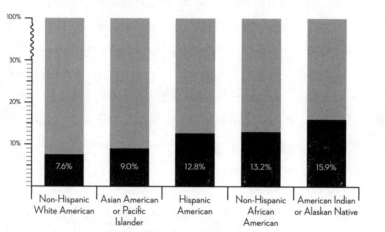

PERCENTAGE OF PEOPLE IN THE U.S. DIAGNOSED WITH DIABETES BY RACE/ETHNICITY, 2014

Information source: American Diabetes Association

While there is also no cure for type 2 diabetes, adults and children with type 2 diabetes do not always need insulin shots or an insulin pump. Like with type 1 diabetes, the precise cause of type 2 diabetes is unknown. However, we do know more about how to prevent it because we know what many of the main risk factors are. Many type 2 diabetics can control their disease with a mix of medicines, a healthy diet and regular exercise, which may help reduce the chances of heart disease and strokes too.

Someone helping her family make healthier—and tastier—choices is Haile from Arizona. When her dad was diagnosed with diabetes, Haile was determined to learn to cook, a passion her parents supported. She was only seven! Today, Haile is fourteen years old and loves creating easy-to-make, inexpensive and yummy meals for herself and her family. And through exercise and diet, particularly Haile's healthy meals, her dad's health has improved and he's managed to control his diabetes. Beyond her family, Haile is working to help other kids become healthy influences and cooks in their own homes and schools. She's even trying to make vacations healthier—she's worked with Hyatt Hotels on making their kids' meals more nutritious (and tastier). I had the privilege of joining Haile on *The Rachael Ray Show* a couple of years ago, where she taught me how to make a delicious blueberry peach quinoa crumble. To learn more about Haile's story—and her recipes—you can visit hailevthomas.com. If Haile can change how kids eat in their homes and even at hotels—and how her own family eats—just imagine what you could do! We'll talk more about healthy eating soon.

*Haile cooked healthy food on* The Rachael Ray Show, *and I was lucky enough to get to eat it!*

Helping parents, grandparents and friends eat a healthy diet, get regular exercise, treat high blood pressure and avoid tobacco (yes, tobacco increases diabetes risk too) are all ways you can help loved ones avoid or manage diabetes. Another way is to ensure that everyone in your life knows his or her diabetes status. More than 8 million Americans have diabetes and don't know it. If people don't know they have diabetes, they may not be making the diet and food decisions necessary to lead healthy—and long—lives. Encouraging a visit to the doctor for a simple blood test and assisting diabetics in managing their blood sugar effectively can literally improve and save lives.

# OBESITY

A major risk factor for diabetes, heart disease and many cancers, including breast cancer, is obesity. In the U.S., one of every three kids is overweight or obese, which means very overweight. Even more American adults are overweight or obese, two out of every three. And this isn't only an American challenge. Around the world, more than one out of every four people are overweight or obese. Someone is overweight or obese if they weigh more than what doctors and nurses consider healthy based on their height, age and whether they're a boy or a girl. Doctors and nurses often use a calculation called body mass index, or BMI, to help figure out if someone is at a healthy weight or not. Generally, a BMI between the fifth and eighty-fifth percentile is considered healthy. If you have questions about your BMI or your weight, talk to your parents and your doctor or school nurse. And it's never okay (or helpful) to stigmatize someone for being overweight or obese. It's important we all support our family and friends in their efforts to be healthy—and ask that they do the same for us.

Kids who are obese are more likely to be obese when they grow up and face all the health challenges adults who are obese face today. But childhood obesity isn't just a risk factor for heart disease when kids grow up. A child who is obese has a higher risk of heart disease as a kid, including an increased risk of having a heart attack or stroke. Kids who are obese are also more likely to develop asthma, as excess weight can make breathing more difficult. Children who suffer from severe asthma are also more likely to be overweight, another example of how it's hard to separate out cause and effect.

RATES OF OBESITY IN THE U.S., 1980-2011

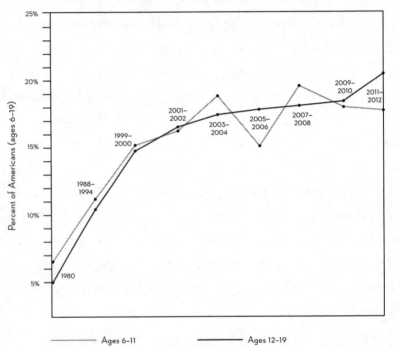

Information source: Centers for Disease Control and Prevention (CDC)

As is clear from the chart, the childhood obesity rate has increased dramatically in my lifetime—for some age groups it's four times as high now as it was in 1980. Why? Kids started eating more and exercising less, often because unhealthy food options were more available and exercise less available than ever before. Thankfully, we know what we need to do to help kids, families and communities be healthier today and in the future.

# EATING HEALTHY

The American Heart Association estimates that less than one percent of American adults eat ideal heart-healthy meals, and almost no kids do. Wow. We saw earlier what Haile's doing for the health of her dad and other kids. We've all heard the rules about healthy eating—eat more fruits, vegetables, whole grains and lean proteins like low-fat dairy, chicken, fish, beans, tofu and eggs. We know we're supposed to stay away from too much sugar, salt and fat, especially saturated fat and trans fat. All important advice, but . . . how?

Eating a healthy diet isn't simple or necessarily easy. It's much harder for some families, depending on where they live, the money in their family budget that they can spend on food and how much time they have to think about healthy food, shop for it and prepare it. As mentioned in $32 a Day, it's hard for any family that lives in a food desert to find healthy, affordable options. If there isn't a store near you that sells fruits and vegetables that make sense for your family budget, consider teaming up with your family, friends and neighbors to let your mayor, local council person and other elected officials know how important you think it is to have a store that does just that. One resource that may be helpful in making the case, even though it's geared toward adults, is The Food Trust, found at thefoodtrust.org.

Given how much time most of you spend in school, it's important that schools provide healthy lunch options and in general are healthy places for you to be. You can work with your principal, teachers and friends to help evaluate how healthy your school environment is (though I bet you already have a good sense of the answer) by using tools from the Alliance for a Healthier

Generation, a partnership between the Clinton Foundation and the American Heart Association, found at healthiergeneration .org. The Alliance has tips on everything from healthier vending-machine options to healthier lunches and snacks. Lots of little changes can make a big difference in helping kids avoid becoming overweight and in losing extra weight (and that's true for adults too).

What happens around a school can help kids and families be healthier too. Katie realized this one day when she was in third grade. She brought home a cabbage seedling from a gardening program at her school in South Carolina. Katie tended it and watched it grow to an astonishing forty pounds! She knew that such a special cabbage needed a special home and so she donated it to a local soup kitchen. When she realized that her cabbage would help con-tribute to providing people at the soup kitchen a healthy meal (and possibly their only meal), Katie knew she couldn't give only one cabbage—she wanted to do more. She pledged to, as she said, "end hunger one vegetable garden at a time." So she got her school to allot some land for a school garden and eventually started an organi-zation called Katie's Krops, which helps kids all over the country grow healthy food to donate to people in need. Today there are eighty-one gardens run by kids

Courtesy of Stacy Stagliano

*Katie helps kids all over the country grow food to donate to people in need.*

in thirty-one states! To support Katie's Krops or learn about starting your own garden, please visit katieskrops.com.

Outside of school, even if your family can afford a variety of healthy foods, knowing what's in your food can be challenging given how confusing food labels sometimes can be. But food labels also can be helpful in comparing two foods to see which has more protein or more fat so you can choose the better option. And while you can never go wrong if you go straight to nature's source—fruits and veggies and other ingredients that come from a farm—that's not an option for many families who live on a tight budget or live far from farms, farmers' markets or other places where fresh food is sold. Thankfully, healthy fruits and vegetables come in many forms—they can be frozen, canned or fresh, provided not too much salt or sugar has been added. Frozen vegetables in general are just as healthy as fresh vegetables and often cost a lot less.

There are all sorts of tools and apps to help kids figure out how to build healthy, affordable meals, like choosemyplate.gov. Most doctors agree the key for almost all of us is balance in what we eat and how much we eat. You love Cheetos (like my

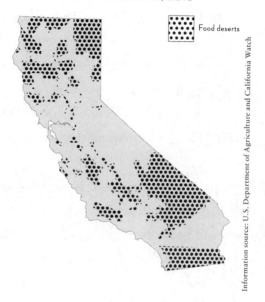

ABOUT 1 MILLION PEOPLE IN CALIFORNIA LIVE IN FOOD DESERTS, 2015

Food deserts

Information source: U.S. Department of Agriculture and California Watch husband, Marc) and can't imagine giving them up? Don't! Just eat them once a week instead of daily. Your sweet tooth won't let up until you have some chocolate? Okay, but choose a couple of Hershey's miniatures for a snack instead of a large chocolate shake. It's important to be aware of how much we eat. Sneakily, portion sizes for food and sodas have grown everywhere—in restaurants, in grocery stores, in vending machines and even at home. Research has found that when people, including kids, are served larger portions, they tend to eat or drink more without even realizing it!

Ideally food is both fuel and fun, good to eat and good for you. You shouldn't feel ashamed about how you eat, and eating should never be a chore or something you dread. Admittedly, I learned this from my grandmother Dorothy, who was very careful to never eat more than three Girl Scout Thin Mints cookies in one day (we'll come back to Girl Scout Cookies later in the book). While you may have heard of "super foods," and certain foods have been proven to help reduce cancer risk or heart disease risk, most doctors say that it's more important to eat fruits, vegetables and whole grains generally than any one specific food—and that candy, ice cream, chips and cake are fine once in a while.

Since my mom was adamantly opposed to having junk food in the house, I learned early on that treats were reserved for special occasions like birthdays and holidays. I was allowed to have candy only when we went to the movies. Thankfully, we went to the movies a lot when I was little—on average at least once every other week—so there were plenty of opportunities for me to eat gummy bears and Sour Patch Kids. I have very happy memories of devouring unlimited ice cream whenever I went to either of my grandparents' homes (Dove bars were a go-to my grandmothers shared) . . . I always justified it with the argument that going to Grandma's was by definition a special occasion. All in all, I'm very grateful now that my parents instilled good eating habits in me, and that I actually love vegetables and only crave sweets (like dark chocolate . . . or Dove bars) once in a while.

For all the cookies I don't crave and the chocolate I sometimes crave, I love French fries and basically anything with salt. All the time. Everyone needs to be wary of too much salt. It's hard to imagine that too much of something so small can be so dangerous, but too much sodium—a main component of salt—can lead to high blood pressure. Eating more salt is a main reason why high blood pressure is increasingly common in kids. There are certain foods that have been found to have high salt concentrations. Cold cuts (like what often goes on a sandwich), most prepared pizza (what you buy in the freezer section at the grocery store), lots of fast foods (like fried chicken) and prepared canned soup are just a few. You don't need to avoid these foods altogether, but rather be thoughtful about what's in what you're eating, even if you can't see it (like is often true with salt). On average, eight to eighteen year olds eat more than twice as much salt as the American Heart Association suggests. Wow (again). Our bodies need sodium, but not too much of it and definitely not twice what doctors recommend.

## UP AND ABOUT

Ah, exercise! Everyone who can move around should—to get healthy, stay healthy, live longer. But we never seem to get enough, no matter our age. While most physically able American teenagers do some exercise, a majority don't exercise enough. Yet we know exercise helps keep our hearts healthy, helps reduce our risk for certain cancers and may even help cancer patients get back to health. We also know exercise is easier for some families and kids than for others.

One hour of exercise a day is ideal for everyone, but every bit matters, whether it's on a sports team, a track, a playground or taking the stairs instead of the elevator. Did you know that sports like soccer and basketball are terrific for your health and for your grades? Research has shown over and over again that kids who exercise during the day learn more, remember more and perform better on quizzes and tests! But sports aren't an option for many kids, because there aren't always sports teams or because, even if there are, it's too expensive to participate. I think every kid should get to move around during the day in a physical education (PE) class, whether or not they ever step on a field or court. If you agree, work with your parents to make sure your school districts, cities and states know exercise is a priority—for your body and your brain—and urge them to make giving you daily PE classes their priority too. PE classes used to be standard. When I was in elementary school we had PE class every day. That's rarely true today. In the U.S., less than 10 percent of elementary, middle and high schools offer daily PE classes, making it hard for kids to get the sixty minutes of daily physical activity that doctors recommend.

PE class is so important partly because kids today are less active outside of school than kids were a few decades ago. Three out of four kids don't even get a half hour of physical activity a day. This may be because there are fewer safe places to play, or their parents are working and so there's no one who can watch them outside. And let's face it, if you're home, you're more likely to be watching or playing on a screen than doing jumping jacks. (My parents understood this, and it's why they didn't allow me more than thirty minutes a day to play a computer game or watch TV—it was one or the other, not both, and never for more than thirty minutes, unless we were watching TV or playing a game together as a family.)

Even if you have PE class, it's important to get moving outside of school too. That's easier in some places than others. Just like there are food deserts (discussed in $32 a Day and earlier in this chapter), there are also physical fitness deserts, places where it's really hard to find somewhere safe to run around or toss a football back and forth. If you live in a place with few or no safe options for exercise or if you care about this issue, you can work with your family, friends and community to encourage your city and state to invest in building more safe places for people to walk, run and ride bikes so that it's easier for everyone, regardless of income, to make exercise a part of daily life. You can also encourage local businesses to be part of these efforts, for example, by sponsoring parks or sports teams. My softball team when I was a kid was

ALL STAR 87

*Courtesy of the Author's Parents*

*This is me in 1987, when I played on the Screamin' Eagles softball team in Little Rock.*

sponsored in various years by a local dental practice (we were the "Molar Rollers") and a funeral home. If you can't go outside because it's not safe, there's nowhere to go or it's really cold or really hot, blast some music and organize an indoor dance party, lead a jumping-jack competition or see which of your friends can do the most push-ups. Sports and other physical activities are good for your bodies and your minds. They also should be FUN, whether they're inside or outside. Hopefully that's something everyone can agree on.

Someone determined to make exercise fun for her classmates and her community is fourteen-year-old Danyel from New Mexico. She runs cross-country and plays basketball and baseball—yes, baseball, not softball. A few years ago, her appendix ruptured and she had emergency surgery. It was her first brush with poor health. Although she bounced back fast, she

*Danyel lobbied her school for a Navajo-themed field day so kids could get exercise and learn about their culture at the same time.*

started noticing how many people in her Navajo community, especially other kids, were unhealthy and struggling with obesity. Danyel wanted to help more of her friends and neighbors start to exercise and get healthier, and to help people realize that not everyone had to be an athlete like she was to enjoy moving around. She lobbied her school to have a Navajo-themed field day, so that kids could spend the day running around having fun while also learning about their culture and heritage. Her school agreed, and that first field day was only the beginning of Danyel's ongoing work to help people in her community get healthy while celebrating Navajo traditions, language, stories, dancing and singing. I've never met Danyel, but I hope to, and if I'm ever near the Navajo reservation during one of her field days, I hope she'll invite me to join the fun.

## NO SMOKING

Smoking-related diseases will kill an estimated 1 billion people across the world this century. That's an eye-popping number—it's ten times higher than the number of Americans expected to get cancer—but it's sadly not a surprising one. In 2012, there were close to a billion smokers in the world, a number that continues to rise as the world's population increases and more people make money and spend some of the extra cash they earn on cigarettes. More than 7,000 chemicals have been identified in tobacco smoke. The most famous is nicotine, the chemical that makes tobacco so addictive. Close to seventy of the chemicals are known to increase the risk of getting a variety of cancers, including lung cancer, mouth cancer and throat cancer. In addition to cancer, smoking can cause lung disease, such as emphysema, where lung tissue is so damaged it becomes impossible to breathe; gum disease; heart disease, including heart attacks and strokes; and as mentioned earlier, diabetes. It doesn't only make you sick or kill you, tobacco can also make you a worse athlete, stain your teeth and give you wrinkles around your mouth. None of that is fun, it's certainly not attractive and all of it's dangerous.

There is no safe way to use tobacco, whether in cigarettes, cigars, chewing tobacco or dissolvable tobacco. Yet close to one in five American adults use tobacco in some form, most of them by smoking cigarettes. People can get addicted to cigarettes within days—meaning their bodies *need* the nicotine in tobacco to feel normal—and by people, I largely mean kids. Almost every adult smoker started before his or her eighteenth birthday. Many smokers in the U.S. become addicted at around fourteen, having tried their first cigarette at eleven.

## NEARLY ONE OUT OF FIVE AMERICAN ADULTS USES TOBACCO*

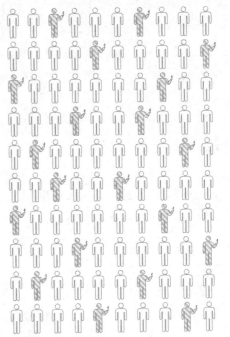

*Data based on years 2005–2013.

Information source: Centers for Disease Control and Prevention (CDC)

Smoking isn't just a U.S. challenge but a global one. Almost all of the world's smokers live in the developing world and most of the people who will get sick and die from smoking are in poorer countries. It's not only Americans who need help quitting, or better yet, avoiding tobacco in the first place.

The good news is that quitting smoking allows your body to return to normal. Although it's unquestionably better to never smoke, once a person quits smoking, that person's body immediately starts to heal itself, repairing smoke-damaged lung and heart tissue. Literally immediately. The risk of a heart attack drops even twenty-four hours after the last cigarette, is cut in half a year after quitting, and after fifteen years is about the same as someone who never smoked. Two to three months after people quit, their lungs work better, which means they can run longer distances without getting short of breath. Twenty years after quitting, a person's risk of dying from all cancers with one exception is the same as a nonsmoker. That one exception? Lung cancer. So, while quitting is good, never starting is better, for you and for the people around you.

*I'll never forget when, in fifth grade, I first saw a picture of what a smoker's lungs looked like (in case you were wondering, the smoker's lungs are on the right). Can you believe the contrast?*

 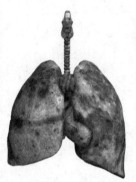

Courtesy of Stocktrek Images, Inc./Alamy
Courtesy of Valentyna Chukhlyebova/Alamy

Smoking threatens a smoker's family, friends and other people who are nearby through secondhand smoke. Children who live with smokers get sick more often with things like colds and ear infections than those who don't. If you know an adult who needs extra help quitting, explain to them that quitting is good for *your* health as well. And it's not just about health. Smoking deadens the sense of smell and taste; nonsmokers or those who have quit can taste and smell better. Smoking is also expensive. A smoker in the U.S. will spend more than $1,800 a year on average just on cigarettes. In 2014, the average movie ticket price was $8.17— not smoking would buy 220 movie tickets every year!

While smoking isn't contagious in the same way infectious diseases are, if your parents, siblings or friends smoke, you're more likely to smoke. Helping your parents or friends quit smoking is good for their health and good for your chances of never becoming a smoker. Most smokers say they want to quit, so it's likely the smokers you know want to break their habit. You can help them by making your home less smoker friendly by removing ashtrays and lighters and not permitting anyone to smoke (you can even put up No Smoking signs—before I asked my grandma Ginger to quit, I'd threatened to do that . . . in her own home!).

It can be really hard to quit smoking and it might take a couple of tries until someone never lights up another cigarette (or chews tobacco again). It's important to be supportive if a family member or friend "slips" and picks up a cigarette or chewing tobacco, reminding them why they wanted to quit in the first place. Helping people quit can even be fun. I remember my grandmother Ginger and I played cards, cooked and laughed a lot while she was quitting. People are more likely to quit permanently with the support of loved ones. I remember how proud Ginger was when she'd quit and how proud I was to have helped her quit. It's a big deal when someone stops smoking and that's important to celebrate. When Ginger stopped craving cigarettes, we celebrated with her favorite German chocolate cake and an Elvis movie marathon. For more suggestions on how to help people stop, or never start, smoking, particularly friends your own age, teen.smokefree.gov is a good resource, as is the information on how to help a smoker quit at cancer.org. You can also call the toll-free national hotline number 1-800-QUIT-NOW for free advice on anything quitting-related and to find what local support programs are available to help you or the smoker in your life quit.

If you're thinking of smoking, you deserve to know all the risks to your health, your family and friends' health and your wallet. What's discussed here are only a few. So ask yourself: "Is it worth it?" And if you're thinking about using electronic cigarettes or e-cigarettes (sometimes this is called "vaping"), ask yourself the same question. Like conventional cigarettes, electronic cigarettes have nicotine in them, which is dangerous for anyone's health. There's not been enough research yet to determine what the long-term health effects of e-cigarettes are, but doctors agree they're not good for anyone.

Sometimes, while encouraging people to quit smoking (or not start), you can work to make healthy food more widely available at the same time, just as Magi, from Florida, did. Her picture is at the beginning of the chapter. Magi was named the 2014 Campaign for Tobacco-Free Kids National Youth Advocate of the Year, and it's pretty clear why. When she was a freshman in high school, Magi joined Students Working Against Tobacco. She helped get passed a countywide ban of any tobacco on school campuses and even at school events off campus. She pioneered a selfie campaign in which young people (and some older people) took pictures of themselves standing against tobacco use and tobacco companies using the #NotAReplacement hashtag. Check out the campaign gallery at kickbuttsday.org.

Courtesy of the Twitter account of the U.S. Surgeon General

*U.S. Surgeon General Dr. Vivek Murthy joined Magi's #NotAReplacement campaign.*

Magi also worked with United Way, AmeriCorps and other partners in an event called Tobacco-Free Farm Share. Their collective effort provided five tons of free healthy food to people in her county. No tobacco was allowed at the event, and in addition to the food they took home, the 1,200 families who attended also left with smoking cessation and tobacco prevention materials. To learn more about Magi's story in her own words, check out her awesome video on the Campaign for Tobacco-Free Kids website, tobaccofreekids.org.

## (OTHER) HEALTH MATTERS

### *Accidents and Allergies*

There are many, many chronic diseases and other health challenges that I've not mentioned so far this chapter. I'll talk about a couple here briefly. In no way are those that aren't included or only touched on any less important. As one example, road accidents are a major cause of injury and death for adults and kids, in the U.S. and around the world, and I hope you always wear your seat belts and talk to your parents about safe driving. That's incredibly important, even though I don't talk about road safety in this chapter beyond these two sentences. Drowning and fire also pose great risks to kids across the globe, whereas for older people, falling down a couple of stairs is too often a death sentence. Far too many kids never learn to swim, putting them at real risk of drowning. Learning how to swim, encouraging other kids to learn how to swim and working with parents and other adults to use fire and fireworks safely all go a long way toward protecting your own and other kids' health. Many cities offer free swimming lessons for kids, so look online with your family to find the right option for you if you don't know how to swim. Injury—from things like car accidents or fires—is the leading cause of death around the world for kids over nine. You can help change that. To learn more about road safety, drowning prevention and what you can do against these and other causes of preventable injuries, please visit safekids.org. It's a resource for adults but has safety tips we can all learn from.

One type of "accident" you can help people in your life avoid is accidentally eating things they're allergic to. An estimated 6 million kids in the U.S. have food allergies. Some kids have minor food allergies—maybe they cause a rash, and some have very serious allergies—they may be deadly. Some common foods kids are allergic to include various nuts, milk, eggs, wheat and shellfish. I'm very allergic to certain shellfish, so I have to be careful not to eat something that many people would find delicious, but to me would be dangerous. My husband and friends help me do that while ordering in a restaurant. You can help your family and friends in the same way. It's important to ask friends what allergies they have so you don't share foods that could make them sick. For friends with severe allergies, make sure you don't have anything around them that could make them sick—and be sure to wash your hands with soap and water, in case you've eaten something recently with things in it they're allergic to (like cookies made with peanuts). Yes, hand-washing can help protect people with allergies. If you think you might have allergies (for example if you get rashes or a scratchy throat after eating), ask your parents to call your doctor and talk about allergy testing. And, as ever, if there's an emergency and someone is having a severe allergic reaction, call 911.

## Mental Health

Mental health encompasses our emotions, how we think and feel about ourselves, our family, our friends and everything around us as well as how we behave and function in the world. We all have emotions (are we happy today? are we sad today? are we stressed today?). If someone you know is particularly sad or tired, wants to be alone a lot of the time, often is in fights or otherwise out of control or doesn't want to eat or eats too much, it's important to encourage that person, whether a friend or family member, to talk to their parents, a doctor, a teacher, a religious advisor—really any adult they feel comfortable being open and honest with. If any of those things are true of you, please follow the same advice. Mental health challenges are nothing to be ashamed of.

Like is true with heart disease, people living in poverty in the U.S. and around the world face a higher risk of mental health issues, in part because of the stress poverty brings (how to pay for rent, how to pay for food). People with chronic mental health issues often have a harder time getting and keeping a job, making them more vulnerable to poverty and the stresses of poverty. The relationship between mental health and poverty once again demonstrates how hard it can be to separate out a cause from the effect.

Substance abuse or misuse—abusing illegal drugs, prescription drugs or alcohol—is a worldwide problem and one also linked to mental health. People with mental health issues are more likely to abuse drugs and alcohol, and people with substance abuse problems are more likely to have mental health challenges. But most people manage and deal with their mental health issues without ever turning to drugs or alcohol. If you have concerns about a specific person in your life (especially if it's a friend around your age, younger or older) who is abusing drugs or alcohol or thinking about abusing drugs or alcohol, it's important to talk to adults you trust and ask for their advice. It's often hard for people who are struggling with substance abuse to recognize that they have a problem, which is why it's so important that friends and family are there to support them during their recovery.

Helping people treat mental health problems as early as possible is important to their future health and vital to preventing self-harm and suicide. No young person—or anyone—should feel like suicide is an option. If you have questions about how to help prevent suicide broadly in your community or how to help friends you're worried about, a good resource is halfofus.org from the Jed Foundation. Your doctors, teachers and religious leaders also likely have more mental health resources that they can share. If you or a friend doesn't feel like there is an adult you can talk to or trust or if you'd just rather talk to someone else, Crisis Text Line offers counseling and referrals through texting. To learn more about Crisis Text Line, including how to use it, go to crisistextline.org. This is far, far too short a discussion of the serious hardships a lot of young people face and their right to feel valued and supported, but it's too important not to mention at all.

## Bullying

No one should be harassed because of who they love, who they are or what they look like. It's important to stand up against bullying, whoever the bully is and whatever he or she is using to justify the bullying. Whether it's directed at people because of their race, gender, sexual orientation, what they're wearing, what their hair looks like, what they did in school today, what they may do after school, whether they're artistic or athletic, overweight or underweight, if they have two moms at home, two dads at home, one mom at home, one dad at home, or don't have a permanent home—there is never an excuse to physically intimidate someone, use profanity, call someone bad names, hit someone, or make anyone feel like they are less worthy, less valuable, or simply less. Never. There's also never an excuse to intimidate someone online—it's no more okay if the person is on the other side of a Facebook page, Twitter account, Snap-Chat, WhatsApp or Ask.Fm question. And standing by and doing nothing is not a noble option—either step in and stop the bullying if you can do so safely, or go and get, call, text, email or message a teacher, parent, religious leader or other trusted adult to stop the bullying so no one gets hurt further. Bullying hurts the bully too—it's not good for anyone's mental health to be angry or violent. That's as true online and on social media as it is in person. For tips on how to stop bullying, whether you're the one being bullied or you see bullying, on how to help prevent bullying and on how to help bullies get the support they often need, please visit stopbullying.gov.

Young people who are lesbian, gay, bisexual, transgender or questioning (LGBTQ) are still, even in the 21st century, more likely to be bullied or harassed. Tragically, experiencing persistent bullying has been linked to some LGBTQ young people harming themselves and even taking their own lives. The Trevor Project works to prevent self-harm and suicide specifically in LGBTQ young people and to provide a safe space online for LGBTQ young people to connect with and support one another. To know more about how you can participate and support LGBTQ friends, please visit thetrevorproject.org.

## *Autism and Alzheimer's*

I want to briefly (and again, too briefly) mention two other health challenges you may come across in your classrooms, communities and possibly families. Autism (short for autism spectrum disorder) is generally thought of as a childhood condition, because it typically arises in very young children. Alzheimer's disease generally affects older people, often people who are your grandparents' age or older, but can affect people your parents' age or even, in rare cases, younger people. Both autism and Alzheimer's affect the ways in which the brain works and how people interact with family, friends and others.

Children with autism often have trouble communicating. They may sit quietly and play by themselves to the exclusion of everyone else and may avoid eye contact, or they may interact with others in a way that might feel awkward to you. They might be unable to have a conversation or might say the same things over and over again, possibly quite loudly. Autism has become more common in the U.S. in recent years for reasons that aren't yet well understood. What we do know is that anyone of any age can support family and friends with autism. Being patient and accepting, even if it's hard when your friends or family can't communicate with you in the same ways you can communicate with them can help all of us be good friends, family members and neighbors.

The same is true for our loved ones with Alzheimer's disease. Over time, adults with Alzheimer's experience increasing memory loss and may reach a point when they're unable to remember anyone's name or anything about their own lives. They may not be able to recognize their loved ones, even their own children and grandchildren. Again, being patient and accepting is part of being a good friend or grandkid. We know how we treat those around us even if those around us may not always know. Alzheimer's has become more common as adults are living longer lives. As with so many challenges that affect the brain, we don't yet understand Alzheimer's well, though lots of research is being done on how to prevent and treat it.

Both Alzheimer's disease and autism deserve more space than given here and I hope that you will visit the terrific resources that exist to describe in depth what Alzheimer's disease and autism are, what research is being done and what you can do to support loved ones confronting Alzheimer's and autism. The Alzheimer's Association has a section for kids that you can find on alz.org. You can learn more about autism, including how to be a good friend to someone with autism, at autismspeaks.org.

If we make healthy choices for our bodies, hearts and minds, and support our family and friends to do the same if and when they can, we're all likely to lead longer and healthier lives. That means more time together—and more time to make a difference in the world.

# Get Going!

- Share the information and tips in this chapter with family and at least three friends
- Get an annual checkup that checks your blood pressure

- Make sure the grown-ups in your life do the same
- Exercise any way you can (and try for an hour a day)
- Encourage your family and friends to take walks together
- Ask your doctor about any medical questions you have
- Start learning about CPR online
- Take an in-person CPR class
- See if you can organize a CPR class in your school
- Donate hair to Locks of Love or Children With Hair Loss
- Volunteer at a hospital (if you're old enough)
- Stay away from secondhand smoke
- Encourage people you know who smoke or use other forms of tobacco to quit
- Write to your elected officials about the importance of lessening pollution in your neighborhood, making healthy affordable food more available and getting exercise back into schools
- Find out your diabetes status and make sure adults in your life do too
- Help grown-ups plan and cook healthy meals that work for your budget, including by using helpful apps
- Raise awareness about food deserts
- Check out Haile's healthy-cooking tips
- Compare food labels and buy the healthier foods
- Work with your principal to find out how healthy your school is— and what you can do to help make it even healthier, especially at lunchtime
- Start a garden through Katie's Krops or on your own
- Participate in the Campaign for Tobacco-Free Kids' Kick Butts Day
- Have an indoor dance party
- Lead a jumping jack competition
- See which of your friends can do the most push-ups

- Organize a field day of activities you think would be fun at your school, like Danyel did at hers
- Get an allergy test (if you think you need one)
- Learn to swim
- Stand up to bullies online and in real life and support kids who are being bullied
- Support friends who are having a hard time and talk to a trusted adult about getting friends the help they may need
- Be patient and kind to anyone you know with autism, Alzheimer's or any challenge that may affect how people communicate and interact
- If you're at least thirteen, use social media to follow organizations (like the American Cancer Society) and leaders (like Michelle Obama) who are working to help more people be and stay healthy

Courtesy of Jose Luis Pelaez/Corbis

CHAPTER SIX

# VIRUSES AND VACCINES

After school, on Thursday, November 7th, 1991, when I was eleven, I was in my father's campaign office in downtown Little Rock. On October 3rd, my father had announced that he was running for president. A little more than a month later, there was already so much happening, and I loved being amid the people talking about policy ideas and political strategy, phones ringing, notes being scribbled down on yellow pads and most of all, the energy from people who had come from across the country to be part of my dad's campaign. A lot of energy was concentrated in that office because people had to physically be together to work together—it was before most people were using cell phones or the Internet (or had even heard of the Internet). I wasn't there that often because of school, homework and ballet, but when I was there after school and on weekends, I loved listening to all the banter. I tried to be useful—often stuffing envelopes—and I tried to stay out of the way.

That November Thursday, I remember the office got completely quiet when the nightly news came on with footage from a press conference earlier that afternoon in Los Angeles in which Earvin "Magic" Johnson announced that he was HIV positive. Like many kids in the late 1980s and early 1990s, I was captivated by the great basketball players of the era: Magic Johnson, Michael Jordan, Larry Bird and Arkansas' own Scottie Pippen. I had vaguely heard of HIV and AIDS, but until Magic Johnson put a face on the epidemic for me and many Americans, I didn't know what HIV was or how it related to AIDS. I had no idea how horrible it would be for our world or how many lives it already had claimed. I certainly didn't suspect I would spend much of my adult life thinking about, studying and supporting the global fight against AIDS. I didn't know how drawn I would be to advocating and

*This is Magic Johnson in 1991, when he announced at a press conference that he was HIV positive.*

Courtesy of Ken Levine/Getty

working for more people around the world to have access to clean water, improved sanitation and the same high-quality health care we have, at our best, in the United States.

Today in the U.S., HIV is no longer a death sentence, if it's diagnosed early enough and treatment started immediately. Magic Johnson is known today more for his basketball commentary and business success than his HIV status. He looks as healthy now as he did when I

*In this picture taken twenty-two years after he announced he was HIV positive, Magic Johnson is still looking healthy—and is healthy—thanks to antiviral therapy.*

watched his press conference speech more than twenty years ago. But that's not the reality in much of the developing world where millions of people aren't diagnosed early enough, if at all, and millions aren't on the treatments that could save their lives, in part because they and their governments can't afford them. And it's not only about HIV. Far from it.

One of the leading causes of death around the world for young children is severe dehydration due to diarrhea, but it's almost only deadly in the developing world, not in wealthier countries. That wasn't always true. In 1900, severe dehydration due to diarrhea was one of the leading causes of death in the U.S. Again, I am reminded of the saying "There but for the grace of God, go I." You or I might have gotten many of the diseases discussed in this chapter and the next one if we'd been born in a different part of the world or even lived in the U.S. in a different century. Like in the last chapter, in this chapter and the next, we'll talk about specific diseases and what each of us can do to protect ourselves, our families, our friends and to help protect people across the world from these infections, many of which we've been fighting for a very long time.

For much of human history, people generally believed diseases were caused by an imbalance in our bodies (sometimes blamed on our parents or ancestors, though DNA wasn't identified until the 20th century). Another historical theory was that we got sick when we breathed in bad smelly air, often reeking because of rotting food or polluted water nearby. We now know that while some diseases and risk factors are inherited by children from their parents, some of the smallest organisms on earth—viruses, bacteria, parasites—cause some of the most frightening and deadly infections, from pneumonia to HIV/AIDS to Ebola. Although bad air or stinky water alone doesn't make people sick, the things that can infect us and make us sick may be transmitted through air, flourish in dirty water or make themselves at home in spoiled food.

## A LONG TIME AGO . . .

Infectious diseases have been killing people forever. A 9,000-year-old skeleton buried in the Mediterranean off the coast of Israel showed evidence of tuberculosis (TB). The first-known mention of malaria appeared in a Chinese medical text that's approximately 4,700 years old. Evidence of smallpox has been found in 3,000-year-old Egyptian mummies and was mentioned in 1,700-year-old writings from India.

What do you think the deadliest infectious disease of all

time is? Did you say malaria? Some research estimates half of all deaths throughout human history were caused by malaria, which would mean that more than 50 billion people have died from the disease, making it a matchless villain. Even if it's half that number, it would still be a staggering statistic. Smallpox killed an estimated 300–400 million people in the 20th century alone, more than the number of people who died in World War I and World War II combined. Influenza, also known as the flu, was particularly nasty in the 20th century, killing an estimated 30–50 million people in less than a year from 1918 to 1919. Human history is in part the history of our struggle to prevent, stop and recover from infections.

## A FEW DEFINITIONS

Before we go any further, I want to define a few terms so you'll know what I'm talking about in this chapter (and the next). When a new disease emerges or an old disease comes back with surprising strength, infecting more people than expected, that is what's known as an "outbreak." If a disease is widespread in a particular community at a particular point in time, this is known as an "epidemic." When a disease affects more than one country, or even many communities within a country, it stops being referred to as an epidemic and becomes known as a "pandemic." That word comes from the Greek words *pan*, which means "all," and *demos*, which means "people." So it makes sense that a pandemic is a situation when a disease affects many people. (If you're interested in this sort of thing, "epidemic" comes from *epi*, which means "upon," and *demos*, again, so the word literally means "upon the people.") The 1918 to 1919 flu mentioned above is an example of an outbreak that became an epidemic and ultimately a global pandemic. The "case fatality rate" is relevant to any disease. It's the proportion of people who die out of the total number of people who get a disease.

## WHAT WE KNOW NOW

Across the 20th century and the beginning of the 21st century we made a lot of progress against infectious diseases, but they remain a leading cause of death in many of the poorest countries on earth and a leading cause of death for children globally. While people in America are living an average of thirty years longer than they did at the start of the 20th century, around the world, far too many kids and adults still get sick from diseases we know how to prevent and treat. There are still many places around the world where it's all too common to die of pneumonia, malaria or severe dehydration due to diarrhea.

One of the ways we have made progress is by interrupting the paths by which infectious diseases travel from one person to another. Various illnesses, like the flu, are transmitted through direct skin-to-skin contact (like shaking hands) and through coughing or sneezing. Some germs can also hang out on a surface like a table or computer keyboard or basketball waiting for someone else to pick them up so they can make themselves at home inside yet another person's body. Other illnesses—malaria, for example—rely on animals or insects (for malaria it's mosquitoes) to carry them while they wait to infect their next human victim. Still others thrive in bad food and dirty water.

We have learned that keeping hands and surfaces clean prevents countless cases of the flu or the common cold. This is why your parents and teachers (and I will too) nag you to wash your hands. Using bug repellent and bed nets to thwart mosquitoes has helped control malaria in some areas. Better food storage methods, including refrigeration, have helped avoid incalculable cases of stomach bugs and diarrhea that are particularly deadly to children. And improved sanitation systems that keep drinking water clean and free of the germs that live in the stuff we flush down the toilet have saved millions of lives. Infectious diseases are scary, but we know that we can fight and defeat them by keeping our communities and ourselves germ-free, healthy and vaccinated—and treating them when they do occur. That's all much harder to do in developing countries and poorer communities in every country, but it's not impossible, and we'll talk about some specific solutions later in this chapter.

# VIRUSES

Viruses are among the smallest creatures on earth, even smaller than bacteria (discussed in the next chapter), and they cause a variety of infectious diseases, including the common cold, the flu, HIV/AIDS and diarrhea (though bacteria can cause diarrhea too). Scientists compare viruses to hijackers, because they invade our bodies and use our own healthy cells against us by forcing them to produce more unhealthy viruses, eventually killing the healthy cells or the virus's hosts in a vicious cycle. Viral infections are especially tricky because medicines we rely on to treat other types of diseases, like antibiotics for bacterial infections, do not work against viruses. Antivirals, drugs designed to treat viruses, are pretty new. And while a lot of research on antivirals is being conducted around the world, so far they've mainly been used to treat HIV/AIDS, the flu and a few other select diseases. What follows is a discussion of just some of the most common viruses that impact people, particularly kids, worldwide and what we can do—and are doing—to defeat them, with vaccines, antivirals, hand-washing and more.

## *Smallpox, Vaccines . . . and Measles*

Let's start with a success story. Smallpox is the only major disease the world has ever defeated, but in its heyday it was highly contagious and quite deadly. Smallpox made people really tired and gave them high fevers, aches and horribly painful (and ugly) sores, often all over their bodies. Although many people who got smallpox eventually recovered, it killed more than a quarter of its victims (its case fatality rate was about 30 percent) and left terrible scars on its survivors, sometimes blinding them. (That happened if people got sores in their eyes.) Viruses, like other germs, act in their own self-interest—

they want to keep on living, just like people do. If viruses killed 100 percent of the people they infected, the viruses themselves would die out. Since most people who got smallpox lived, the virus could live on and on, traveling the world, claiming victims and shaping history along the way.

The Spanish, English, French and Portuguese explorers and colonists brought smallpox

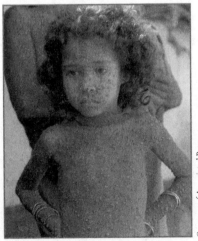

*This young Indian girl was infected with smallpox in 1974.*

along with their ships, animals and tools when they arrived in the Americas. Some Native American tribes were almost completely killed off and others were severely weakened by the virus; smallpox is estimated to have killed half of the North American Cherokee population around the Carolinas in 1738 alone. Multiple smallpox epidemics are believed to have killed tens of thousands, if not hundreds of thousands, of people in Brazil in the 16th and 17th centuries alone (the 1500s and 1600s). In a tragic sense, smallpox might have been the European colonizers' greatest help in conquering the Americas.

Smallpox didn't discriminate between a king or a peasant. Tsar Peter II of Russia is one of its famous victims and Queen Anne of England one of its famous survivors, but smallpox was deadliest for children. For example, in London in the late 1880s, eight out of ten children infected with smallpox died. It's fitting then that what is known as the world's first vaccination was given to an eight-year-old boy. But I imagine it was quite scary for James Phipps, that eight-year-old, to be part of this brand-new science. In 1796, Dr. Edward Jenner inserted cowpox virus under James's skin through a couple of shallow cuts (injections hadn't been invented yet). Jenner believed that the use of a much less dangerous virus—cowpox—would protect James against the far more deadly small-

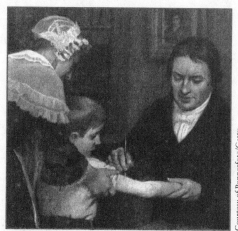

Dr. Edward Jenner and James in 1796.

pox. A month and a half later, Jenner repeated the process with James, but this time he inserted smallpox under his skin (an experiment that would never be allowed today!). Thankfully, James didn't develop smallpox. The immunity (or defense) he'd developed against cowpox protected him from smallpox too. And while there were definitely people who were skeptical about vaccines in the late 1700s and early 1800s, within four years, 100,000 people had received the smallpox vaccine in Europe, and large-scale vaccination efforts had begun in the United States.

General George Washington believed in vaccinations too. Even before Jenner's discovery that a less powerful virus could protect against a more powerful one, Washington inoculated American troops during the Revolutionary War, instructing army doctors to use the same procedure Jenner would use, but with smallpox instead of cowpox (which was even more dangerous). Soldiers would have small amounts of smallpox inserted into skin cuts. This process, known as variolation, generally led to milder forms of smallpox that, once soldiers had recovered, provided immunity against more serious cases. Some historians believe Washington's decision (initially widely opposed) was crucial to the United States' victory in the Revolutionary War.

President Thomas Jefferson believed in vaccinations too. President Jefferson wrote Jenner praising his discovery and basically said vaccines were the greatest medical advancement ever. Given how many lives vaccines have saved over the last couple of centuries, it would be hard to argue with Jefferson's conclusion (though Dr. Alexander Fleming, who we'll meet in the next chapter, may also have a fair claim!). Even the case of smallpox vaccinations alone would arguably support Jefferson's enthusiasm. Smallpox eradication, or getting rid of the virus completely, became an official priority for the world in 1966. Through a well-coordinated combination of vaccination efforts and the rapid identification of any smallpox cases, smallpox was eliminated in a decade. The last-known case of smallpox was in 1978 and the world declared victory against smallpox in 1980. The role of cowpox in vaccine development isn't forgotten either; the word vaccine comes from *vacca*, the Latin for "cow"!

# GIVE IT A SHOT!

Do you know anyone who likes getting shots? I don't think I do. I remember my friend Elizabeth once telling me in elementary school she'd threatened to jump out of her doctor's window rather than get a shot. But regardless of how we feel about shots, we can all be grateful that vaccinations today look very different from what Jenner used more than 200 years ago when he inserted cowpox pus into open cuts on James Phipps' arm. Today, most are shots that take only seconds to deliver, and some vaccines even come in the form of a nose spray or a drop of liquid on your tongue.

When you get a vaccination, you're more likely to avoid the specific virus guarded against and you're also contributing to "herd immunity." Like cattle in a herd (not the most flattering image for us, but bear with me please), people live together in communities, and when almost everyone in a community is immunized, or protected against a disease, that group protection acts as a shield, keeping those who can't get vaccinated—like infants and people with severe illnesses—from getting sick too. The more dangerous the disease, the more individuals need to be vaccinated to ensure herd immunity works. And because we live in a society where people travel and move around so much, it's especially important that everyone who can get vaccinated does—because our germs go with us.

Right now in the United States, there are fierce debates about vaccines and whether or not they are safe or necessary, particularly in the context of what is known as the MMR vaccine, which covers measles, mumps and rubella (hence the name MMR)—all viruses that can make people really sick and can even be deadly. These are not new debates. George Washington had to convince a skeptical Continental Congress that inoculating American troops against smallpox had more benefits than risks. More than a hundred years ago, in 1905, the U.S. Supreme Court decided that American states could require that everyone get the smallpox vaccine. Less than twenty years later, in 1922, the Supreme Court decided that school districts didn't have to let kids who had not received mandatory vaccinations into their schools. These cases hardly settled the issue. In 2014, the U.S. had record high rates of measles for recent years, tied to low vaccination rates.

Adults choose not to get themselves or their children vaccinated for many reasons that have no basis in science. One reason people say they won't get the flu vaccine is that it gives them the flu. This is not actually possible. There is no live virus in the flu shot, so it's impossible for the flu vaccine to give anyone the flu. Scientists do their best to predict which strains of flu will be the most common in a given year and to create a flu vaccine to protect against those strains. But they don't always get it right. In part because the flu shot only protects against certain flu strains, it's possible to get the flu by being infected by a strain the vaccine didn't guard you against. It's also possible that your body failed to develop immunity against the flu strains included in the flu vaccine. That's rare, but it happens. What's important to understand is that it's impossible to get the flu because you've gotten a flu shot.

A particularly troubling misconception about vaccines is that they cause other diseases, like autism. There is not one virus-sized piece of scientific evidence to back up this claim. Another reason people say they're not getting themselves or their kids vaccinated is because they think the disease in question is not so serious, whether it's the flu or measles. Let's go back to measles, part of the MMR vaccine—the one vaccine most commonly believed to cause autism, despite there being no evidence to support such a link. Someone who gets measles will have a high fever, cough, sore throat and a full-body red rash. At best it's uncomfortable. But at worst, it's lethal. Both the flu and measles can be very serious, even deadly, particularly for small children or older adults. Recent research also shows that measles weakens our systems long after we recover (if we recover), making us more vulnerable to other infections. Both measles and the flu spread through the air by coughs and sneezes, making them hard to avoid in places where there are a lot of people close together, like schools or transportation systems (if you live in New York like I do, think of our subway system!), so prevention through vaccines is all the more important, since hand-washing is at best not easy and often impossible to do on a bus, plane or train.

Yet another reason often offered against the use of vaccines is that improved hygiene and sanitation are responsible for the decline of disease rates in developed countries like the United States. While it is absolutely true that housing with more space and better ventilation (not overcrowded), cleaner water, improved sanitation (no more mixing of poop and water) and safer food have helped people stay healthy, not get sick and recover from sickness more quickly, there is no doubt that vaccinations have also helped. This is particularly true with measles.

Before the vaccine was introduced in the 1960s, there were hundreds of thousands of measles cases in the United States. Within a decade, the cases were measured in tens of thousands, and by the time I was born in 1980, in the thousands. In 2000, there were only eighty-six confirmed cases. From hundreds of thousands to less than a hundred in forty years: that is the power of vaccines.

MEASLES CASES IN THE U.S. OVER TIME, 1950–2014

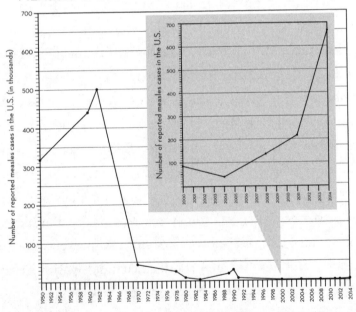

Information source: Centers for Disease Control and Prevention (CDC)

So why are we starting to see an uptick in measles cases in the U.S. now? The recent rise in measles sadly demonstrates the power of fear and the ability of misinformation about the

MMR vaccine and autism to travel as quickly as any email or Facebook post. There's a clear link between lower vaccination rates and more people getting measles today than a few years ago. There are things in this book where there is not one clear answer. On vaccines, there is.

We shouldn't have to worry about measles anymore, but we do and will until vaccination rates go back up. Thankfully, we don't have to worry about smallpox any longer. For the flu (which we'll talk more about below), we can protect ourselves by getting vaccinated, washing our hands with soap and water and avoiding touching our eyes, nose and mouth (in other words, places that provide great opportunities for germs to walk right into our bodies). All of that protects our family and friends too. If we do get sick, we should stay home from school or work, drink lots of fluids and rest—all things many of us hear from our parents and our doctors. Why? Because keeping our bodies hydrated and getting enough sleep helps us heal faster. I am thirty-five years old and I still get that advice from my mom on a regular basis!

## Influenza & Pneumonia

Every year, up to half a million people around the world die of influenza, more commonly known as the flu. Unlike many diseases that are equally common throughout the year, flu has a season, one that largely coincides with football season in the U.S.—autumn into winter and sometimes lasting through early spring. There are many different flu strains, some of which you may have heard of, like H1N1, also called swine flu because of its similarity to a virus found in pigs. Although there are some diseases you can get from eating meat infected with something nasty like the E. coli bacteria, you can't get swine flu from eating bacon or pork chops. Flu symptoms are similar to those of the common cold but generally worse, often including a high fever, sore throat, achiness and tiredness. Part of what makes the flu so dangerous is that it, like measles, is highly contagious. Another part of what makes the flu dangerous is that it can weaken your immune system, making it easier for pneumonia to take hold, especially in kids and older people.

Pneumonia is a lung infection that usually brings with it a fever, coughing and difficulty breathing; it can be fatal. Although plenty of people with the flu never get pneumonia, you can, so it's important to get vaccinated against pneumonia too (which generally you have to do only once). However, to make it more confusing, pneumonia can result from either viruses or bacteria, and the vaccine only protects against the viral kind. Still, some protection is better than none. In 2013, flu and pneumonia together killed more than 50,000 Americans. Who wants to be part of that statistic? Once again, being vaccinated is an easy (and not-too-painful) way to help avoid getting sick or worse.

## Rotavirus

You may not have heard of this before, but you were probably vaccinated against it (my daughter Charlotte got her rotavirus vaccination when she was only months old). Rotavirus is the leading cause of extreme diarrhea among children five years old and younger, including infants. There are still more than 750,000 kids who die every year around the world because of severe water loss, or dehydration, due to diarrhea, often the result of a rotavirus infection. I think it's horrible that in the 21st century so many kids still die from diarrhea, something we know how to prevent and treat. Until a rotavirus vaccine was developed, most kids in the United States would have gotten a rotavirus infection at least once, and some would have died. In fact, at the beginning of the 20th century, severe dehydration because of diarrhea was a leading cause of death among

*Rotavirus may be small, but the danger it poses to children is huge.*

American kids, just like it is today in many developing countries.

Gavi, The Vaccine Alliance, is a global partnership focused on closing what's known as the "vaccine gap," so that kids everywhere—and not just in relatively wealthier countries like the U.S.—are vaccinated against the greatest infectious disease threats to kids' health today, like pneumonia and rotavirus. Since 2000, Gavi has helped vaccinate 500 million children around the world. If you're interested in knowing more about Gavi's work, you can visit their website, gavi.org. And once you've learned more, if you want to help kids everywhere get the vaccines most American kids get, you can urge your senators, your congressperson and our president to continue providing American support for Gavi's work (since most of Gavi's funding comes from donor governments). You can write letters, send emails, make phone calls and sign petitions. If you're thirteen or older, you can tweet, post on Facebook and otherwise engage social media to make sure your elected officials know that you— as a young person—believe no young person anywhere should die from something a vaccine can prevent. You can even share the

247

story of James Phipps, or talk about how increasing access to vaccines is as American as George Washington!

It's important to treat severe dehydration (whether caused by rotavirus or something else) while working on increasing vaccination rates around the world. Severe dehydration is best treated through something called oral rehydration solution, a precise mixture of clean water, salt and sugar, in combination with zinc. It helps our bodies recover, and literally rehydrate, more quickly. In India, kids your age act as sort of "health ambassadors," learning about diarrhea prevention and treatment at school, and then taking that information home to share with their parents, all in an effort to help them take care of themselves and their younger siblings. The Clinton Health Access Initiative—an NGO affiliated with the Clinton Foundation that my father started—is one organization working with young health ambassadors. As of early 2015, it had equipped 500,000 kids with the facts about diarrhea, including how to prevent it and how to find affordable treatments. It's a program that's helping kids save their own lives.

As with all diseases, it's better not to get sick in the first place. Thankfully, every year, more and more children around the world receive the rotavirus vaccine, in large part thanks to Gavi and its partners.

RISE IN BASIC VACCINATION RATES AROUND THE WORLD*

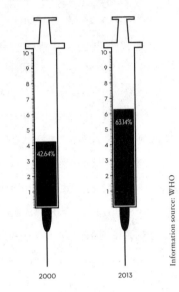

2000 — 42.64%
2013 — 63.14%

Information source: WHO

*Includes Diphtheria, Hepatitis B, Hib, PAB, Measles, Meningitis, Pertussis, Polio, Rotavirus, Tetanus, Tuberculosis, Yellow Fever

# HIV/AIDS

As I shared at the beginning of the chapter, I didn't know a lot about the human immunodeficiency virus (HIV) before learning Magic Johnson was HIV positive (another way of saying that he had HIV). Now it feels like I can't remember a time before HIV or the acquired immune deficiency syndrome (AIDS), the final stage of the HIV infection. As AIDS is the advanced form of HIV, I'll refer to HIV/AIDS in most of this section to describe the disease.

An estimated 35 million people are living with HIV/AIDS around the world—that's about the population of Canada. Since the first cases were reported in 1981, HIV/AIDS has claimed the lives of even more people worldwide, 39 million and sadly counting. In the U.S., more than 650,000 people with HIV/AIDS have died and currently more than 1.2 million people are living with the disease. HIV/AIDS is on every continent but it has hit Africa the hardest where it currently is the number one cause of death in adults. Unquestionably, HIV/AIDS is the cruelest new virus of the past few decades measured by the number of lives it has taken and the lives affected—particularly the millions of children it has orphaned.

Thankfully, antiviral medicines now exist that enable people with HIV/AIDS to live healthy, full lives. These medicines work by stopping the virus from replicating (or making more copies of itself) inside an HIV-positive person's cells. In 2015, with the right treatment started early enough, an HIV-positive person can have a reasonable expectation of living an otherwise healthy life.

The number of new HIV cases is going down as prevention

## PEOPLE WITH HIV/AIDS AROUND THE WORLD, 2013*

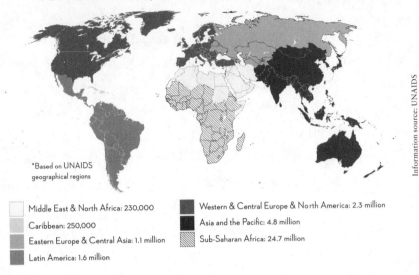

*Based on UNAIDS geographical regions

Information source: UNAIDS

Middle East & North Africa: 230,000

Caribbean: 250,000

Eastern Europe & Central Asia: 1.1 million

Latin America: 1.6 million

Western & Central Europe & North America: 2.3 million

Asia and the Pacific: 4.8 million

Sub-Saharan Africa: 24.7 million

and treatment efforts become more widespread and effective. At the end of 2013, almost 13 million HIV-positive people were on antiviral treatment around the world, the vast majority (11.7 million) in developing countries. The Clinton Health Access Initiative has helped expand HIV/AIDS treatment by working with drug companies to dramatically lower the cost of treatment so that more people can get the medicines they need. What used to cost thousands of dollars per person per year now costs $100–200 per adult each year (and even less for children). Because treatments cost so much less, developing countries and donor countries (like the U.S., which is the number one donor to HIV/AIDS treatment efforts in the world) are able to purchase more medicine to help more people.

Someone today who's receiving the less expensive—and just as effective—treatment is a boy named Basil. When I first met him in Cambodia in 2013, Basil was an almost seven-year-old

PEOPLE RECEIVING ANTIVIRAL THERAPY IN LOW- AND
MIDDLE-INCOME COUNTRIES AROUND THE WORLD COMPARED
WITH TOTAL NUMBER OF HIV–POSITIVE PEOPLE AROUND
THE WORLD, 2002–2013

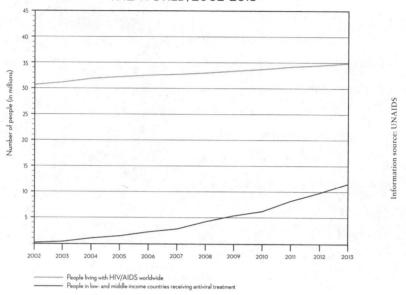

Information source: UNAIDS

People living with HIV/AIDS worldwide
People in low- and middle-income countries receiving antiviral treatment

full of energy who showed me (or more accurately, ran me) proudly around his school, playground and clinic at New Hope for Cambodian Children, a residential facility for orphans and abandoned children living with HIV/AIDS. He didn't look sick at all. But when Basil was just a month old, he was left at a health clinic. He was very, very sick with tuberculosis (discussed in the next chapter). His mom had just died of HIV/AIDS and he was HIV positive. That day, no one thought he'd live such a healthy life. No one thought he'd be alive at all for much longer. Basil became the youngest HIV-positive child in Cambodia, at the time, to receive treatment and now, nine years later, he's healthy and still running around. We've made progress as a global community against HIV/AIDS but still have a long way to go before every HIV-positive person is getting the medicines needed and has a story like Magic Johnson's or Basil's, in which HIV/AIDS is a chronic disease to be managed, not a death sentence.

HIV/AIDS is different from viruses like smallpox or measles because it attacks the body's immune system and it never quits. Our immune system keeps our bodies healthy by fighting off every infection that comes our way (like measles or pneumonia). Under the onslaught

*Here I am with Basil, a super energetic kid, who has been on antiviral medication almost his entire life.*

of HIV/AIDS, our immune system stops working. A common cold could prove deadly to someone with untreated HIV/AIDS. Without treatment, HIV/AIDS is almost always fatal.

HIV is transmitted from person to person through the sharing of blood or other bodily fluids, often through sex. Another common way it can be transmitted is by so-called dirty needles, or needles that have been used before by someone with HIV/AIDS. If a hospital, for example, uses a needle to draw blood from an HIV/AIDS patient and then uses the same needle to draw blood from someone who doesn't have HIV/AIDS, that person faces a major risk of getting HIV/AIDS from the used needle. Don't worry—using new, sterile (a fancy word for super clean), safe needles is a required practice in the United States and around the world for hospitals, clinics and doctors' offices. Another way doctors and nurses protect patients and themselves from HIV/AIDS is by wearing proper protection when they come into contact with blood—it's one of the reasons you've probably noticed the latex gloves your doctor or nurse wears when drawing blood or giving you a shot.

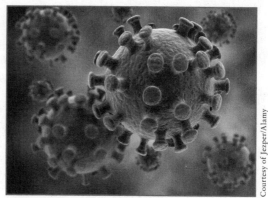

*The HIV virus is very deadly even at only .000005 of an inch.*

Courtesy of Jezper/Alamy

While needles can pass HIV/AIDS, mosquitoes thankfully cannot. Tragically, mothers with HIV/AIDS can pass the virus to the babies growing in their bellies. This is called mother-to-child transmission and it is the most common way in which kids have been infected with HIV/AIDS around the world. To protect babies born to mothers with HIV/AIDS, infected women must take antiviral drugs while pregnant. Children cannot get HIV/AIDS from hugging their moms (or being hugged by them). You cannot get HIV/AIDS from touching or hugging or holding hands with someone who has HIV/AIDS. You cannot get HIV/AIDS from touching something that someone with HIV/AIDS touched.

Currently, no HIV/AIDS vaccine exists. Generally, vaccines are developed from dead or weakened viruses, and those research efforts are often helped by studying people who've recovered from the disease. Unfortunately, thus far, no one has a record of long-term recovery from HIV/AIDS (though there are a few long-term non-progressors, people who have HIV and remain healthy without taking medicines). The common methods for developing vaccines have proven too dangerous or ineffective. Even with these challenges, there are many people around the world who are working tirelessly on an HIV/AIDS vaccine.

The way people look, whether they're boys or girls, what religion they practice, where they live and who they love does not offer special protection from HIV/AIDS. You cannot tell if people have HIV/AIDS from looking at them—unlike some other illnesses that have obvious characteristics like rashes or sores. Someone's HIV/AIDS status only can be known through an HIV/AIDS test. If people don't know their status, they can't start the treatment their bodies need. It's estimated that millions of people worldwide, including hundreds of thousands in the United States, don't know their HIV status. In many communities around the world, including across the U.S., confidential and free HIV/AIDS testing is available (confidential means only the person getting tested knows the results). If you know people who have questions about their HIV/AIDS status, please encourage them to get tested. Anyone can visit aids.gov to find a local clinic that offers free, confidential HIV/AIDS tests. If you have questions about how people protect themselves from HIV/AIDS during sex or in any situation, please talk to your parents, teachers, doctor, school nurse or another trusted adult. The quicker someone is tested, the quicker treatment can start if found HIV positive; that's good for that person's health and for all of us. Someone who is on antiviral treatment is less likely to pass on the HIV virus to another person.

It's especially important to be educated about HIV/AIDS so you can help teach others about how it is transmitted and how it isn't. Why? Well, in addition to helping people know how to protect themselves from HIV/AIDS, it's also important because sadly in many places people are still discriminated against because they or someone they love has HIV/AIDS. In some countries, discrimination against an HIV-positive person is still legal. Around the world, fear of stigma remains a key reason why people are reluctant to get tested and even to take the antiviral therapies that would

*In marches like this, both HIV-positive and -negative people wear HIV-positive T-shirts, showing there's no shame in HIV-positive status. Here they're marching with Treatment Action Campaign, an organization on the front lines of fighting for HIV/AIDS patients in South Africa to get the treatment they need and the respect they (and all people) deserve.*

Courtesy of Gideon Mendel/Corbis

help them lead healthier and longer lives. Part of treating people with respect and dignity regardless of their HIV/AIDS status is ensuring that no one feels any shame for being HIV positive or worried about getting tested. It's also standing up for kids who are bullied because they or someone in their family has HIV/AIDS. This is something we all can do.

One way you can help kids like Basil (and adults too) in the developing world with HIV/AIDS (or tuberculosis or malaria—discussed in the next chapter) is by supporting organizations like UNITAID and the Global Fund to Fight AIDS, Tuberculosis and Malaria. Both are working to get people in developing countries the medicines and care they need to lead healthy and long lives, and to prevent people from getting sick in the first place. You may already be supporting UNITAID if you've ever taken a flight out of Cameroon, Chile, Republic of Congo,

France, Madagascar, Mali, Mauritius, Niger or South Korea. How? Well, those countries each decided to put a small levy, or tax, on airline tickets. Generally it's a $1 or €1 (the € or euro is the currency in much of Europe) for an economy flight ticket. Over time, that adds up. From 2006 to 2014, UNITAID raised almost $1.5 billion from airline taxes alone. To learn more about UNITAID's work, please visit unitaid.org.

If you've ever bought a (RED) product, you're already supporting the Global Fund. There have been (RED) Gap shirts, Apple computers and FEED bags—often, but not always, (RED) products are literally the color red. Companies who sell (RED) products contribute a portion of the proceeds to the Global Fund, specifically to support efforts to protect babies from getting HIV/AIDS from their mothers. From 2006–2014, companies participating in (RED) contributed more than $275 million to the Global Fund, because of the purchases individuals like you and your parents (and possibly actually you and your parents) made. You can find out more about the Global Fund and (RED) by visiting theglobalfund.org. Unlike UNI-TAID's funding, most of the Global Fund's support comes from donor governments, so if you believe in its mission and its work (once you've learned more), urge your senators, congressperson and our president to continue U.S. support for the Global Fund.

## Ebola

If you had to pick the disease right now, at this very minute, you were the most scared of, what would it be? Maybe Ebola? Ebola is a scary disease, partly because it's highly contagious and partly because it's proven very deadly. By May 2015, Ebola had killed more than 11,000 people in Liberia, Sierra Leone and

Guinea, the West African countries hit hardest in the recent outbreak that started in earnest in early 2014. But there's also lots of misinformation swirling around it (including who is at risk of getting Ebola), a situation somewhat understandable given that it was first identified only a few years before HIV/AIDS.

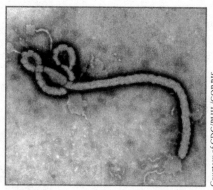

*Not all viruses look as threatening as they are. Under a microscope, the Ebola virus looks just like a snake.*

Courtesy of CDC/PHIL/CORBIS

Ebola first attacks the immune system, weakening a person's defenses before moving out more broadly into a person's body. It attacks quickly and very often lethally, bringing fevers and other symptoms often common with viruses, as well as hemorrhaging (severe bleeding). Because of how extreme Ebola's symptoms can be, how deadly it often is and how little we still know about it, this virus has made a lot of people afraid, and all too often that fear has been directed at the people who are sick. The fear of Ebola and the widespread stigma against Ebola patients contributed to an underreporting of Ebola cases to health authorities in the most affected countries, meaning a lot of people who had Ebola didn't tell anyone that's why they were sick (it's also why we're not sure how many people died—and why there's such a wide range of 50–80 percent in the case fatality rate). Underreporting, if it happens, is a serious challenge when trying to control an infectious disease—if doctors, nurses and other health workers don't know who's sick, it's hard to get people the help they need and to prevent them from infecting others. Fear also all too often leads to stigma around victims and survivors of a disease. In April 2015, I was honored to meet a group of Ebola survivors in Liberia and was heartbroken to hear how many hadn't gotten their

*Here I am with my dad, meeting with Ebola survivors in Liberia in May 2015.*

jobs back or their friends back, because people were still afraid of them, even long after Ebola had left their bodies.

Ebola is spread through contact with an infected person's blood or bodily fluids and it can be transmitted through something that an infected person has touched or worn or a bed they've slept in (which makes it very different from HIV/AIDS). Ebola is not transmitted through the air. Unlike what's true for many viruses, however, Ebola can infect others even after a victim's death, at least for a few days. Because Ebola is so powerful, the protective gear (full-body suits, goggles and gloves) you may have seen in the news is important for doctors, nurses and others working to treat people with Ebola—so that people with Ebola can receive the medical attention they need to get better and health-care workers can be protected while doing their jobs—it's also important for those working with the bodies of Ebola victims. The absence of enough safe, full-body protective gear for everyone on the front lines of the recent Ebola outbreak helps explain why Ebola has taken such a tragically heavy toll on doctors, nurses and other health-care workers, killing more than 500 in 2014 alone. Ebola's ability to spread in so many different ways helps explain why it can move so quickly within families and communities, infecting along the patterns of love, care and support that normally sustain us. Many people have lost multiple family members to Ebola, as those who had cared for the first Ebola victims didn't have the necessary protective gear and became victims themselves.

There is currently no approved vaccine for Ebola, though different groups are working on developing one, and active tests (technically known as trials) of potential Ebola vaccines are occurring in Sierra Leone and Guinea (and there may be a vaccine by the time this book comes out). There are also active tests ongoing to determine which experimental antiviral treatments for Ebola might prove most effective. The absence of approved and broadly available medicines has meant that most treatment of Ebola patients relies on what is known as "supportive care"—making sure people who are sick don't get dehydrated and treating other infections if they happen so that a patient's immune system has the breathing room and strength to fight off the Ebola virus.

In the U.S. and other countries with strong health systems, we have built-in protections against something like Ebola that people living in places like Sierra Leone, Guinea and Liberia don't have yet. We have a robust network of government health officials, hospitals, clinics, lots of doctors and nurses, people who are trained to look out for diseases at airports, seaports and other border crossings—in other words, we're much more prepared to spot possibly scary infectious diseases quickly so that people can get the treatment they need in a safe environment, increasing their ability to get better and decreasing their ability to infect anyone else. That's why in the U.S. we've only had four cases of Ebola, and three of the people recovered. Lots of people are still scared of Ebola in the U.S., because it's scary—but it's far from our greatest infectious disease threat. A core part of our robust network is what's known as the CDC, or the U.S. Centers for Disease Control and Prevention. If you have more questions about Ebola, including how to protect yourself from Ebola (if you're ever in an area with an Ebola outbreak), please visit cdc.gov.

## *Polio*

This chapter on viruses started off with the greatest defeat of an infectious disease in the world's triumph over smallpox, and it ends with an almost-defeat. Hopefully, the effort against polio will not prove the saying "snatching defeat from the jaws of victory." In 2015, polio has been eliminated from most of the world but remains persistent in Afghanistan, Pakistan and Nigeria (and has shown up elsewhere, including in Syria). Polio is highly contagious, and a case anywhere truly poses a threat to people, particularly kids, everywhere. In the most severe cases, polio can cause extreme muscle weakness,

*Franklin Delano Roosevelt, our thirty-second president, was paralyzed by polio when he was thirty-nine. Here he is with his granddaughter Ruthie Bie and his dog, Fala.*

Courtesy of Everett Collection Historical/Alamy

sometimes leading to permanent paralysis (loss of the ability to feel all or part of the body) and even death. Some people, like President Franklin Delano Roosevelt (FDR), survive severe polio and go on to lead successful and otherwise healthy lives. Others do not survive and many who are stricken cannot get the kind of care FDR received.

Throughout its history, polio has had an outsized effect on children, pregnant women and those with weakened immune systems (because they can't fight off the polio infection). It's transmitted mainly when people unknowingly ingest tiny, invisible bits of poop from people who have polio through drinking contaminated water, eating contaminated food or touching something carrying the polio virus and then putting their hands in their mouths. Because polio is so contagious, people who live, work or play with a recently infected person have a very high risk of catching polio.

There is no cure for polio, so the polio vaccine is crucial to ensuring people stay safe from polio's worst effects, or even its mild ones. The most commonly used polio vaccine today is an oral vaccine. People need to take multiple doses over a few years to be fully protected. Tragically, in Pakistan, Afghanistan and Nigeria at different points over the past few years, various community and religious leaders have spoken out against polio eradication efforts. They often falsely accuse polio workers—most of whom are from their own communities in Pakistan, Afghanistan and Nigeria—of being part of an American plot to prevent local children from having children once they grow up, which makes no sense at all. From December 2012 to November 2014, at least sixty-five anti-polio health workers were killed in Pakistan alone. Nine anti-polio workers were tragically killed

*Polio vaccine workers face violent attacks while working to rid the world of this disease.*

Courtesy of Asianet-Pakistan/Shutterstock

in northern Nigeria on one day in 2013. Children now infected with polio are the invisible victims of those attacks. In Pakistan there were four times as many polio cases in 2014 as 2013.

Unlike many diseases, polio cannot survive for long outside of humans and it cannot thrive in animals. The vaccine is effective and relatively cheap to make, though at the moment it's clearly dangerous for health workers to give it to the kids who need it the most. Hopefully, newer strategies from the brave people and organizations who work against polio will help lessen the fear about the polio vaccine so that all kids can be vaccinated and polio can then follow smallpox into the history books. If you want to learn more about polio vaccination efforts across the world, polioeradication.org is a good place to start.

As always, the first and most important thing you can do is to try to keep yourself healthy, at home, at school and when you travel. If you can do that, you help prevent others from getting sick. If you make sure your vaccinations are up to date, it protects you and your friends (and strangers) from getting diseases like measles and the flu. And although this has come up many times already (and I did warn you I would nag you about this), it's impossible to overstate the importance of washing your hands with soap and water after you go to the bathroom and before you eat, which may sound completely obvious, but too often people forget or don't want to bother. You can use an alcohol-based hand sanitizer as a back-up option if soap and water aren't available. This may also sound obvious, but if you see blood or vomit or anything that looks like it came out of a person or animal (yes, I just wrote that), find an adult to help safely and appropriately clean it up.

Another way to help protect yourself and others is by sharing what you know about good hygiene and healthy behaviors. Without even thinking about it, we often take for granted that other people know what we know, and sometimes they don't. One thing you can do is to remind (nicely) or even tell someone for the first time about the importance of vaccines, hand-washing, bug repellant (more on that in the next chapter), good hydration and other proven strategies to help prevent specific diseases and to generally keep yourself virus-free and healthy.

Someone who's doing just that is Shaba (whose name is changed for her protection) from Pakistan. When she became a school leader with Right To Play, an organization that helps teach kids important life lessons through sports and play, she was in sixth grade. Shaba lives with mental and physical disabilities and for many years, she was teased and bullied, often responding the only way she knew how, by fighting back. She was socially isolated when she started to work with Right To Play volunteer Coach Aisha (whose name has also been changed for her protection).

Coach Aisha gave Shaba the opportunity to use sports and games to help teach her classmates about the importance of

*Right To Play helps kids learn about good hygiene through games like this one.*

hygiene, making learning about hand-washing fun (focused on, you guessed it, the right way to wash hands). Shaba taught kids hand-washing games they could do together before meals at school and at home. Over time, she's grown more confident, which is great for Shaba and helps people see beyond her disabilities to the person she is. She's teased less and doesn't think fighting back is the only response, even when she is bullied.

Shaba's confidence has also helped make her a more effective leader and peer educator, which means more people know how to better protect their health and why hand-washing is so important. That's good for everyone—the kids in Shaba's school, and the families they go home to who now know more about hygiene, good health and hand-washing games too! To learn more about Right To Play's work with kids like Shaba on hand-washing and other health fronts as well as its very cool founder (and my friend) Johann Koss, please visit righttoplay.com.

When talking about health risks and prevention, whether it relates to hygiene or anything else, it's important to stick to facts. You can share fact sheets and helpful infographics from reliable sources like the U.S. CDC at cdc.gov and the World Health Organization (often referred to as WHO) at who.int about everything from specific diseases (what they are—and what they aren't) to why vaccines are safe, to how best to wash our hands (yes, there is a "right" way). It's also important to be aware of what are *not* immediate health risks, like Ebola was not an immediate health risk to almost all Americans during the recent outbreak in West Africa, and what are more immediate health risks, like the flu during flu season. It doesn't help anyone anywhere if we panic unnecessarily in our own minds, homes or schools. If you're traveling outside the U.S. for any reason, it's good to check the CDC website's travel section to be aware of what additional precautions (like extra vaccines) you may need to take so that you're protecting your health away from home just as well as you do at home.

That doesn't mean you shouldn't still pay attention and be concerned about what's happening elsewhere, even if you have no plans to travel outside the U.S. Quite the contrary. That's a polite way of saying that I believe we must support efforts to improve health everywhere—it's good for all of us. If every country had a health system more like ours than not, more people in more places would be less likely to get sick—and we'd be less likely to get sick too. We would never worry about an Ebola outbreak in another country because we would know any Ebola patients would be quickly identified and treated, hopefully leading to their recovery and stopping Ebola from spreading even to their neighbors, much less other countries.

If you want to help fight infectious diseases in other communities and countries (even if you can't go there yourself!), it's important to first understand what the challenges are and aren't (in some places HIV/AIDS is the main concern, in others it's heart disease, in many places it's both). It's important to know what has been proven to work and recognize that some things that work in one place may not work in another. And it's crucial to be aware of what the communities combating infections think the best and right methods are for preventing and treating various diseases. Imagine how you and your family would feel if someone showed up telling you to do A, B and C without ever asking how you felt about A, B or C.

North Carolina–native Erin is a terrific example of someone who felt a connection to a specific place—Haiti—and issue—access to health care after Haiti's devastating 2010 earthquake—and wanted to do something to help. Erin also found an organization—Partners In Health (PIH)—that works, as its name implies, in partnership with local communities in Haiti and elsewhere to provide high-quality health care in places that often have had none (they've never had a doctor or a nurse). Erin first learned of PIH and its work to help Haitians fight HIV/AIDS, get vaccinated, get cardiac care and much, much more in 2009.

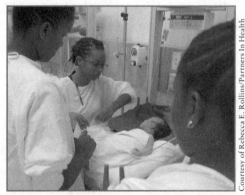

Courtesy of Rebecca E. Rollins/Partners In Health

*PIH has facilities all over Haiti, like the one shown in this picture. It's a place where anyone would feel good getting care.*

After the 2010 earth-quake hit, then-seven-year-old Erin gave her mom the $3.08 she had saved so that she could donate it to PIH for Haiti. Although Erin had given all the money she had, she wanted to do more. So Erin decided to sell handmade bookmarks

*Erin raises money for PIH to help Haitians get high-quality health care.*

at the local farmers' market. As she recently told PIH, her first goal was $10, but that goal quickly swelled to $100, then $1,000.

Erin could have stopped long ago—she's been raising money for PIH for five years now—and still have accomplished a lot, but she knows she can do even more, so she continues to sell her bookmarks and now, additionally, sells greeting cards to ensure that people she may never meet don't have to die of malaria or HIV/AIDS or cholera (more on cholera and malaria in the next chapter). To learn more about PIH, visit pih.org. I'm on PIH's board of trustees because I believe so strongly in PIH's mission and work, and I'm also grateful for the opportunities the Clinton Foundation and Clinton Health Access Initiative have had to work with PIH in Haiti and across the world. Paul Farmer, one of PIH's founders, is one of my heroes and someone I'm proud to call my friend.

Erin also did something important in addition to raising money. She showed that a girl in North Carolina cared enough about PIH to first make greeting cards and bookmarks and later to travel to Boston to meet some of the PIH team to say thank you. That's the sort of support any of us can provide—by saying thank you to people on the front lines doing research to fight diseases, providing support to communities to prevent diseases and caring for those who are sick. You can send emails or letters to say thank you, whether to PIH, or any of the organizations or people mentioned in this book, or really anyone you think is doing important work. I remember my mom and grandmother Dorothy explaining this to me when I was little as the discipline of gratitude—if we're thankful to someone for something, we should say thank you so they know it. It's not a notion either of them originated (far from it—the idea is in the Bible) but I always think of my mom and grandma in connection to the discipline of gratitude because of all the conversations we had about it over the years. And I try to practice the discipline of gratitude every day. Thank you to Dr. Jenner and Dr. Farmer and all the doctors, nurses, community health-care workers, teachers, parents and more who've helped me lead a healthy life and are continuing to help people around the world lead healthier lives too.

# Get Going!

- Make sure your vaccines are up to date and get a flu shot each year
- Cover your nose and mouth with a tissue or your elbow when you sneeze
- Stay home from school if you're sick
- Wash your hands with soap and water after you use the bathroom and before you eat—every time

- Tell at least three friends about the importance of vaccines and hand-washing
- Help educate your friends about what the causes and treatments for various diseases are (and what they're not)
- Never discriminate against or stigmatize any person with any disease, or a survivor of any disease
- Send emails or letters to say thank you to any NGOs and charities doing important and lifesaving work (like Erin did with PIH)
- Write to elected officials to tell them how important vaccines and supporting vaccine efforts around the world are
- If you're traveling outside the U.S., make sure you know what vaccines and precautions you need to take by visiting cdc.gov
- Help raise money for organizations that are fighting diseases you want to help defeat or helping build stronger health systems
- Start an online petition about vaccines or to support various patients and survivors of different diseases
- Talk to your family about buying (RED) products if and when you can to support the Global Fund
- Support family members and friends fighting any of the diseases mentioned here as well as those that aren't
- If you're at least thirteen, share stories on Twitter, Facebook or other social media channels about vaccines and viruses, about patients and survivors of various viruses
- If you're at least thirteen, use social media to follow organizations (like PIH and Right To Play) and leaders (like Elton John through the Elton John AIDS Foundation) working against infectious diseases and the stigma that, too often, patients have to fight along with their infections

CHAPTER SEVEN

# BUGS AND BACTERIA

**W**hat's the first thing you learned about in school that scared you? Really, really scared you? Maybe this hasn't happened for you yet. For me it was the Black Death, or the bubonic plague. I'll never forget learning about the Black Death for the first time in my ninth grade history class and remember to this day Mrs. Morin's vivid and terrifying descriptions of people dying in their homes, in streets, in churches—everywhere—across Europe hundreds of years before. I have always loved learning about history, in and out of school. I love the subject so much I chose to major in history and literature in college. My trips as a kid to the library I mentioned earlier? They were often to check out books about actual historical figures that fascinated and inspired me, like the medieval Eleanor of Aquitaine (the only person to ever sit on both the thrones of England and France), or fictional historical characters that similarly captured my imagination, like the American Revolutionary War era Johnnie Tremain (a resilient silversmith apprentice). I used to dream I was riding alongside Eleanor in 12th-century France and Johnnie in 18th-century Boston. To say I had a romanticized view of the past would be . . . accurate. Then came that day in Mrs. Morin's class. Hearing that whole families and even towns had died gruesome, horrible deaths because of a bacteria made me very grateful to live in the then-late 20th century, to have wonderful doctors and to live after Dr. Alexander Fleming discovered penicillin, which paved the way for modern antibiotics.

Viruses have been around a long time. Bacteria have been around even longer. This is all relative! Along with parasites, they've tormented people for thousands of years (and likely tormented our pre-human ancestors for millions of years). It's important to understand the differences between the viruses, bacteria and parasites that make us sick so we can have a better chance of protecting people today and defeating the diseases in the future. As antivirals are used to treat viruses, antibiotics are used to treat bacterial infections, though they work very differently. Specific antivirals work only against specific viruses (because viruses use our own cells to reproduce and nobody wants a medicine that kills all the healthy cells in our body while killing the virus). Antibiotics historically have worked against many different bacteria by attacking bacterial cells' walls (that's safe for our healthy cells because human cells don't have cell walls). But these days, antibiotics are getting less effective at doing their job because too many people aren't taking the right antibiotics for the right things in the right way and the wily bacteria are growing resistant to them.

Still, while researchers work on new antibiotics and new strategies to help people take antibiotics appropriately, we should all be grateful to mold (yes, mold, the green stuff that grows on fruit or bread left out too long) and messiness (yes, truly, messiness). In 1928, Dr. Fleming was cleaning his lab and found penicillium mold—but no bacteria—on part of one lone petri dish (a shallow dish where bacteria are grown). All the other petri dishes had bacteria and no mold. Something in the mold had killed the bacteria. Dr. Fleming and his team quickly realized how powerful the mold extract penicillin could be ("penicillin" is from the Latin for "paintbrush"). While it took almost fifteen more years for researchers to figure out how to mass-produce pen-

icillin, it's hard to imagine the last seventy-plus years without it. Penicillin and newer antibiotics have helped me get over strep throat and other infections more than a few times throughout my life. I'm sure you have similar stories. Thank you, Dr. Fleming. We'll

*Dr. Alexander Fleming discovered penicillin due, in part, to his messy lab.*

come back to antibiotics, but let's talk first about why we need them at all.

## BACTERIA

Bacteria are single-celled organisms that can reproduce on their own—they do not need to barge into our healthy cells like viruses do. They also, as mentioned above, don't look like our cells, so arguably they're not as sneaky as viruses—though this does not mean some of them can't be very deadly. Yet, unlike viruses, most bacteria are helpful, living in our stomachs for example and helping to digest what we eat. In fact, we're learning more and more about how good bacteria help keep more than just our stomachs healthy. New research links brain health, heart health and more to bacteria in our stomachs (often called by scientists—seriously—our guts!) and elsewhere. Less than one-percent of all bacteria cause diseases in humans, but those that do are dangerous. As judged by the number of people killed, bacteria caused the single most-devastating infectious disease outbreak in history.

## *Plague*

When you think of the plague, you might think of the Black Death (like I do), the bubonic plague outbreak that devastated the world in the mid-1300s. More than 750 years ago, over the course of approximately four years, the plague killed an estimated one-half of all the people in China, one-third of Europe and one-eighth of Africa, making it the largest pandemic in history judged by the percentage of the total population who died. And we don't know how many more people got sick and survived. Unfortunately for the world, that was neither the first nor the last time the plague wreaked havoc.

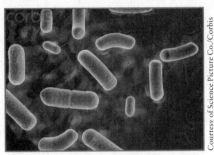

*This is what the plague bacteria looks like in humans and rats.*

There are various types of plague, with bubonic plague being the most common (many deadly diseases have names that don't sound particularly threatening, but I've always thought "bubonic" sounded appropriately very scary). It causes swelling of the lymph nodes—glands that filter out germs like viruses and bacteria—in a person's neck and in other places in their body, which visibly seep blood under the skin. Pneumonic plague is an advanced stage of bubonic plague that infects the lungs, sometimes so powerfully and painfully that an infected person's lungs disintegrate—they just disappear. It is the most contagious form of plague and one of the most contagious diseases around, period.

The plague bacteria live in small animals—particularly rats—and their fleas. The plague is highly contagious, spreading first from animals to people (largely through fleas, which bite rats and then people) and then from person to person. It spreads through many ways, including coughing, sneezing and touching an infected person or a contaminated surface. Part of what makes the plague so terrifying and unique is that it can move from person to person in multiple ways, and move from animals to people back to animals and back to people. Left untreated, bubonic plague kills about half of those infected, with untreated pneumonic plague killing almost all of its sufferers.

Plague vaccines exist but they've not proven to be very effective. Antibiotics can be effective if given early (soon after someone is infected). Not surprisingly, prevention is again key. The plague has been eliminated almost everywhere through improved sanitation and pest control, particularly rat control. But the plague isn't completely gone. As I write in early 2015, Madagascar currently is fighting a deadly plague outbreak and the U.S. recently had four rare cases of plague in which thankfully everyone recovered (because of early diagnosis and the right antibiotics).

The plague bacteria are so tough that scientists recently found what they believed to be traces of plague DNA on the New York City subway system (they also found lots of other nasty bacteria). Thankfully, the researchers were also quick to say that it didn't pose a risk to the 6 million people who ride the subway every day. Phew. Other scientists disputed that what was discovered was even the plague. Still, I try to not think about the plague when I ride the subway. (Sometimes, I fail).

## Cholera

Cholera was arguably the first disease of early globalization in the 19th century. At the start of the 1800s, as sea travel and trade became easier and more widespread, cholera began appearing in different seaports around the world, including in the United States. In New York City alone, there were terrible cholera epidemics throughout the 1800s, striking hardest in the city's crowded poor areas, where recent immigrants and freed slaves lived. In 1854, in London, Dr. John Snow discovered that cholera moved through water (by realizing that people who drank water from one well were more likely to get sick than people who drank water from another well . . . or who drank beer). This and later discoveries about the cholera bacteria provided a major catalyst for the development of public water and sanitation projects. It's hard to believe now (and it sounds gross), but in the U.S., sewage, or the stuff we flush down toilets, was not always separated and cleaned out of drinking water. That it is now means that cholera is very rare in the U.S. and other developed countries.

Sadly, cholera remains too common in the developing world, where there are far fewer robust clean water and sanitation systems (it's just as gross in other countries today as it was here long ago—and people everywhere want and deserve clean water and toilets, like we have in the U.S.). Approximately 750 million people around the world still lack reliable access to clean water and more than 2.5 billion people lack access to improved sanitation, meaning a place where someone can safely go to the bathroom and not have to touch poop (or more likely, invisible residue from poop, including possibly nasty cholera bacteria and other dangerous things).

Cholera infects an estimated 3–5 million people and kills 100,000–120,000 people each year. Most people who get cholera are infected through dirty water (even if it looks clean), but contaminated food is also a risk. Shellfish can carry the cholera

## CLEAN WATER ACCESS

DID YOU KNOW?

One out of nine people on earth lacks access to clean water.

One out of three people has no access to safe toilet facilities.

Information source: Water.org

bacteria and must be avoided in areas with high cholera rates. Cholera cases have risen in the past few years as more and more people move from rural areas into cities or flee violence by moving into slums and refugee camps. In other words, more and more people are living in crowded places without clean water and sanitation systems and so there are more and more opportunities for poop and water to mix.

While most people infected with cholera do not develop symptoms, for those who do it's a devastating, painful and often fatal disease. And it strikes suddenly. Diarrhea and vomiting occur first, leading to severe dehydration since a sufferer's body can't hold on to the water needed to survive. Without treatment, people cannot replace quickly enough the fluids their bodies are losing and they die. Cholera can kill someone in less than a day. Children and those with weakened immune systems, such as people with HIV/AIDS, are most at risk.

Like with all infections that cause diarrhea, the best treatment for people with cholera is to help them get and keep the fluids and water their bodies need, plus antibiotics to fight the cholera bacteria. Given how quickly cholera takes hold of someone's system, the sooner people get treatment, the better off they'll be. The most effective way to prevent cholera's spread is to build and maintain systems that keep drinking water safe, clean and separate from where people go to the bathroom. Generally governments do that work, sometimes in partnership with companies. But places like SHOFCO, which we talked about in We're Not There Yet, aren't waiting for the government or anyone else. They're building their own.

It's impossible to be overly dramatic about how important clean water is. Water comes up a lot in this book because we all

*SHOFCO's great work in Kibera has included providing improved sanitation and water for their students and community.*

Courtesy of SHOFCO

Courtesy of SHOFCO

need water to live. And, too often, water itself brings death. Certain parasites (like malarial mosquitoes, which we'll talk about in a bit), nasty bacteria (like cholera) and viruses (like rotavirus) all live and thrive in dirty water, particularly when poop and water aren't safely separated. One of these so-called waterborne diseases kills at least one child under five every minute.

As mentioned in the first chapter, there are lots of organizations working on the water crisis. Some, like Water.org, charity: water and Living Water International, work with local partners to help finance, drill and build wells or other safe water systems that work best for local communities so that it's easy for those communities to maintain the water systems into the future. This is important. Imagine if someone gave you a pump, but it needed electricity to work—and there was no electricity around. These organizations make sure there's not a mismatch between the water systems they finance, drill or build and what communities want and can maintain. To learn more about how they think about their work and where they've done their work, please visit their websites, listed in $1.25 a Day. As one example, charity: water has a terrific visual map showing all their projects across the globe.

Through its Children's Safe Drinking Water program, Procter & Gamble (the company that makes everything from Crest toothpaste to Tide detergent to Pampers diapers) provides families with a clean-water solution while they wait for safe water and improved sanitation systems to be built (or are building their own). It makes water purification packets that turn ten liters of dirty water into water that's safe to cook with and even drink—enough to last a family of four one to two days. One water purification packet costs ten cents to make and deliver. Partners like the NGO World Vision distribute the packets to families who need them most—in areas with no clean water or where natural disasters have ruined what clean water did exist (as happens after a hurricane or earthquake).

The ten-cent packets are clearly less expensive than the wells or water systems that can cost as much as $10,000 or more, but

*Procter & Gamble provides purification packets that make any water— even the dirtiest—safe to drink.*

those systems, once completed, can often provide communities enough clean water for many years. In the best scenario, the water purification packets from Procter & Gamble or others help families today while water systems are being built or wells drilled. All of these efforts are vital (literally about life: the word "vital" comes from *vita*, Latin for "life"). If you care about clean water, you can raise awareness or money (like Matti, who we met in $1.25 a Day), or share your support and gratitude for the people on the frontlines, like at World Vision (similar to Erin and PIH). To learn more about the Procter & Gamble Children's Safe Drinking Water program and what you can do to support it and its partners, go to csdw.org. Every drop of water—just like every vaccine or every bed net, which we'll talk about in a bit—can help save a life.

## Tuberculosis

According to the World Health Organization, more than 2 billion people carry the tuberculosis (TB) bacteria. That's more than one out of every four people on earth, making TB one of the most common diseases on the planet. For most people with TB, their infection is latent, meaning it's effectively sleeping, not hurting them and not contagious to anyone else. Active TB makes a person sick and contagious. TB generally attacks a person's lungs, leading to coughing, chest pain, fatigue and fever, among other symptoms. Less commonly, TB attacks the brain, spine, kidneys or other organs. In 2013, there were more than 9 million new cases of TB, and more than 1.5 million people died from it.

Clearly, TB is very contagious—otherwise more than 2 billion people wouldn't have it. It's a disease most likely to travel between family members, friends and work colleagues, in other words, the people we spend the most time around. That's because it's spread through the air (unlike via rat fleas or poop-polluted water) and only by inhaling TB germs can a person become infected. It remains far more widespread in some places than others, notably parts of Asia, Africa and Latin America. Across the world, it is the number one killer of people with HIV/AIDS.

TB MORTALITY AROUND THE WORLD, 2013

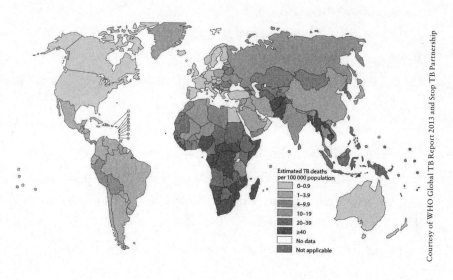

Estimated TB deaths
per 100 000 population
0–0.9
1–3.9
4–9.9
10–19
20–39
≥40
No data
Not applicable

Courtesy of WHO Global TB Report 2013 and Stop TB Partnership

There is a TB vaccine, but like the plague vaccine, it's not very effective. TB is curable, however the treatment is not as easy as taking antibiotics for a few weeks. Treating TB means taking a series of different antibiotics for six months or longer. Many people infected with TB don't take their antibiotics appropriately or for as long as they're supposed to. It bears repeating: bacteria are very clever. If given the chance, they mutate (or change), having learned how to resist the antibiotics used to fight them. This has happened with TB. It's gotten stronger and learned how to outwit traditional antibiotics; this is known as drug resistance. Newer antibiotics have been developed to treat the drug-resistant strains of TB and researchers are searching for even

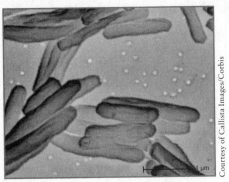

*Tuberculosis got its name in part because of its tubular shape.*

more-powerful new treatments and better ways to aid patients in taking all their antibiotics correctly, and for as long as needed.

It's vital that people take the medicine to rid their bodies of TB infection, because not only is it good for them, it's also the most effective way to stop the spread of TB to other people. A crucial part of this is ensuring people know whether or not they have TB. That may sound obvious, but lots of people with TB don't know they have it. TB is very rare in the U.S. If you travel to a country with extensive TB (which, again, the CDC can tell you), try to avoid being in closed spaces with people who have TB or with strangers (because it's close contact with TB patients that can make you sick). That definitely doesn't mean you should avoid countries with extensive TB, but rather, take precautions. I've traveled to lots of places with TB and thankfully never gotten it. Most people who are exposed to TB don't wind up becoming infected, but it's better to be on the safe side and to get tested if you ever suspect you might have TB. It's also likely you'll have to take a TB test if you ever want to volunteer or work at some of the places mentioned in this book (like the

Packard Children's Hospital, where I volunteered in college). That's also nothing to be scared of.

# PARASITES

## *Malaria*

The term "malaria" comes from the Italian words for bad air (*mal* or *mala* = "bad," *aria* = "air"). As I said at the beginning of the last chapter, until the 19th century when scientists realized germs—whether bacteria, viruses or otherwise—caused people to get sick, many people (including scientists) believed that illnesses came from bad air, which was called miasma (from the Greek for "pollute"). Given how many diseases are transmitted through the air, this theory was understandable (if mostly wrong). Although it was realized that germs (some of which traveled through the air) were actually to blame for everything from cholera to "consumption," as TB was called in the 19th century, malaria had already become the name of a particular and all-too-common illness.

Malaria exists in close to 100 countries today (though this is changing as we'll see—and not for the better) and threatens almost half the world's population every year. In 2013, there were close to 200 million cases of malaria, and more than half a million people died from the disease. But a hundred years ago, even fifteen years ago, malaria was more prevalent and more deadly. The number of kids who die from malaria in Africa has dropped by more than half since 2000. That's a big deal because nearly all malaria deaths occur in Africa and most of those who die are children under five. But we still have a lot of work to do

## MALARIA RATES AROUND THE WORLD, 2013

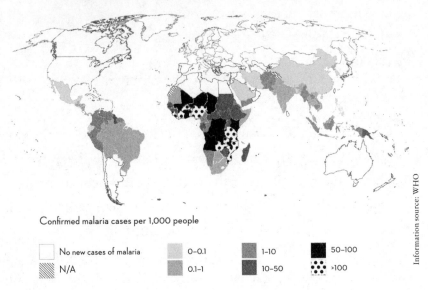

Confirmed malaria cases per 1,000 people

| | | |
|---|---|---|
| No new cases of malaria | 0–0.1 | 1–10 | 50–100 |
| N/A | 0.1–1 | 10–50 | >100 |

Information source: WHO

until all children are safe from deadly mosquitoes. In 2013, a child died of malaria every minute.

There are five different parasites that cause malaria in humans, all of which spread to people through the bites of infected mosquitoes. The types of mosquitoes that carry malaria generally bite at night and breed in standing water, sometimes in places as shallow as a footprint. Mosquitoes love stagnant water—it's where adult mosquitoes lay their eggs to hatch more baby mosquitoes that can infect even more people. That's why ongoing efforts to refresh or get rid of standing bodies of water, whether outdoor watering holes for animals or indoor vases for flowers, are so important. When there are more mosquitoes, after the rainy season in the tropics for example, malaria risk and infections go up. As the earth's average temperature grows warmer and warmer as is currently happening, malaria-carrying mosquitoes can survive, breed and infect more people in more places.

This is particularly concerning for places that have never had to deal with mosquitoes (because they're less likely to be prepared) and for places like the U.S. that eliminated malaria decades ago.

In the 1940s, the U.S. made eliminating malaria a priority. The large-scale national effort centered on the thirteen southeastern states where it still lurked (including Arkansas, where I was born). Through extensive use of insecticides on and around homes as well as through draining swamps, by 1951, the U.S. declared victory over malaria. But as the earth warms, higher temperatures could make it easier for malaria mosquitoes to reinvade the U.S. Thankfully, as discussed in Viruses and Vaccines, we have a strong public health system, so while we hope malaria doesn't come back, we're better prepared in case it does. Other countries aren't as well protected—which is why the number of countries with malaria could sadly soar far past 100 if we don't keep fighting malaria and do something to stop global warming (talked about in the next chapter).

Malaria's first symptoms can often be mistaken for the flu or a cold: fever, headache, chills and vomiting. Symptoms can worsen in people of all ages, but young children are particularly vulnerable, in part because they lack the immunity (or protection) adults have often developed to malaria (by repeatedly surviving infections). But mild malaria symptoms aren't something to celebrate; they often cause people to miss work or kids to miss school. As discussed in $1.25 a Day, malaria is expensive for families and countries.

The progress the world has made against malaria is the result of a combination of efforts over time, including getting people the medicines they need to cure it and getting people the bed nets and other tools they need to prevent it. An insecticide called DDT played a major role in the U.S. campaign against malaria in the mid-20th century. That strategy certainly worked in eliminating malaria from the U.S., but it also hurt bald eagles (discussed in Too Close to Gone), so while other insecticides are used to guard against malaria, the world doesn't use DDT anymore. Additionally recent research has found a probable link between long-term DDT exposure and certain cancers. Still, some people think we should use DDT given how powerful it is against mosquito-borne diseases. As on all debates, this is one where you'll have to weigh different evidence, even as it's evolving, and make up your own mind.

Today, the main tools used to fight malaria are insecticide-treated bed nets—just like the one in the picture at the start of this chapter. They're exactly what their name implies: nets with insecticide in them that mosquitoes can't get through. The nets block the mosquitoes; the insecticide kills them. When the nets are used appropriately, people sleep under them at night. Nearly half of the people in Africa who live in places with malaria either have a net to cover themselves and their children while sleeping or can afford one. It's particularly important kids sleep under nets because of how vulnerable they are to malaria. Medicines also exist that people can take to help prevent malaria. While somewhat similar to vaccines, they're not the same and they're generally expensive to make and not very easy to use—which is why we still need a malaria vaccine. While there's never been a vaccine against a parasite like malaria, scientists and researchers are working hard on developing one.

Because there's no vaccine and millions of people aren't yet sleeping under nets, early diagnosis and treatment are important in controlling malaria. This is so people can recover more quickly. That seems obvious—and it is. But it's also vital to treat people quickly so they're less likely to pass on the malaria parasite, via a mosquito, to someone else. We think of mosquitoes infecting people, and they do, but mosquitoes are first infected with malaria by biting someone who has the disease. It's a very nasty cycle that can be broken only through appropriate treatment—including drugs called artemisinins—and prevention. There's also growing concern about malaria becoming resistant to artemisinins—an area being closely watched by health officials. To learn about malaria, including its economic impact as discussed in $1.25 a Day, Malaria No More is a terrific resource, which you can find at malarianomore.org.

Pennsylvania-native Katherine first learned about malaria in 2006, after she and her mom, Lynda, watched the PBS documentary *Malaria: Fever Wars.* They decided to help as many people as they possibly could get bed nets to protect themselves and their kids from malaria. They thought everyone should know that at that time malaria was killing a child in Africa every thirty seconds—statistics that could change, and have, with something as simple as a bed net. Katherine and Lynda started by working with their church and local community to raise awareness about malaria and to encourage people to think about giving nets as Christmas gifts. That first year, Katherine and her mom raised more than $10,000, including from the sale of more than 600 gift certificates that they hand-decorated and which showed up in stockings and under Christmas trees. The gift certificates were for purchasing bed nets in honor of the recipient, who then knew that a life had been protected, even saved, from malaria. That was only the beginning of their work to raise awareness and to raise funds. By 2011, when Katherine

*Katherine used a diorama at her church to raise awareness about malaria and the bed nets that help protect families and kids from malaria.*

was ten, she and her mom had spoken at the White House, the Annual Conference of the United Methodist Church and the United Nations. They'd been in the *Philadelphia Inquirer* and the *New York Times*. Lynda had traveled to Uganda to participate in a bed net distribution program. As of 2015, they've raised more than $300,000, enough for tens of thousands of bed nets, working with Nothing But Nets. When Katherine started, she was just five years old. You're never too young to make a difference. For ideas on how to raise awareness about malaria and raise funds to get people the bed nets they need for malaria prevention, and also to learn more about Katherine and Lynda's work, please visit nothingbutnets.net.

Malaria shouldn't stop you from going anywhere in the world. If you're traveling to an area where malaria is common, talk to your doctor about which medicines you and your family should take, which bug spray to use and what else you should do. What you'll likely hear is how important it is that you sleep under an insecticide-treated bed net. Like with TB, I've traveled to lots of places with malaria, followed my doctors' advice and never gotten sick (knock on wood).

Malaria is not the only mosquito-borne illness that's becoming more common in more places as the earth warms. Dengue fever is another. While it's not a parasite (it's actually a virus, so it's an interloper in this chapter!), like malaria, dengue is passed from people to mosquitoes and back to people. It's rarely fatal but it's increasingly common, particularly in Latin America and the U.S., which is why it's included here. Over the past few years, it's infected hundreds of millions of people every year. People who get dengue suffer from high fevers, pains, headaches, rashes and bleeding from the nose and gums. It's the bleeding that gives the more severe form of dengue— dengue hemorrhagic fever—its name (*hemorrhagic* means bleeding a lot—the word *haima* means "blood" in Greek, and *rhage* means "a breaking"). Dengue is one of the rare diseases in which younger children generally don't get as sick as older kids and adults. Preventing dengue largely looks like preventing malaria—using bug spray and insecticide-treated bed nets, and removing stagnant water mosquitoes love. Treatment for dengue is similar to treatment for the flu or a cold: lots of fluids and rest. Thankfully, most people who get dengue don't suffer the hemorrhagic kind and most recover. We've made a lot of progress around bed nets, but we're still far from 100 percent coverage. Preventing malaria and dengue are two very good reasons we should keep working on the goal of getting every family that needs one an insecticide-treated bed net.

## Guinea worm

Time for another (almost) success story: the defeat of the guinea worm (sounds like a summer movie—and definitely one I would go and see). The technical name for guinea worm disease is dracunculiasis, yep, like Dracula (though the disease wasn't named after the vampire legend). Guinea worm is spread through drinking water containing minuscule water fleas that carry guinea worm larvae, or baby guinea worms. Once the guinea worm larvae are inside someone, they hatch and start growing. Over roughly the next year, the guinea worms can grow up to three feet (as tall as an average American two-year-old!). Scientists compare them to very long, thin noodles, without the benefit of being fun to eat, or fun at all. Quite the opposite.

*After a year of growing inside someone's body, guinea worms like this one emerge painfully.*

Guinea worms also mate inside their host—the person originally infected by guinea worm larvae—and it's as horrifying as it sounds. When a pregnant adult female guinea worm wants to leave her host, she starts to burrow out, creating a blister as her exit door through a person's skin, often through feet or legs. The blister generally burns and to alleviate that feeling, people stick their legs into water. When the worm exits, she releases (or gives birth) to more guinea worm larvae—right into the water that some other unsuspecting victim will drink.

In 1986, there were approximately 3.5 million people suffering from

*There are special straws that filter water to stop the spread of guinea worm.*

guinea worm disease every year. In 2014, there were an estimated 126 cases. In close to thirty years, guinea worm has been almost eliminated. As there is no vaccine or cure for guinea worm, progress has been made through prevention. This includes educating people in areas with guinea worm to filter water to remove the larvae, and helping people who are infected understand how important it is to avoid putting their legs in water (so that larvae can't get out and reinfect the water). A vast majority of the world's countries are now guinea worm–free. This is another real (almost) success story, one made possible by an international partnership led by the Carter Center, founded by former President Jimmy Carter. To learn more about the heroic work against guinea worm, go to cartercenter.org.

## NEARLY ALL COUNTRIES ARE GUINEA WORM-FREE, 1996-2014

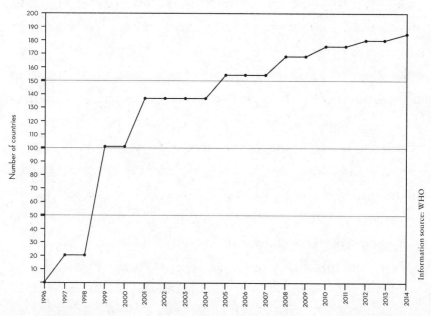

Number of countries

Information source: WHO

# BEATING THE BUGS

Thankfully, there's a lot we can do to protect ourselves against infection and try to help communities more effectively protect themselves against even age-old scourges like malaria. Bug spray. Bed nets. Be wary of standing water (and safely empty it out). Also, before you travel, talk to your doctor about what additional precautions you should take, like taking medicine to help prevent malaria. We're fortunate in the U.S. that we have public health officials who monitor (or watch closely) places like swamps where diseases can hide out, but you might visit places where that's not true, so it's better to be cautious (and curious!).

In addition to what was discussed in the last chapter—supporting groups working to improve health care (like PIH) and healthy habits (like Right To Play)—you can focus on helping fight a specific illness, like Katherine and malaria, through raising awareness and raising funds. There are also online and app games to help you and your friends learn about malaria (and other diseases too, but I think the coolest games at the moment are about malaria). The most sophisticated, fun (in my opinion) and scary game is Nightmare: Malaria. It's available for free through iTunes, the Apple app store or Google Play, all accessible at nightmare.againstmalaria.com. The only way we'll end the nightmare of malaria or TB or cholera is by ensuring we're keeping ourselves safe and healthy and helping others do the same, in our homes, our schools, our communities and around the world.

One organization doing just that is Project C.U.R.E., the world's largest provider of donated medical equipment (like hospital beds) and supplies (like bandages) to developing countries. At its collection centers across the U.S., Project C.U.R.E.

accepts donations of excess supplies from U.S. hospitals, clinics, manufacturers and individuals. It then works with hospitals and clinics in the developing world to determine what their
needs are so that what Project C.U.R.E. sends will be put to
immediate and very good use, like to help care for new moms
or patients suffering from dehydration. It also donates tons (literally) of soap and other things to help families, particularly
following natural disasters, keep themselves and their kids safe
from water-borne and other infections. There are lots of jobs for
volunteers, including kids, to do at Project C.U.R.E., from helping separate out donations into various categories (like sterile
gloves versus medical tubing) to bagging and boxing what will
ultimately be donated. You can also support Project C.U.R.E.
by donating any excess medical supplies you might have (like if
you grew out of smaller Band Aids that were never opened) and
encouraging doctors and nurses you know to do the same. To

*With Project C.U.R.E. Brownie volunteers and others after packing
supplies together in Denver, Colorado.*

find out how to get involved, please visit projectcure.org. Every bandage and bed net—and every hour of volunteering—makes a difference.

# Get Going!

- Encourage people who are sick to finish all of their antibiotics or other medicine, even if it takes months (or longer)
- Use bug spray
- Check the CDC travel website before you travel to know if you need to take extra precautions (like the bug spray mentioned above)
- Wash your hands (it's so important that, like the CDC travel website check, it gets mentioned two chapters in a row)
- Sleep under a bed net if you're going somewhere with malaria (or dengue fever or any scary mosquito-borne illness)
- Empty out containers of standing water regularly (which helps avoid mosquitoes generally—who doesn't want that?)
- Raise awareness online or offline about malaria, cholera and other diseases
- Play the game Nightmare: Malaria and share it with friends
- Raise money, like Katherine did, for groups like Nothing But Nets that help people get the bed nets they need to protect themselves
- Talk about the importance of clean water with your friends
- Raise money for groups like Living Water International, charity: water, Water.org and others working to provide clean water to families around the globe
- Support groups like PIH providing treatment to people with severe dehydration due to diarrhea
- Help efforts to get clean water to people quickly (while waiting for

wells and water systems), like the Procter & Gamble Children's
Safe Drinking Water partnership with NGOs like World Vision

- Donate excess first-aid supplies and encourage any doctors, nurses
  or hospitals you know to donate excess medical supplies to Project
  C.U.R.E.

- Don't stigmatize anyone for any disease, and support family
  members and friends fighting any of the diseases mentioned here
  and those that aren't

- If you're over thirteen, use social media to follow organizations
  doing work you support (like Water.org) and individuals too (like
  Bill Gates, who is a tireless champion of fighting so many of the
  diseases discussed in this chapter and the previous one, from HIV/
  AIDS to polio to malaria and more)

# PART IV

## It's Your ENVIRONMENT

Courtesy of Marc Fiorito, Team Rubicon

CHAPTER EIGHT

# WEATHER REPORT

What's your favorite class? Along with history, I always loved science class. Every year, every grade, it was one of my favorite subjects, partly because of the science reports and projects I got to do. In elementary school, research for my projects mainly consisted of hunting through books and magazines in my school library and the big library downtown near my church. I also talked to local experts at the planetarium and elsewhere depending on the subject. There was no Google or Wikipedia, no online magazines or websites; they hadn't been invented yet. Science class took place on chalkboards, on tabletops doubling as labs and, most of all, in our imaginations.

*Science was one of my favorite subjects, in part because of reports like this one on Jupiter. (I promise I enjoyed it far more than the serious expression on my face implies!)*

Courtesy of the Author's Parents

The science reports and projects from elementary school that still stick out in my mind involved honeycombs and coral reefs (and Jupiter, as seen in the picture—but admittedly that one doesn't fit as well into this chapter!). I loved learning how honeycombs and coral reefs played vital roles in keeping our planet healthy and was so sad to learn how both were under severe stress because of climate change. The coral reefs' spectrum of colors captivated me. I'd heard about their colors fading and their very lives being threatened as oceans warmed. That really worried me. As part of my project in fourth or fifth grade, I made what I hoped resembled coral reefs out of clay and Popsicle sticks that I then painted and superglued onto poster board. While my artistic abilities were questionable at best (okay . . . pretty awful), I loved learning about life in the depths of the ocean and felt a responsibility to share with my classmates and teachers why I thought we all should be concerned about what happened to the reefs, even in Arkansas, very far away from the nearest coral or ocean.

I also loved knowing I could do something about climate

change. Around the time of my coral reef project, I was proud to be part of a group Mrs. Eilers and Mrs. Huie, two teachers at Booker, formed to help start our school's first paper recycling program. My concerns about climate change have only intensified in the twenty-five years since I accidentally glued, along with my model coral reefs, part of my T-shirt to the poster board (I then had to cut that part off and cover it with more clay). Our planet continues to warm, our weather patterns are changing, and life on the earth, in the sky and in oceans, lakes and rivers, all are being altered because of these shifts, possibly forever. And most frightening? None of the changes, as we'll see, are good ones.

Scientists tell us that floods and extreme storms, like Hurricane Sandy that hit the East Coast so hard in 2012, will become more common. The homes and lives of millions of people who live on or near the ocean will be threatened, even destroyed. Storm cleanups like the ones I participated in after Sandy will be regular parts of our lives. Droughts will become more common too, making clean water even harder to come by for millions of people, some who don't have to worry about clean water today but will in the future. All of that will make farming harder in more places, making food more scarce and more expensive, possibly for everyone.

I realize all of that may be a little (or a lot) scary and that much of what we'll talk about in this chapter may feel overwhelming. But there's also a lot you and all of us can do to help out. The first step is to be aware of what climate change is, why it's happening and what we can do to slow or even reverse it when possible. And to be aware of what climate change isn't, what isn't causing it and what doesn't work to fight it (like waiting). This all may sound obvious, but it still isn't to lots of people.

The overwhelming scientific agreement across the world is that the choices humans (that's us) make about how we run factories, fuel cars, power buildings, use air-conditioning, raise livestock and cut down trees (deforestation) are all driving climate change and global warming. Yet only around half of American adults recognize that human choices fuel climate change (bad pun intended). The majority of scientists also consistently label climate change a very serious problem. But in recent surveys, only a third of American adults agreed. The gap between what scientists know based on their research and examination of the earth's climate and temperature patterns over many years and what the public believes hasn't changed much over time.

Just like most scientists, most eighth graders in a recent poll also recognized human activity as driving climate change and global warming. Many of you already know the facts, understand what isn't true and can help your parents and families become aware and informed about what climate change is (and isn't) and what we can all do to help fight it. Many of the free videos and games about climate change created for kids could be just as fun for families. PBS LearningMedia has terrific videos on climate change topics (Marc and I love watching these because we always learn something, even though many of them are terrifying). You can search by subject and grade level at pbslearningmedia.org. Bill Nye's Climate 101 video is another great resource (you can find it at climaterealityproject.org) and his Lab Dash game is also a lot of fun and informative too. You can find it at billsclimatelab.org.

There's a little bit of science in this chapter, but not much (no charts on the carbon cycle). If you're really interested in the science behind climate change—and the science behind stopping climate change—I hope you'll visit the National Aeronautics and Space Administration (better known as NASA, the part of the U.S. government

*Bill Nye's Lab Dash game is a great way to learn more about climate change (and it's a lot of fun).*

focused on space!) and the Environmental Protection Agency websites on climate change specifically for kids. They're both free (and also arguably as helpful for adults as for kids). You can find them at climatekids.nasa.gov and epa.gov/climatestudents. Your science teachers and any local museums that are focused on natural history, science and exploration are also terrific resources.

As I shared at the beginning of the book, I believe lots of small actions add up to big actions, including big changes. This is particularly true in relation to climate change. The actions we take in our own homes, schools and neighborhoods matter to the health of our communities and our planet.

## CLIMATE AND CLIMATE CHANGE

Climate refers to what the weather is like on average in a given place—that could be the community we live in, our country or the earth itself—over a period of time. Climate change means exactly what it sounds like—all changes relating to climate across the world, including shifts in weather patterns, ocean currents, wind currents and average air and water temperatures. It includes what is happening with hurricanes and torna-does, rainfall and snowfall, whether those occur in the Arctic, near the equator or in our own hometowns.

Over the course of the earth's long history, the climate has fluctuated. The average temperature and rainfall have gone up and down . . . up and down . . . up and down over time. But the climate has never changed as quickly as it's changing now. Most scientists think these changes are different from the ones that have occurred historically, mostly because the pace of change is so fierce and unprecedented. And the vast majority of scientists point to us, humans, as the cause of today's climate change, not to the natural phenomena that explain why temperatures or rainfall rose or fell hundreds or thousands of years ago. The main culprits? The burning of fossil fuels, largely coal and oil in factories and cars, as well as deforestation (cutting down or burning lots and lots of trees quickly).

## Why Is the Climate Changing?

Where does light come from (besides the sun)? Or heat? People have been burning coal for light, heat and other uses for thousands of years. Starting with the Industrial Revolution in the late 18th and 19th centuries—that's the 1700s and 1800s—coal increasingly became the go-to fuel to power ships and trains, to heat homes and buildings and to help electrify, well, everything that could be lit up, like streets, homes and buildings. From the beginning, coal helped do much more than power lights. The electricity it produced lit up innovation in extraordinary ways. From light bulbs to train engines, from factories to stoves, it's hard to imagine the last couple of hundred years without coal and all it helped enable. And it's impossible to imagine our daily

## RENEWABLE VS. NON-RENEWABLE ENERGY

| RENEWABLE SOURCES* | NON-RENEWABLE SOURCES |
|---|---|
| Wind | Coal |
| Water | Natural gas |
| Solar (the sun) | Crude oil |
| Geothermal (heat brought up from underground) | Uranium |
| Biomass, which includes leftovers from agriculture/forestry and processed waste (sanitized poop) | *We didn't recently "discover" renewable energy. People have been using wind and water for energy for hundreds of years. |

Information source: U.S. Energy Information Administration

lives today without electricity, which we rely on in so many ways—like keeping the lights on in our homes, milk and eggs fresh in our refrigerators and our laptops and phones powered so we can be connected to the world and our friends. The same is true of oil, which helps power most of our cars, buses and airplanes, and gets most parents to work and you to school, the movies or over to a friend's house. In many places, coal remains a major energy source, including in the U.S., and in most places, oil remains the main fuel for transportation. The major sources of greenhouse gas emissions and drivers of climate change today are electricity, transportation and industrial uses (think factories), largely because they still depend on coal and oil.

Yet, in the 21st century, more so than ever before, there are a variety of renewable ways beyond coal and oil to generate energy. What makes these forms of energy renewable is that they come from sources that will never run out—the wind will always blow, the sun will always shine and the ocean's waves will never cease to rise and fall. There's also lots of work being done on what's known as clean coal, or coal used for energy in a way that doesn't add (at least not as much) greenhouse gas to the atmosphere.

When traditional coal is used to generate energy and electricity, or oil is used to power a car, carbon dioxide is emitted. Lots and lots of carbon dioxide. More carbon dioxide, or $CO_2$, is emitted for every unit of coal used than from any other major fuel source. This is important because the increase in carbon dioxide in the atmosphere over the past couple of hundred years, and particularly the last few decades, is a major reason our planet is warming. While there are many natural sources of carbon (including our breathing out), most of the carbon that's been put into the atmosphere in the last decades and even centuries is from how we make and use energy.

Scientists estimate that one-third of all carbon dioxide emissions every year come from burning coal alone. Plants take in carbon dioxide and sunlight to produce food for themselves and they emit oxygen in the process. This makes them perfect partners for humans—we breathe in oxygen and exhale carbon dioxide. Historically, our forests, plants and oceans absorbed all the carbon (from carbon dioxide) we put into the atmosphere. That's no longer true. Carbon emissions—from more and more factories, utilities, cars, planes, buildings and many other uses—have tipped the scales way out of whack. At this point, the plants on land and under the ocean can't keep up with the amount of coal and fossil fuels we're burning. That would be true even if we weren't cutting down trees. But we are. And we're cutting them down at faster and faster rates around the world so there are fewer and fewer to absorb carbon dioxide.

Trees are being cut or burned down for lots of reasons—so that the cleared land can be used for farming (often in a way

*In the Amazon, deforestation by burning.*

*Reforestation is one of the ways we can help combat climate change. This is a reforestation project in the Andes.*

that's not sustainable, meaning it won't work well for very long) and so the wood can be used for fuel or to make furniture or for construction. Deforestation poses a particular threat to indigenous, or native, people around the world who live in forests. In the Amazon, indigenous people are working to secure the densely forested land on which they have hunted and lived for generations. Indigenous activists are fighting to stop people from cutting down trees illegally and working for more responsible tree-cutting policies and practices. They're also advocating for their right to own the land they've lived on for centuries. Illegal deforestation can be very profitable, and the people making a lot of money don't want to stop cutting down trees. Illegal loggers have threatened people throughout the Amazon. Even worse, in 2014 in Peru, illegal loggers killed four indigenous activists. That tragedy hasn't deterred the people working for more sustainable logging practices and more reforestation—or replacing trees that have been cut down—in the Amazon; if anything, they're working even harder for their forests and future.

Reforestation isn't happening everywhere, or even in a lot of places where lots of trees have been cut down. At least, it's not happening yet. We need to be replacing the trees that are being cut down through deforestation as well as promoting responsible timber or tree farming. And we need to plant even more trees to try to keep up with the, at least for now, increasing amounts of carbon being released by burning fossil fuels. How best to do that looks very different in the Amazon than it does in Canada, China or Kenya. When planting trees around our homes or in our communities, it's important they're the right kind of trees for our local environments so that they'll grow well, fit in the local ecosystem—and are likely to live healthy, long lives to fight climate change into the future.

Wangari Maathai is one of my all-time heroes. One day she planted a tree to compensate for deforestation in her native Kenya. And then she planted another tree. And another. Then she recruited people to help her plant more trees and she built a movement, appropriately named the Green Belt Movement. Wangari inspired Kenyans to plant 30 million trees and people across Africa to plant millions more.

*Here Wangari is with one tree. Her Green Belt Movement inspired Kenyans to plant 30 million trees.*

She also inspired a kid more than 5,000 miles away in Germany named Felix. In 2007, when Felix was nine years old, he decided the world (and kids) couldn't wait on adults to fight climate change and that he would follow Wangari's example and fight climate change and deforestation one tree at a time. That year he launched Plant-for-the-Planet with a goal of planting 1 million trees. He recruited friends and strangers alike to his effort and they reached that goal in 2010. Their new goal? Planting 1 trillion trees by 2020. To find out more and how you can get involved, check out the website plant-for-the-planet .org and to learn more about Wangari's amazing legacy, please visit the website greenbeltmovement .org. If you want to start your own effort

*Felix started Plant-for-the-Planet when he was nine years old. Here he is speaking at the UN urging everyone to plant trees.*

close to home in the U.S., the Arbor Day Foundation can help you find out which trees are best for your neighborhood—and fight climate change at the same time. You can learn more at arborday.org.

## Life in a Greenhouse

Turning back to fossil fuels, what do you think of when you hear that term? Dinosaurs? Well, fossil fuels are called fossil fuels because they are formed from the remains of prehistoric plants or animals (but not dinosaurs) that lived hundreds of millions of years ago. Coal is a major fossil fuel and, as mentioned earlier, a big source of carbon dioxide, the number one greenhouse gas. Greenhouse gases got their name because they trap energy close to the earth, just like a greenhouse traps heat close to plants, flowers and trees to help them grow, even if the weather is cold outside the greenhouse. Carbon dioxide is the main greenhouse gas, but it's far from the only one. Methane, nitrous oxide and ozone are the other major greenhouse gases, all of which have increased in the atmosphere since before you were born and even before I was born. It's important we work on limiting those too, in part because some of them—like methane—disappear from the atmosphere more quickly than carbon dioxide does.

Just like with carbon dioxide, there are natural and man-made sources of methane, nitrous oxide and ozone. Livestock farming (think cows and sheep), oceans and wetlands all contribute methane to the atmosphere. Though oceans give off most of the nitrous oxide emissions in the atmosphere, human activity generates a lot of nitrous oxide, too, especially in farming through the use of fertilizers to help crops grow. The ozone

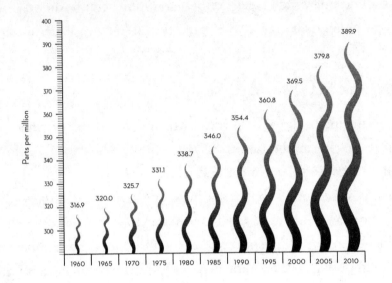

Information source: NOAA

close to the earth, most famous for being a component of smog, is all man-made. We'll talk more about ozone and smog in a bit.

Hydrofluorocarbons, or HFCs, aren't yet one of the major greenhouse gases, but they're on their way. That's not a good thing. HFCs can trap more heat than carbon dioxide, somewhat ironic as they're used mainly in refrigeration and air-conditioning. They're so worrying that they're known as "super greenhouse gases." Before HFCs, chlorofluorocarbons, or CFCs, were used for similar purposes—and caused similar concerns. Because the world was so worried about CFCs, every country committed in 1987 to phasing them out. Today, there are almost no CFCs used. That's a good thing and it shows what can happen when the world works together. It's unfortunate CFCs' replacements weren't much better. Many scientists think similar action is needed to phase out HFCs (and find a greener alternative) or global warming will rapidly accelerate.

The atmosphere, which is made up of layers of gases, acts like a blanket over the earth. Some amount of greenhouse gas in the atmosphere is necessary to make sure we don't all freeze at night when the sun goes down. But, in the last ten to twenty years, greenhouse gases have increased to such high levels that they have trapped more and more heat close to the earth's surface, turning our planet into a global greenhouse.

## Global Warming

A consequence of living in a global greenhouse (and one of the most worrying aspects of climate change) is something that's already come up in this chapter: global warming. It's another phrase that means exactly what it sounds like: an increase in the earth's average yearly temperature. Since 2000, the world has seen nine out of the ten warmest years ever recorded, including the warmest ever: 2014. All ten of the warmest years on record have occurred since I graduated from high school. While that

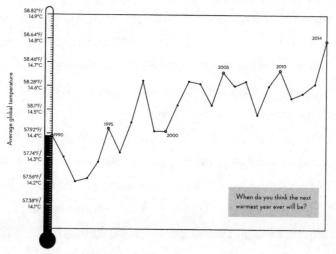

AVERAGE GLOBAL TEMPERATURE, 1990–2014

When do you think the next warmest year ever will be?

Information source: NOAA and NASA

makes me feel old, it also makes me more worried about what increasingly warm weather will mean for life on earth.

Global warming does not mean that everywhere on the earth gets warmer, but rather that the earth's average temperature is increasing. Since it's an average, that means that some places could be—and actually are—experiencing even colder weather. Depending on where you live, you may have noticed this. In 2014, parts of the East Coast, including New York, where I live, and parts of the Midwest experienced a colder year on average, while California experienced its warmest year ever.

It's not only temperatures that are growing more extreme, weather is too. Floods and droughts that used to be rare are now expected. As the earth warms, more glaciers and ice caps are melting, and because of that, sea levels are rising. This is happening at the top and bottom of the earth. At the top of the globe, the Arctic and Greenland ice sheets are both melting, and at the bottom of the globe, the Antarctic sea ice is melting and thinning out. A chunk of ice about the size of Washington, D.C. melts away from Greenland each year. Wow (not in a good way).

Even more worrying than the warming we've had so far is that if nothing changes in the current rates of pollution (more greenhouse gases) and deforestation (less ability for the planet to absorb those greenhouse gases), the earth's average temperature is projected to rise at least four degrees Fahrenheit by 2100, and some scientists say it could rise by as much as twelve degrees. That's mind-boggling. Scientists predict that even if we all did everything we could to halt climate change (like using more renewable energy and less coal), the temperature would still go up by at least two degrees Fahrenheit. Maybe those predictions don't sound like big jumps, but all are. Even seemingly small changes in temperature have huge consequences for life on earth. Think about when you get a fever. A two-degree fever can leave anybody feeling awful and groggy, and a four-degree fever starts to be dangerous (particularly for kids). A twelve-degree fever would be fatal. Seemingly minor changes matter.

While it's true that global warming doesn't mean warmer weather everywhere, the places that do get warmer will stay warmer for longer, increasing the risk of dangerous heat waves. Older people are particularly vulnerable to heat waves. In Chicago's 1995 heat wave, an estimated 750 people died from heat-related causes in only five days, dying of heat strokes, heart attacks and dehydration. People living in poverty are more vulnerable to heat waves. Many of those who died during the Chicago heat wave lived in buildings without air-conditioning, meaning they had no ability to cool off, even when temperatures soared well above 100 degrees. Many also lived in neighborhoods

*Courtesy of Keystone/Getty*

*Not the most water-efficient way to cool off, but it's understandable that when, in the 1950s, temperatures soared into the 100s, kids opened a fire hydrant.*

where they weren't comfortable opening a window at night because they felt unsafe.

A 2003 heat wave across Europe was even more deadly, claiming more than 50,000 lives, including many elderly and people living in poverty, in cities and rural communities, and in different countries across the continent. Climate change falls hardest on people living in poverty across the world, but it affects all of us, today and into the future. Some scientists predict that in the longer-term future, parts of the planet could become unlivable because it will be too hot year-round (that's a pretty scary vision). Others think life as we know it will become impossible almost everywhere (that's truly terrifying).

## *Small Changes, Big Challenges*

Are humans the only ones threatened by climate change? No, not at all. As the earth heats up, animals and plants are also at risk (and that also isn't good for us because we rely on animals and plants for lots of things, especially food). Animals that need temperate (relatively cooler) climates are forced to migrate (or move) to find more comfortable environments. Sometimes those migrations take animals far away from their homes. This isn't good for those animals and it's not good for other animals or plants that are part of their ecosystem, the community of organisms that live in an environment and are dependent on one another in obvious and hidden ways. One animal species moving away can have a domino effect, hurting other animal species (even forcing them to leave too or risk dying out), plant species and humans—particularly those who rely on them to fill out their diets.

Plants are feeling the direct effects of climate change too.

Certain crops only grow well at certain temperatures, and foods that have been staples in people's diets for centuries may become impossible to grow as the earth warms. A warmer earth also means more droughts, leaving less rain and water to help crops grow. Scientists estimate that if the average world temperature rises 3.6 degrees Fahrenheit, corn production in the U.S. would decrease by 10–30 percent, both because corn couldn't grow in as many places and because there would be more droughts, hurting crops even in the places where corn could continue to grow. Once it's above 95 degrees, corn can't really grow at all. This means more than just missing out on popcorn at the movies. We actually depend on corn for a range of uses in addition to food, including fuel, animal feed, plastics (yes, seriously), soaps and even medicines.

While looking to lessen the effects of climate change, we'll possibly need to alter what food we're growing, where we're growing it and how we're growing it to make sure we have enough to feed everyone, including people who don't have enough to eat today. Thankfully, there are lots of "low-tech" and "high-tech" solutions that are already proving to work, and scientists and farmers are experimenting to find even more. These include everything from mixing trees and crops through something called "ecological agriculture" to growing a wider variety of food in cities (on rooftops and elsewhere) as well as developing new types of seeds that can grow in much hotter temperatures and need less water.

Seeds like those that grow in hotter temperatures, need less water or are able to withstand wild swings in temperature and rainfall are often genetically modified organisms, or GMOs. You may have heard of GMOs—they've received lots of attention recently. While many scientists and health experts think vegetables and fruits grown from GMO seeds are safe to eat, some don't, and most Americans remain opposed to GMOs, or at least unconvinced of their benefits. Many people don't know that it's likely most of us are already eating food (and wearing clothes) made from GMO crops. In the U.S., about 90 percent of the corn and cotton, as just two examples, are grown using GMO seeds. What almost everyone agrees on is that more research needs to be done on GMOs to understand all the health and economic benefits and risks to people and farmers over time.

*Droughts alter what food we can grow and where we can grow it.*

The United Nations has said world food production will need to double by 2050 for everyone to have enough nutritious food to eat, while at the same time it's expected to be harder and harder, because of climate change, to keep growing the types of crops we grow today in the way we're growing them. If you're interested in how we address that challenge, it's important to become familiar with the GMO debate and decide what you believe the role of GMOs should—or shouldn't—be in helping the world feed itself. If you want to know more about GMOs, including understanding more about why they have such strong supporters and opponents, you can start at pbs.org and search for "harvest of fear."

## *"Water, water, everywhere, Nor any drop to drink"*

Yes, water again. Water scarcity—when there's not enough clean water to go around—is also a challenge the world is already facing and one that is expected only to worsen if current trends continue. If we don't change how we use water, there simply will not be enough water for everyone in the world. The United Nations predicts that by 2050, just like we'll need a lot more food for the world, we'll need 40 percent more water than will be available if the earth continues to warm at current rates and droughts become more and more normal. That's a lot more water—and it's a challenge we as a world have to solve.

COUNTRIES FACING WATER SHORTAGES
AROUND THE WORLD, 2013

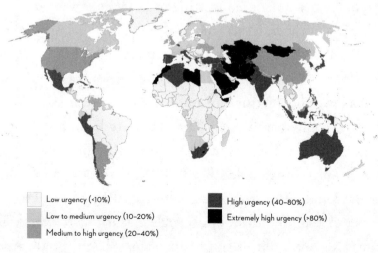

Low urgency (<10%)

Low to medium urgency (10–20%)

Medium to high urgency (20–40%)

High urgency (40–80%)

Extremely high urgency (>80%)

Information source: World Resources Institute

Imagine if you could drink only about half of the water you wanted a day or only brush your teeth once a day instead of twice. Or if you couldn't get the food you wanted because there wasn't enough water to grow crops or for animals to drink. To avoid this scary future, while fighting climate change, we need to make major changes in how we collect and use rainwater, clean and reuse water and water crops (whatever type of seeds they're grown from) and even how we water our plants at home. That's all in addition to what we need to be doing today to help people access the water they need and to ensure it's safe and clean. This is another area where there are lots of different views about what the world should be doing and where there is lots of work being done to find the right solutions.

Governments, companies, NGOs and entrepreneurs are already changing how we as a world use water—and what we use it for. As one example, Coca-Cola has pledged to be water neutral by 2020, meaning for every liter of water Coca-Cola uses to produce their sodas and other products, they'll give back the equivalent amount to people and nature. Governments and companies alike are investing in desalination technologies so that it's cheaper, easier and more cost- and energy-efficient to turn salt water from the oceans into drinking water or for irrigation use to water crops. Some companies are even experimenting with how to turn air into water. Yes, seriously.

Other companies and entrepreneurs are looking to change technologies that use lots of water so they require less or even none at all. For example, they're looking to develop washing machines and dishwashers that would need a lot less water and still get clothes and dishes just as clean. Or toilets that would be just as sanitary but require less water or none at all. And I recently heard of an entrepreneur working to build a waterless car wash. Truly.

Governments and others are also looking at how golf courses, parks and other green spaces can stay beautiful and fun while maybe being a little less green and needing a little (or a lot) less water. Flood irrigation—literally flooding croplands with water redirected from rivers or pumped in from underground sources—is still a main method for watering crops around the world, but one that often wastes water because crops get more than they actually need. Farmers, academics, companies and others are experimenting with different ways for crops to get the water they need but no more (and how to avoid flooding fields).

You and your family can make water-conscious choices at home by turning off the water when you brush your teeth, taking shorter showers, making sure your toilets and faucets aren't leaking, using reusable water bottles when you're out of the house (instead of buying a new plastic one)—and those are only a few ideas. In our house, we try to do all that, every day. Some days we do better than others, and we're constantly reminding ourselves to bring water with us so we don't resort to buying plastic bottles. Sometimes, I forget. So I definitely have work to do too.

Where you choose to shop, what you chose to buy and what you choose to eat can all help fight climate change and global warming. If your family can afford to make choices about what you buy and where you shop, you can choose to support companies that are "green," which means they may use less water or get more of their energy from renewable sources or recycle a lot and in general are working to lower their overall negative effect on the environment. Every year, *Newsweek* ranks companies in the U.S. and around the world on their greenness. You can find the 2014 list at newsweek.com; it's a diverse list, including companies focused on everything from technology to shoes. Companies listen to their customers. Supporting their green efforts by buying what they're selling (instead of buying something similar from a different company that isn't as green) helps prove that you think their extra efforts to care for the environment are important.

## A Rise in Ocean Temperature

DID YOU KNOW?

On average, ocean temperatures have increased about 0.18 degrees Fahrenheit in the last century.

In the top 2,300 feet of oceans across the globe (where most of sea life lives), the average temperatures have increased more than 0.3 degrees Fahrenheit and only since 1969.

Rising ocean temperatures may not sound like a lot but it's having a big impact.

Information source: NASA and National Geographic

Warmer temperatures and less rainfall don't pose a risk only to how we currently grow food and think of our drinking water, they also increase the risk of droughts and fires. In 2012, many parts of the U.S. experienced droughts, because of the warmer-than-average summers of 2011 and 2012 and decreased rainfall leaving soil and plants parched and dry. Not surprisingly, more drought leads to less fresh water as there's less rain and snow to refresh water sources. Less rain and higher temperatures also mean that in addition to the ice sheets melting, as mentioned earlier, glaciers are shrinking around the world,

from the Rockies in the U.S. and Canada to the Himalayas in
Asia to the Alps in Europe and the Andes in South America.
This "glacial retreat" leads to less and less fresh water flowing
into rivers and ground tables (the source for wells) that can be
used for drinking, cooking, irrigation and other purposes, such
as fighting fires. Hotter and drier conditions in the western U.S.
help explain why wildfires are more common and more severe
(burning more land and more homes) than even a few decades
ago. Once they've started, wildfires are now burning on average for longer and devastating more land. Unless we stop global
warming, all of this is expected to get even worse.

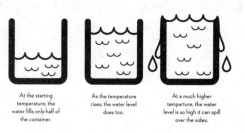

AS THE ICE CAPS
MELT, WATER EXPANDS
ACROSS THE GLOBE

At the starting temperature, the water fills only half of the container.

As the temperature rises, the water level does too.

At a much higher temparture, the water level is so high it can spill over the sides.

Information source: EPA

As temperature rises (and ice caps melt), water expands across the globe.
This doesn't look deadly, but it can be for people living on or near water.

Global warming leads to oceans warming too. Warmer water
leads to more water, as zany as that may sound. The water melting off ice caps and glaciers gets added to the ocean; warmer
water also literally expands, taking up more space than cooler
water. All of this causes the sea level—the actual height of the
oceans in relation to the shore—to rise. By 2012, global sea levels had already risen by eight inches since 1870. Of those total
eight inches, close to seven had occurred in the previous 100
years. This is another seemingly small change with big consequences. Sea levels are expected to continue to rise, and islands
and coastlines are already disappearing under higher waters.

Across the United States, almost 5 million people live less than four feet above their local ocean's, bay's or waterway's high tide. They—and their homes—are in danger of being swept away because of rising sea levels, especially during floods and strong storms like Hurricane Sandy, which took the lives of at least fifty-three people and destroyed thousands of homes and businesses across the East Coast, including in New York City.

Today, some communities are still recovering from Hurricane Sandy, and different people from across the government, along with scientists and others, are thinking about how the East Coast and anywhere can prepare for "next time," so that no one dies, homes aren't destroyed and everyone's better off. This is so important because researchers who study weather patterns and climate change say it's more likely than not that more superstorms such as Sandy are in our future.

Whole cities are at risk as sea levels rise from melting ice and glaciers. If we don't act on climate change, parts of New York City could disappear permanently. New Orleans and Venice, Italy, could disappear entirely. In Calcutta, India, 14 million people could lose their homes if sea levels rise by only a little more than 1.5 feet. Similarly, close

*Hurricanes and superstorms like Sandy, pictured above, can be devastating when they make landfall—and even out at sea. They're as dangerous as they look.*

Courtesy of NG Images/Alamy

*Rising water levels may cause some cities, like Bangkok, pictured here, to flood completely.*

to 5 million people each in Shanghai, China; Ho Chi Minh City, Vietnam (which you may have heard called Saigon in your history books); and Miami could lose their homes. In Alexandria, Egypt, more than 4 million are at risk; in Amsterdam, The Netherlands, more than 1 million. Remember, lots of the world's biggest cities sit on water. Across the world, on almost every continent, rising sea levels threaten the homes of millions and millions of people. In some places, whole countries are threatened. The Maldives and other island nation-states could disappear underwater if sea levels rise and rise and rise.

Stronger, fiercer and more frequent tropical storms and hurricanes (like Sandy) are another consequence of warmer average ocean temperatures. Storms literally draw more energy from warmer oceans—another thing that sounds zany but is true. This matters because stronger storms (like Sandy was) are more likely to cause serious and longer-lasting damage on land and in the ocean too (like Sandy did). Bigger storms can ruin freshwater by turning it brackish, or making it salty, and consequently

323

deadly for the fish that need fresh, non-salty water to survive. That's also bad for people who rely on those fish as a source of food. Stronger storms are also more likely to wreak havoc on crops, hurting what's growing now and changing the makeup of the soil, often making it saltier and impossible to farm for years. All of this is already happening. Over the past thirty years, stronger and stronger hurricanes in the Atlantic Ocean have battered North America and the Caribbean, killing fish and crops alike. Many scientists predict this is only the beginning, unless we stop climate change and global warming.

## Coral: The Rain Forests of the Sea

If you think about coral reefs, what comes to mind? I see bright, bold, colorful coral reefs teeming with fish (and my science report from elementary school). Sometimes referred to as the rain forests of the sea, coral reefs make up a significant part of the world's biodiversity. An estimated one-quarter of all marine life lives in, on and around coral reefs. They play an important role in helping to keep ocean floors healthy and provide safe spaces for fish and other marine life to live. Because of that, coral reefs are also important to the people who live around them, for fishing and as an attraction for visitors who want to snorkel or scuba dive. I love to snorkel and scuba dive and the most beautiful scenery I've seen underwater has been around coral reefs.

Additionally, coral reefs protect coastlines and communities, acting as a break against rising water levels and storms (the storms basically trip over the reefs so they're weaker by the time they reach land). But weaker reefs mean that storms that start over the ocean are likely to be even more intense when they make landfall than warmer water alone would make them. That's not good for anyone.

As the little green plants that live in oceans absorb more carbon dioxide, the oceans become more acidic. Warmer ocean temperatures and ocean acidification affect coral in many damaging ways, including leading to what's known as coral bleaching, when reefs' vibrant shades fade to chalky white shells (like what happens if you use bleach when washing a white shirt to get a stain out). Although it doesn't always lead to the reefs dying out, bleaching frequently is only one step in a fatal chain of events for coral. What's deadly for coral is also deadly for the fish that depend on the reefs. As one example, reefs near the Seychelles, a country made up of islands off Africa's east coast, suffered terrible bleaching after ocean temperatures and acidification skyrocketed in 1998. In 2006, only eight years later, a study found that half the fish species around the coral had disappeared.

Coral reefs aren't the only marine life affected by warmer temperatures and acidification. Just like on land, as ocean tem-

*When coral starts to bleach, like is happening here, the reef's whole ecosystem is vulnerable.*

Courtesy of Helmut Corneli/imageBROKER/Corbis

peratures warm, new species migrate into water that before would have been too cold for them. These invaders often disrupt ecosystems that had been perfectly balanced beforehand. The consequences of these disruptions are not yet clear, but what is certain is that life on and under the sea is continuing to change and many fish, coral and other species are being lost or permanently altered because of climate change.

Oyster reefs also play an important role as brakes on storms, and they help with water quality by filtering the water around and above them and removing nasty pollutants. With more intense storms expected, oysters can help blunt the impact from those storms, even in places not normally associated with oysters, like New York City. In 2011, at the Clinton Global Initiative (a meeting of leaders across governments, businesses, NGOs and foundations working together to try to solve big world problems),

Courtesy of the Billion Oyster Project

the New York Harbor School committed to producing 10 million oysters per year by 2015 (which they're on track to do). That goal marked a big expansion of its then-current work, but clearly was only part of the school's vision, as they named their effort the Billion Oyster Project.

The New York Harbor School wanted to re-create the healthy oyster reefs that used to be common in New

*New York Harbor School students hauling out Harbor School–spawned oysters to check on their growth.*

York Harbor, restore water quality and fight the effects of climate change all at once. Today, high school students at the New York Harbor School are engaged in oyster breeding and helping to feed and care for the oysters. And they're recycling old oyster shells from restaurants in Brooklyn and Manhattan into homes for the new oysters that students are breeding. That's all far cooler than anything I got to do in high school or middle school (the Billion Oyster Project now has 100 partners across New York City, including forty-six middle schools).

Wherever you live—in a desert, near the mountains or by a lake—whether you live in a big city or small town, you are part of an ecosystem and can work with your teachers to identify which animal or plant species is most key to the health of your area and develop a curriculum around it similar to what the Harbor School has done with oysters. If there were more programs like the Harbor School's, more students would learn about their local environments and climate change while at the same time helping to protect their local environments and fight climate change. All in the same school day! To learn more about the New York Harbor School, how to support its programs or how you could possibly start something similar in your own school, check out billionoysterproject.org.

## CLIMATE CHANGE AND HEALTH

### *Air Pollution*

The warmer the earth's average temperature becomes, the worse the consequences are for our health. Heat waves are not the only climate change–related threat to our health. Air pollu-

*This picture was taken during the Great London Smog in 1952. It's daytime, but you can't tell.*

tion is anything in the air that can hurt humans or our global ecosystem. Similar to global warming, it's often the result of using coal and oil to fuel factories and cars. What's in air pollution can weaken our lungs, making us more vulnerable to catching things like colds. It can also lead to asthma, particularly in kids, and worsen asthma in people already suffering from it.

Currently, more than 20 million Americans have asthma, including more than 6 million kids and teenagers under eighteen. You likely know someone with asthma or may have asthma yourself and recognize the telltale symptoms of wheezing, shortness of breath and coughing. Asthma, if left untreated, can permanently damage a person's lungs and even lead to death (which is why a lot of kids with asthma carry inhalers with them wherever they go). Dust and pollen from trees and flowers are often pointed to as key triggers for asthma attacks. So too are ozone, carbon monoxide and other pollutants generated from cars, factories and power plants, all significant contributors to air pollution. In addition to helping fight climate change, making different choices about where our energy comes from (like using solar instead of coal) will keep the air clean and safe for all who need to breathe (that's all of us!).

## Ozone

Thinking about ozone can be confusing—ozone is good up in the atmosphere (often referred to as "good ozone"), but harmful close to the Earth's surface (referred to as "bad ozone"). It's the main ingredient in smog, which is why the two terms are often used interchangeably. There's no question it's bad for us to breathe in, whatever it's called. Besides worsening asthma and causing long-term lung damage, breathing in smog can kill, and kill quickly.

In 1952, during the so-called Great London Smog, thousands of people died in less than a week. In an effort to prevent similar future tragedies, the United Kingdom enacted a series of laws changing the ways factories were built and where they could be built so that there would be less pollution, especially in and near cities where more people lived. The air became cleaner and people started worrying less about smog. The U.S. passed similar laws—and other countries did too. These are often called "clean air acts" or "clean air laws" because of their focus on regulating air pollution. In the U.S., these laws have made a big difference.

Companies have also made changes on their own, often prompted by people asking for, or even demanding, they emit less ozone, carbon monoxide, carbon dioxide and other things that pollute our air (and land and water). In 2013, our cars, factories, buildings and power plants emitted two-thirds less carbon monoxide than in 1980. But there's so much in the atmosphere already, and so many other greenhouse gases, that we have a lot more to do to prevent pollution from hurting people's health today and in the future. We also need to fight pollution and global warming for yet another health-related reason: to prevent mosquito-borne diseases (like malaria) and tick-borne diseases (like Lyme disease) from spreading into new areas and from living longer throughout the year (and making more people sick). If you're curious about air pollution and smog in your community, visit stateoftheair.org, a site run by the American Lung Association, to see what you can do to help lower air pollution in your community and protect your and your family's health.

## CLIMATE CHANGE AND FUN

It's not only our homes and our health that are impacted by climate change, it's also how and where we play, vacation and what sports we can do. As sea levels rise, beaches are eroding across the world (you may have noticed this if you live near the ocean) and some beaches could disappear entirely under the ocean. During the 2014–2015 winter, massive amounts of snow fell on the U.S. East Coast and notably little snow fell in parts of the western U.S. Changing snow patterns mean less skiing in some parts of the world. If there's less snow in the winter, that means there is less snowmelt in the spring, and that means that rivers are lower. Lower river levels mean fewer places to fish and fewer rapids to enjoy while rafting or kayaking. Glacial retreat over time has the same consequences of lower rivers and fewer places to ski. Climate change is definitely un-fun.

# WINNERS (OR AT LEAST NOT LOSERS) AND ... LOSERS

Coral are far from the only animals threatened by climate change. Many species are already adapting, or attempting to adapt, to climate change. They're moving north searching for cooler climates or swimming into new waters looking for the same. Scientists talk about the likely winners and losers as the climate continues to change and the earth warms. Winners will include the animals that can move to new areas and are able to eat new and different foods, as well as those that can survive and thrive in a variety of temperatures. Admittedly, it's hard for me to think of these as true "winners," as they'll still have to make huge shifts to even have a chance of survival in a warmer, drier world (even if where they're living is getting much colder and wetter).

The clear losers will be the animals that can neither adapt to different temperatures nor move to different areas, such as koalas, whose diet consists principally of eucalyptus. Koalas' habitat (or where they live) is limited to areas where eucalyptus is easily available, like in their home country of Australia. If warmer temperatures threaten eucalyptus, koalas will have a hard time—Australia is massive but it's still an island and currently koalas only live in a relatively small part of the country.

Scientists believe at least one species has already gone extinct in part, if not entirely, because of climate change. The golden toad was last seen in 1989. As its native Costa Rican cloud forests disappeared due to severe droughts tied to climate change, the golden toad's habitat also disappeared. Just as humans cannot live for long without a home, neither can animals. In the next chapter we'll talk about endangered species, including some animals, like polar bears, whose lives are also threatened by changes to their home environments caused by climate change.

*The golden toad is likely extinct; it exists now only in photographs like this one.*

## WHY POOR PEOPLE ARE PARTICULARLY VULNERABLE

In addition to people who live in areas below sea level, who else do you think is particularly vulnerable to climate change? People living in poverty all over the world, and not just because of the heat waves talked about earlier. As more severe weather makes growing crops more challenging, food prices are expected to go up, making it harder for poor people everywhere to afford the food needed to feed themselves and their families. People with fewer resources are also less able to adapt to climate change. For example, poorer families are a lot less likely than middle-class or wealthier families to have the option of moving to cooler climates or areas with lower risk of floods or heat waves or air pollution. Families with fewer resources are also less likely to have things like air-conditioning that help blunt the worst effects of heat waves (as tragically seen in the Chicago heat wave mentioned earlier). Poor families are less likely to be able to modify their homes to make them more resistant (better protected) to floods and wildfires, even as floods and wildfires are expected to become more common. As just one example, in 2005, the people who were hit hardest by Hurricane Katrina in New Orleans and other parts of the Gulf Coast were twice as likely to be poor and twice as likely to not have a car compared with the national average (meaning they were less able to fortify their homes, to escape before Hurricane Katrina hit, or to seek refuge elsewhere after the storm had destroyed their homes). It's also harder for poorer families to move away from places with lots of air pollution or persistent smog, putting them, and particularly their kids, more at risk for asthma and for other pollution-related health challenges. In fact, kids from poorer families already suffer from asthma at higher rates than the national average.

## WHAT THE WORLD IS DOING (OR AT LEAST TRYING TO DO)

Pollution—like the water and air it moves through—doesn't need a passport to travel from one country to another. Recognizing this, government leaders across the world met in 1992 at a conference called the Earth Summit. They agreed that more needed to be done to reduce greenhouse gas emissions and prevent climate change's nightmare scenarios from coming true (even twenty years ago they were pretty frightening). Since 1992, government leaders have met many times to discuss what should be done. There was a big agreement in 1997 called the Kyoto Protocol in which developed countries (like the U.K., Germany and Japan) pledged to reduce their greenhouse emissions (like carbon dioxide from coal or oil); then–U.S. Vice President Al Gore was a major champion of the Kyoto Protocol. You may know Vice President Gore better as the narrator of *An Inconvenient Truth*, a movie worth watching about climate change and what may well happen if the world doesn't take the type of coordinated action reflected in the Kyoto Protocol.

Since Kyoto, there's been little agreement on what the world should do to prevent further climate change or on what individual countries should do. Most countries have not succeeded in cutting greenhouse gas emissions, but some have. Denmark, Sweden, France and Belgium, for example, have done so in large part because more people and businesses are using less carbon-intensive forms of energy. As one example, in 2014, Denmark generated a lot of its electricity from wind energy. As another, Germany is a leader on solar power and in recycling; Germans recycle almost half their waste.

The United States has not made significant progress in cutting emissions, but has ambitious plans to do so. In early 2015, the U.S. announced a plan to cut greenhouse gas emissions by 2025 (the details of how we'll do this are still being worked out). China and other countries have also announced ambitious plans. Others still are expected to announce plans, while some countries remain focused on their own economic development (back to the energy poverty discussed earlier in the book). The next big climate-change summit (kind of like the grown-up child of the Earth Summit) is in Paris at the end of 2015. We'll know more about what the world will (or won't) be doing on a big scale then. You can work to influence what happens in Paris and afterward by telling your congressperson, senators and our president what you think the U.S. and other countries should do to combat climate change. You can also attend rallies and marches to help raise awareness about the urgent need for action on climate change and join online campaigns to do the same. But remember, as stated at the beginning of this chapter, there's a lot each of us can do on an individual basis that can make a big difference (no matter what happens—or doesn't happen—in Paris at the climate summit).

# WHAT EACH OF US CAN DO!

## *Recycle*

Are you recycling? If you are, great! If you want to and don't know where to go or how to start, you can visit earth911.com to find a place where you can recycle almost anything—paper, aluminum, plastic and more—near your home. Another terrific resource is called iRecycle. It's a website and free app available on iTunes and Android that can help you find local recycling options for your family for everything I just mentioned above plus old electronics, batteries and more. Almost anything can be recycled—paper, plastic, metal, glass, electronics and used batteries are among the most common—and there's probably a place near you where you can recycle all of those (though not every place may recycle every material).

In San Francisco, people are required to separate out what can be recycled from what can't be. Approximately 80 percent of San Francisco's waste is now recycled or gets composted (turned into fertilizer to help crops grow) rather than put in landfills. If you like that idea, you can encourage your family to support similar measures like that in your community or city. If you don't like that idea, you can encourage your family to support measures that make climate-conscious choices, like recycling common materials such as glass, paper, plastic and aluminum, easier but not mandatory. This is another area where change.org may be a good tool to use.

You can also start a recycling program at your school if it doesn't have one and urge your parents to do the same at their work. Marc and I recycle obsessively and I'm grateful New York City makes it pretty easy to do so. Recycling can also be a source of income as some states pay for each aluminum can recycled—so you could even consider starting a recycling business if you live in a place where that's the case.

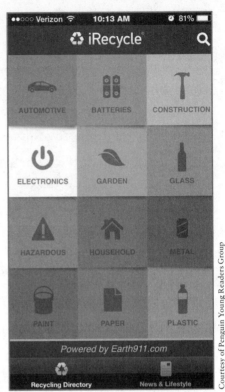

*Here's a screenshot of the iRecycle app, which I have on my phone and find very useful.*

## Reuse! Donate!

Reuse what you can and donate what you can (so someone doesn't have to a buy a new one). Reuse means using something more than once, like bringing your own bag to the grocery store instead of getting a paper or plastic bag each time you go, or bringing a bottle you can refill with water instead of buying a new bottle of water (yes, water again). Donating means giving away things like books (to your local library, homeless shelter, church) so that other people can benefit from them instead of buying new books, for example, which also means (if we're talking about lots of books) fewer trees being cut down, since paper is mainly made from wood. Books are only one example of things we can all think about donating. The U.S. Environmental Protection Agency has a good website, which might not be very kid friendly, but is very straightforward and helpful, at epa.gov. Another idea is to trade books with friends instead of buying new ones (including this one—I hope if you like it, you'll lend it to a friend!).

Reuse can even apply to cooking oil. Yes, cooking oil. When Cassandra was in fifth grade in Westerly, Rhode Island, she learned that used cooking oil could be transformed into clean-burning biodiesel fuel to help heat homes and that doing so wasn't expensive. So, in 2008, Cassandra created Turn Grease Into Fuel. Through Turn Grease Into Fuel, kids recruit local restaurants to donate their used cooking oil to local organizations that can then turn it into home heating oil. That home heating oil is then given to low-income families who otherwise may not be able to heat their homes, especially during really cold winters like the one we had in 2014–2015. By 2014, Turn Grease Into Fuel had helped prevent more than 3 million pounds of carbon dioxide emissions from being released, because families were using biodiesel from recycled cooking oil instead of other sources to heat their homes. As of 2015, Turn Grease Into Fuel had partner restaurants and businesses in three states and had converted over 200,000 gallons of waste cooking oil to help over 400 families heat their homes.

A few years ago, Cassandra and Turn Grease Into Fuel wanted to do even more on top of their work with individual restaurants and families. So in 2011, they wrote legislation that would require all businesses in Rhode Island to recycle their used cooking oil and worked with state legislators to get it passed.

*Cassandra demonstrating how cooking oil can be turned into home-heating oil.*

They succeeded and the law went into effect in 2012. Turn Grease Into Fuel now helps restaurants and households recycle cooking oil across Connecticut, Massachusetts and Rhode Island. If you're in one of those states and want to know how to participate, or if you want to start a similar program in your own state, please visit w-i-n.ws.

## Curb Your Water Use

How much water do you think you use in a day? In a year? The average American directly uses 80–100 gallons of water every day in what we drink (though that's actually only a small part of the total), how we wash (think showers) and the products we use (like dishwashers and washing machines). To put it in perspective, it's as if we each drank up to 1,600 glasses of water a day! And the average American's water footprint, or how much water we use directly and indirectly, is actually much higher: 2,060 gallons a day! That's because of all the water hidden in the food we eat

## TIPS ON CURBING YOUR WATER USE

| |
|---|
| Wait until the dishwasher is full before you run it. |
| Take a shower instead of a bath (and take a shorter shower). |
| Turn off the water while you're brushing your teeth. |
| Ask your parents to check that your faucets and toilets aren't leaking (and wasting water). |
| Use reusable water bottles instead of buying new plastic ones (except when we may have to, like at airports). |
| Put a plastic container full of rocks in your toilet's tank to displace some of the water and trick it into thinking it's full. |
| Make sure your washing machine is set to the right load size so it doesn't use more water than it needs. |

Information source: *National Geographic*

(because it takes a lot of water to help crops and animals grow), the gas that fuels our cars and the stuff we buy (yes, water was probably even used to make the clothes you're wearing). Using less water is something most of us could do a better job of, and, as discussed earlier in the chapter, it doesn't have to be hard. Check out watercalculator.org to figure out how much water you use directly and indirectly each day and what you could do to use less water in a way that makes sense for your family.

Recycling and reusing matter here too; more water won't be used to make something new if something older can be recycled or used again. Similarly, donating excess food and eliminating food waste, which we talked about earlier in the book, helps hungry families get the food they need, would save everyone money and would help us conserve millions and millions of gallons of water every year.

## Use the Power of Your Wallet

Just like you can support green companies by buying their products, if your family can afford to make choices about what food you're buying, think about where your food comes from and how your food choices might affect the environment. Buying "local" generally means there was less pollution emitted in getting the fruits, vegetables, fish and meat to your supermarket—because they didn't travel by airplane or long-haul truck and put a lot of carbon dioxide and carbon monoxide in the air on the way. It also helps create and support jobs in your community. Buying local isn't an option for everyone, but if it is, there's Locavore, a free app available on iTunes and Android, to help determine what food is local and what isn't. There are also likely many more free apps that you may already know about or could find, including ones focused on your hometown that you and your family could use.

You can also work with your parents, friends and teachers to encourage your school district to buy local food. If every school district around the U.S. focused on locally sourced food for the more than 50 million students who go to school every day that would mean a lot less carbon being served alongside the cafeteria pizza. My husband and I buy local fruits, vegetables, eggs and meat whenever we can, and admittedly carbon splurge (as we call it) on coffee, hoping we come out overall with a relatively low carbon level (and water footprint) for our food consumption. Not everyone can make choices about what food is bought for dinner or where it comes from. We're very lucky to be able to make choices about what we eat (and the coffee we drink . . . possibly too much of).

# *Walking, Biking, Carpooling*

If we all changed how we got around, we could stop a lot of carbon from going into the atmosphere. Walking is a great way to fight climate change, if it's safe. Or biking, again if it's safe—and with a helmet on! The only carbon emitted when we walk or bike is whatever we breathe out! Encourage your family to carpool to work or school or to take public transportation (like a subway or bus) if it's a choice where you live so that you're not emitting carbon dioxide and more pollutants if you don't have to. When you're in the car (hopefully in a carpool), think about when you're using your car's air-conditioning unit. It requires using more gas—and therefore emits more carbon dioxide into the atmosphere. So if you can, open a window instead. And when it comes time to get a new car, if your family can afford to consider electric cars (that use electricity instead of gas) or hybrid cars (that generally use a mix of gas and electricity), switching from a traditional car fueled by gasoline to one fueled at least in part by electricity can lower your family's carbon emissions (and water footprint).

It's not always feasible to carpool, and sometimes we have to get on a long flight to visit family or friends who live far away, or because we're going on vacation. Or your parents or I may need to go across the country (or world) for work. Rather than not going anywhere, we need to make the best, most climate-conscious choices we can about how we get where we need (and want) to go. As is true throughout this section, even little choices can make a big difference.

You can also work with your parents to advocate for your

local government to make biking easier. New York City, Minneapolis and other cities have invested in building bike lanes to encourage more biking as a means of commuting to and from work. In Amsterdam, The Netherlands, and Copenhagen, Denmark, biking is a main, if not the main, way people get around. You can ask your hometowns to think about ways to make biking easier and driving to have less of an impact on the environment. As one example, parking meters in Salt Lake City are now solar-powered.

## Protect Wild Places

Depending on where we live, we can help protect and keep wetlands, beaches, forests and other places clean and healthy by volunteering to pick up the trash that too often accumulates from what is tossed into oceans or rivers, out of car windows and left behind by campers. That helps the natural beauty of places shine through and it's good for the environment. Wetlands, like the Florida Everglades, protect seashores, riverbanks, cities and communities from flooding and also help protect important ecosystems for fish, birds, land animals and plants. Scientists consider wetlands the most diverse habitats in the world.

Wetlands help lessen the impacts of climate change; however, they're also at risk from the effects of climate change. Specific threats to wetlands include salt-water flooding, droughts and fires, all of which threaten their very existence. So, in addition to keeping wetlands clean, you can encourage your elected officials to support legislation protecting beaches, wetlands, forests and oceans—the frontlines of fighting climate change—and also beautiful places where many of us like to walk, play and swim.

## Protect Those Who Are Hit Hardest by Storms (or Heat Waves)

Encourage your churches, temples, mosques, schools and other community spaces where you spend time to open during extreme heat waves and provide fans, air-conditioning and other ways for people to remain cool and safe during extreme heat or storms. That will help protect those most vulnerable to more extreme weather, particularly the elderly and people living in poverty. You can also raise money for those efforts or ask people to donate or lend fans and other cooling units to the places that need them.

After storms, you can support recovery efforts like the one by Team Rubicon, shown in the picture at the start of this chapter. Team Rubicon is an organization that harnesses the experience, skills and teamwork of our military veterans to respond effectively to natural disasters. They help determine the extent of the damage, clean up the desctruction and debris after a storm (particularly important following massive storms like Sandy) and organize other people who want to help. To find out more about Team Rubicon, where they've worked and what they do, please visit teamrubiconusa.org. If you want to volunteer immediately after a storm, you can ask Team Rubicon as well as local political, religious and community leaders for how best to get involved.

## Use Less Energy at Home (and Everywhere)

Many climate-conscious bulbs—like LEDs or compact fluorescent ones—today require significantly less energy than the traditional incandescent ones. The U.S. Environmental Protection Agency gives light bulbs ENERGYSTAR® status if they use at least 70 percent less energy than conventional bulbs and last at least ten times longer. Different bulbs are not always a choice for families because they might be too expensive or they might not work in the lamps and light fixtures families have. But if they are, I hope you'll talk to your parents about changing the bulbs in your home. Energystar.gov is a good resource for figuring out which light bulbs would be the best option for your family.

It's not just about what type of bulbs you use, it's also about how often you turn on (or off) your lights. You and your family can turn off lights when you leave for school or work, if you go out on the weekend and before you go to bed at night. Unplug appliances (like lamps) and chargers (for phones, iPads or computers) you're not using. And try to plug in appliances only when you or your family are using them. I plug in our coffee machine only when I'm about to use it and unplug it once I've made my coffee. My husband, Marc, and I unplug our computers every night before we go to sleep. It's also okay to recognize that there are some things it's not practical to unplug (like refrigerators—but we all can probably close the door more quickly). Whatever we can unplug (or not plug in), we should—it's good for the environment and our wallets. The U.S. spends more for electricity to wait around while something is plugged in but not on or charging than when we're actually using a phone, a computer, a light. Wow. And if our homes have the right type of insulation (to keep us warm in the winter, cool in the summer and safe all the time), our homes use less electricity. That means lower carbon emissions and a lower energy bill.

In addition to different light bulbs and insulation, your family may want to consider (if they're affordable) buying more energy-efficient appliances when it's time for a new refrigerator or washing machine, or using different types of windows that help keep your home warmer in the winter and cooler in the summer, so you don't have to use your heat or air-conditioning quite as much. (And again, if they're affordable.)

It's not just about lights, appliances and insulation. Think about where your dishwashing soap and washing machine detergent comes from and if there are more climate-conscious options. GoodGuide is a free app that can help your family find the right products for your household needs and budget that are also climate conscious. The Earth911 website I talked about earlier (earth911.com) can also be helpful here.

Consider visiting energystar.gov with your family and calculating your home's energy efficiency today, and then see what you could be doing to make your home even more energy efficient, hopefully saving money and fighting climate change at the same time. At the risk of sounding too repetitive, small changes in how we live in our homes—and how we leave our homes—can add up to make a big difference. And, as always, you can work with your family to support state and national legislation that sets efficiency requirements for light bulbs, appliances and anything that uses electricity in your home or elsewhere.

You can also encourage your school, church, temple, synagogue, mosque, community center and anywhere else you spend time to look at how much energy they use on energystar.gov. There's even a specific ENERGYSTAR program for schools yours could join. You can encourage your parents to work with their office buildings to monitor their energy use (there's a good chance that's already happening—but your parents could ask just in case). In the U.S., buildings account for approximately 40 percent of all energy use and carbon emissions. Making our buildings (like schools and office buildings) more efficient is crucial to lowering our national energy use and fighting climate change. You can even ask your city to become more energy conscious. Los Angeles changed all of its more than 100,000 streetlights to LED bulbs, good for the environment and over time, good for the city's wallet; so far, Los Angeles has saved millions of dollars in energy bills.

*Courtesy of U.S. Environmental Protection Agency, ENERGYSTAR program*

*ENERGYSTAR light bulbs are better for the environment and last longer too.*

## Use a Carbon Calculator! Earth Day!

How big do you think your carbon footprint is—or how much carbon do you think you're responsible for adding to the atmosphere? Similar to a water calculator, you can use a carbon calculator to help figure out the answer to that question and what you can do to help shrink your footprint. The Environmental Protection Agency has a great one especially for kids—though it's equally useful for adults too (at least it was for me)—just go to epa.gov. It takes only a few minutes to go through, and it shows the impact of various choices (like unplugging electronics) on our carbon footprint. Whatever your results, talk about them with your family and friends and think about what you can do together to reduce your carbon footprints at home, at work, at school and in your neighborhood.

We have a saying in my family that patience is a virtue, but impatience gets things done. Counteracting climate change requires both. The only way to reverse global warming is to dramatically reduce our greenhouse gas emissions, such as carbon dioxide from fossil fuels. Even if we stopped all greenhouse gas emissions tomorrow—impossible to do in practice— it would take at least decades, if not a century or longer, for all our forests and oceans to absorb and digest all the carbon dioxide already in the atmosphere. Even so, every contribution counts and the longer we wait, the harder it will be to clean up our atmosphere and save our planet. This may sound cheesy, but I believe it. Earth Day shouldn't only be April 22nd, but every day throughout the year. We don't have any time to waste.

# Get Going!

- Share what you know about climate change with grown-ups (and friends too), and recycle whatever you can
- Play climate change games with your family
- Plant trees (check with the Arbor Day Foundation first)
- Shop at companies that are doing their best to be "green"
- Fight for a recycling program in your town if there isn't one
- Use reusable shopping bags and water bottles
- Trade books, magazines, video games and more with friends
- Donate used cooking oil to be converted to heating oil, or start a program like Cassandra's if there isn't one in your community
- Wait until the dishwasher is full before you run it
- Take a shorter shower instead of a bath
- Turn off the water while you're brushing your teeth
- Donate books to your local library (or anywhere they'll be read!)
- Buy your food from local, sustainable sources if that's an option

- Consider starting a garden at school or home (remember Katie's Krops from earlier in the book?)
- Walk (or bike or scoot) when you can instead of using a car
- Take public transportation or carpool when you can
- Volunteer to pick up trash from animals' habitats (or anywhere)
- Advocate for places for people living in poverty or elderly people to go to stay cool during heat waves and safe during storms
- Encourage your family to buy an electric or hybrid car next time you get a new one if that's an option
- Calculate your home's energy efficiency and use energy-efficient bulbs if that's an option, and look for the ENERGYSTAR label
- Turn off lights when you leave the house
- Unplug appliances (like lamps) and chargers (for phones, iPads or computers) when you're not using them
- Encourage your school or place of worship or community center to calculate their energy efficiency and to become more efficient
- Set up a climate club at your school or place of worship
- Write letters to your local government officials about what you think your town needs to do to save energy
- Know your carbon and water footprints—and help your family and friends know theirs too; work on lowering them together (by doing the things above and any other climate-conscious ideas you have)
- If you're over thirteen, use social media to follow organizations (like The Nature Conservancy) and people (like Kristen Bell) working to protect the environment and fight climate change

Courtesy of Julie Larsen Maher @ WCS

## CHAPTER NINE

# TOO CLOSE TO GONE
## ENDANGERED SPECIES

What's the first group you joined? I'm not sure what the answer is for me, whether the church choir, my softball or soccer team, my Brownies troop or something else. I know the first big organizations I ever joined were Greenpeace, the World Wildlife Fund and Conservation International. My grandma Dorothy told me one year that for Christmas, she and my Pop-Pop (my grandfather) wanted to give me a year's membership to any organization of my choice that was making a difference in the world. I think I was eight when we had that conversation but I may have been a little younger or older. As mentioned in the previous chapter, at that time I was very concerned about coral reefs and whales (even though I lived far from any ocean). My grandparents first gave me a membership to Greenpeace. I devoured all the Greenpeace materials that arrived in the mail. (This was back when everything came in the mail—there were no websites to visit or email or text updates to receive.)

Over the next couple of years, each Christmas my grandparents gave me a yearlong membership to the World Wildlife Fund and Conservation International, both conservation-focused groups. I'd gotten more interested in helping save elephants from poaching and appreciated the work each was doing in that area. I'd also started reading old issues of the *National Geographic* magazine in our school library, searching for articles on elephants and other endangered species (particularly as I waited for someone else to return various Encyclopedia Brown books I wanted to read).

I loved learning about what we were doing in the United States to save our iconic bald eagle and the California condor, and about what work was being done elsewhere to protect not only elephants, but also other animals under threat, for whatever reasons. I remember being so grateful my grandparents helped me to do what felt like my small part through my organizational memberships to protect animals I had seen only in the local Little Rock Zoo or the pages of *National Geographic*. The hard work, commitment and support of people all over the world have helped save a lot of animals, but sadly, many of the species I worried about in the 1980s are still endangered today, and some are even closer to extinction.

Scientists and other experts who track and study wildlife estimate that one out of every five of the world's animals, including mammals, reptiles, birds and fish, are threatened with extinction. If a species (like the golden toad mentioned in the last chapter) goes extinct, that means every animal in the species has died out and no one will ever see another one, anywhere on earth. Some amount of extinction is expected, even natural. This is what scientists call the "background extinction rate." It should be about one to five species per year for the whole world, but we're currently losing species so quickly that research can't keep up. What we do know is that it's not a small number. Scientists estimate that plant and animal species are going extinct at 1,000 to 10,000 times the natural background rate, meaning we're losing at least 1,000 species a year and likely more.

If current extinction rates continue, in our lifetimes, by the year 2050, we could lose up to half of all species that are alive today. That is a very bleak vision and is referred to as the "sixth great wave" of extinction. The first five waves occurred millions and millions of years ago; most dinosaurs died out in the fifth wave. The sixth wave of extinction is not inevitable. We know what works—and has succeeded in the past—to help lessen the threats facing animals across the world and to make sure we grow up and grow old in a world full of wildlife diversity.

Endangered species should concern everyone, not just those of us who are drawn to certain species (I love wildlife, though I admit I especially love giraffes, elephants, whales and gorillas) or those of us (like me) who love going to the zoo with our families and friends to marvel at the crazy climbing, slithering, flying or acrobatic abilities of the animals. Even if someone doesn't care about wildlife, isn't interested in lions or leopards and never wants to go to the zoo, endangered species matter to all our lives. When a species becomes endangered, it sends a message that things are shifting in its larger environment, and not for the better. Animal species depend on one another, and we depend on them. If just one species is lost, that may mean we're missing an important part of our food chain or an animal that helps keep our oceans, rivers and air clean. Healthy animal species means healthier environments and, ultimately, healthier humans—and who doesn't want that?

Sometimes it's hard to wrap our heads around how small actions like helping save a species in another country can also help fight poverty. This may sound flippant (or smart-alecky), but it's not. Many African countries rely on tourism tied to wildlife (like through safaris) to help their economies continue to grow and to lift people out of poverty. How does this work? Think about your family vacations, when you become a tourist. Your family spends money on hotels or on camping, on purchasing food from local stores or eating at restaurants, on buying souvenirs and when visiting local attractions, whether wildlife parks or amusement parks. All of those places hire workers—to run and staff the hotels, to cook and serve the restaurant meals, to convince you to buy that extra T-shirt and to make sure all the rides run safely. Those people in turn earn money from their work that they use to pay their rent or buy a house, buy groceries or eat out, ride a bus to work or to visit a friend.

If elephants and rhinos disappear, fewer tourists will visit the places where they (used to) live and fewer people will then be employed. If parents lose their tourism-connected jobs, they may not be able to afford to pay for school or food for their kids, which in turn would hurt the income of teachers, farmers and others in the community. Healthy animal populations, including many of the species under extreme threat like ele-phants, attract tourists to Kenya, Tanzania and other countries where these remarkable animals live.

Although this chapter focuses on endangered animals and not endangered plants, over centuries, scientific research on plants has led to many medical breakthroughs. According to the National Cancer Institute, a majority of cancer medicines come in part from rain-forest plants. Our continued reliance on nature for our health (beyond the food we eat, air we breathe and water we drink) has long fascinated me. In eighth grade, my first science report at my new school in Washington, D.C., was a group project on a few such plants, including curare and the Madagascar periwinkle. Curare is a chemical extracted from various plants in Central and South America. Originally used by indigenous people to poison the tips of arrows, after years of experiments, curare is now an ingredient in medicines to help in various surgeries. Medicines from the Madagascar periwinkle are used to fight many diseases, and have helped most kids who now get leukemia survive. My group got to show our poster on the extraordinary properties of these plants, alongside our classmates', at the National Zoo (a perfect setting to be talking about the importance of saving all our species). If we keep losing plants and animals at such a rapid rate, who knows what potential medical break-throughs will never happen?

One of the stars of my eighth-grade science report: the Madagascar periwinkle plant, a source for various medicines in use today.

What do you think has caused most extinctions? Well,

historically, species have gone extinct for many reasons. Diseases, destructive one-time events like volcanic eruptions and asteroid strikes and slow shifts in the climate that made an area unlivable to certain species have all driven various species to extinction. Most dinosaurs, for example, are thought to have become extinct about 65 million years ago because of either an asteroid or volcano. One or the other quickly killed most of the plants and animals that dinosaurs ate and also created a long-lasting darkness that made it difficult for the plants and animals that survived the initial destruction to stay alive. The asteroid or volcano didn't kill all species; crocodiles, for instance, were alive then and clearly survived. Sharks did too! Hopefully, hugely destructive asteroids will only exist from now on in movies and video games and won't be a threat to animals—or us.

Today, competition between animals and people for limited resources, people's appetite for jewelry, decorations, so-called medicines (that have no proven medical value) and other things made from endangered species, plus the effects of climate change are the main reasons animal species are threatened with extinction. Global warming is most immediately threatening to those species that live in environments most vulnerable to climate change, like the Arctic.

Poaching—or the killing of animals illegally—is a risk to any animal perceived to be worth more dead than alive. Poachers today are generally not just a few outlaw hunters trying to prove that they're tough or looking to earn a few extra dollars on their own to help support their families. Poaching has become a massive underground illegal business. Often the same dangerous criminals at the heart of poaching are trafficking illegal drugs and guns. Trade in illegal wildlife and wildlife products, including everything from timber to ivory from a slaughtered elephant's tusks to horns from slaughtered rhinos, is thought to be the fourth biggest illegal enterprise in the world, valued at a staggering $19 billion a year. Around half of that money originates from illegal animal products like ivory.

Killing endangered species is clearly a big business. It's also a deadly one for people as well as the animals being targeted. Protecting endangered species is dangerous work in much of the world. More than 1,000 rangers have died in the last ten years alone across Africa and Asia, brutally murdered by the same poachers who kill animals in cold blood.

In this chapter you'll get to know a few specific endangered species from around the world and the major threats to them as a way to put an animal face on the endangered species crisis. You'll also hear about how we can save endangered species today and for the future. Barring any asteroids, of course.

## WHAT IS AN ENDANGERED SPECIES (OFFICIALLY)?

As of early 2015, more than 1,300 different animal species are currently classified as threatened or endangered by the United States, including species native to the U.S. and those that live in the wild far beyond U.S. borders. As defined by the U.S. Endangered Species Act of 1973 (the law designed to protect such species), "endangered" means a species is facing extinction in all or part of its range, a technical term for where a species lives. "Threatened" means those species that are expected to become endangered very soon if nothing changes to better protect them from poachers, deforestation, climate change or other threats.

# NUMBER OF SPECIES ON THE IUCN RED LIST OF THREATENED SPECIES, 2015

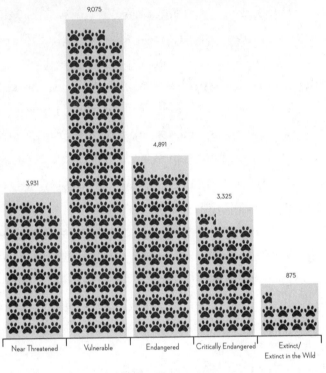

9,075

4,891

3,931

3,325

875

Near Threatened    Vulnerable    Endangered    Critically Endangered    Extinct/ Extinct in the Wild

= 100 species

Information source: IUCN

The International Union for Conservation of Nature and Natural Resources tracks extinct, endangered and threatened species across the world. They regularly update the Red List, an appropriately scary-sounding name for the list of species that have become extinct in the wild and those facing significant threats. It's not all bad news (though admittedly most of it is); the Red List also includes species that are recovering and moving out of the extinction danger zone. As of late 2014, there were thirty-two species listed as extinct in the wild, meaning they live only in captivity (in zoos and parks), with the rest on the Red List labeled critically endangered or facing a very real threat of extinction in the near future, including hundreds of mammalian species, the type (or technically "class") of animal this chapter focuses on. Thankfully, we know a lot about what we—the most powerful mammals on earth—can and must do to help animal species of any class recover and not go the way of the dodo bird, which is sadly famous for having been hunted out of existence in the 17th century.

One thing we know is that if a species loses its habitat, or its home, animals will suffer. In 2007, when they were seventh-grade Girl Scouts, Michigan-natives Rhiannon and Madison decided to found Project ORANGS (Orangutans Really Appreciate and Need Girl Scouts). Inspired by the lifework of the conservationist and scientist Dr. Jane Goodall (another hero of mine) in protecting chimpanzees, Rhiannon and Madison decided to help protect orangutans in their native Indonesia, by working to prevent further habitat loss from palm-oil farming. They started off by checking everything they ate to see if it contained palm oil and encouraged everyone they knew to do the same—and if they found out they were eating something with palm oil, they stopped eating it. When they discovered that the very Girl Scout Cookies they were trying to sell contained palm oil, they started a campaign to get the cookies made with certified rain forest–

*Madison and Rhiannon founded Project ORANGS (Orangutans Really Appreciate and Need Girl Scouts) when they were in seventh grade.*

Courtesy of Sarah Roquemore

safe palm oil. They even enlisted their inspiration, Dr. Jane Goodall, to sign their petition. Their passion and commitment inspired more than 70,000 emails to the Girl Scouts' executives. At the time, the Girl Scouts stuck with their same palm oil. Not every effort meets with the hoped-for success—but every effort matters. Remember the saying "Try, Try Again"? Well, Rhiannon and Madison kept trying and wound up contributing to a much bigger victory: they helped raise awareness beyond the Girl Scouts of the wide destruction wreaked by palm-oil farming and ultimately convinced Kellogg's, which bakes some Girl Scouts Cookies among many other food products (like cereal), to get their palm oil from deforestation-free, rain forest–safe sources.

## THE BALD EAGLE

Sometimes the threat to animals doesn't come from losing their habitats or hunting alone but also from changes in their habitats. The bald eagle became the national emblem of the United States in 1782, even before the U.S. Constitution was drafted! At that time, they could be found throughout the continental United States and Alaska. But being our national symbol didn't protect bald eagles and their population declined throughout the 19th and early-20th centuries. By the mid-20th century, extinction looked like the bald eagle's future. Hunting had become an increasingly serious threat, as Alaskan fishermen worked to kill bald eagles they believed (wrongly as it turned out) were hurting the wild salmon populations. Others hunted for the purpose of making trophies out of the bald eagles they killed (by stuffing them and preserving them). And bald eagles had to compete for food and resources with the growing numbers of Americans living in more and more places (most of the U.S. and Canada are the bald eagles' habitat).

A newer threat in the 20th century was DDT (short for dichlorodiphenyltrichloroethane—now you see why everyone calls it DDT), mentioned in Bugs and Bacteria. In the 1940s and 1950s, DDT was sprayed extensively across the U.S. to prevent and eliminate malaria. It was also

*Courtesy of Julie Larsen Maher @ WCS*

*Bald eagles were one of the first official endangered species in the U.S.—and thankfully no longer are on the list.*

used to protect crops from insects. Unfortunately, DDT didn't just kill mosquitoes or other insects; some DDT found its way into waterways where fish absorbed it into their bodies. Bald eagles, in turn, ate those fish, and although the science isn't well understood, somehow DDT made it so that bald eagles couldn't have safe, healthy eaglets (baby eagles). By 1963, there were only 487 bald eagle pairs in the lower forty-eight states. Trophy hunting, DDT and more had taken their toll.

In the late 1960s, the United States began intense efforts to protect the bald eagle, putting it on the first major endangered species list in 1973, having banned DDT the year before in large part because of how badly it affected bald eagles. Over the past few decades, the U.S. Fish and Wildlife Service has worked closely with conservation groups to protect wild bald eagles and breed bald eagles in zoos and nature preserves to later release into the wild.

Particularly in the 1980s, Americans of all ages got behind this effort, including kids across the country. Kids held fund-raising walks, sold pins and bumper stickers and, in Wisconsin, even sold pickles for bald-eagle conservation. Whatever works! The funds raised through these various efforts (sometimes in the thousands of dollars) helped increase awareness of the how close to extinction bald eagles had come and helped protect bald eagles. Ultimately, no evidence was found linking bald eagles to wild salmon deaths in Alaska and as people grew to understand that, fishermen stopped shooting them. Displaying a freshly killed bald eagle trophy became frowned upon, even taboo, eliminating another reason hunters were killing them. All of those factors helped stop the slaughter and helped populations recover and thrive.

In 1995, the bald eagle was removed from the endangered species list. There are now more than 6,000 bald eagle pairs in the U.S. *National Geographic* has called this a "great conservation story," and it is. It shows that animal species can make a comeback when the government, conservation groups and citizens (including hunters, fishermen and others) all work together. It also shows a reason to be optimistic—we know we can save endangered species with the right partners working together, even if it takes years.

## TIGERS

In a little more than 100 years, the world has lost 97 percent of the tiger population in the wild. From 100,000 tigers in 1900, there are an estimated 3,200 tigers in the wild today. All of the world's tigers would fill about ten large movie theaters (if they could fit in the seats). Although tiger moms give birth to new litters of tiger cubs every 2–2.5 years, about half of all tigers born do not survive past two years old. More tigers are dying because of loss of habitat and poaching than cubs are being born and growing into adulthood. These majestic creatures are, as the chapter title says, sadly too close to gone. Certain subspecies of tigers—like Bali and Javan tigers from Indonesia—have already disappeared.

Let's start with tigers' habitat. The first problem is deforestation, because when forests are cut down, tigers lose the tree cover and land vital to their ability to roam, hunt and lead their lives. Rising sea levels cause similar problems for tigers that live close to the coast instead of deep in the forests. Historically, tigers roamed across much of South and East Asia, from India to Indonesia, across China and into eastern Russia. Today, tigers live in only a small fraction of their range at the beginning of the 20th century.

Poaching also poses a serious threat to tigers. Poachers hunt tigers for their skins and various body parts, including their eyes, bones, claws and teeth, which are used in traditional Asian medicine because people believe that tiger parts can treat everything from malaria to exhaustion. This, of course, isn't true. There's no scientific evidence whatsoever that any

1900                          2010

Information source: WWF

*The tiger population decreased by 97 percent in 110 years. (The tiny tiger represents how much the population has shrunk.)*

tiger part can cure diseases or make people feel less tired. And science has tried. But the lack of proof and the endangered status of tigers haven't stopped people from wanting

*Tigers today live in only a small fraction of the area they lived in 100 years ago.*

to buy tiger parts and poachers from serving that market. Tragically, you can still find so-called medicines and other things made from tiger parts in markets and stores across Asia and even illegally in the United States (including in New York City, where I live).

Tiger protection means preserving their habitats, monitoring populations so we can keep poachers away and ending the demand for tiger parts and products by educating people that there's no such thing as tiger medicine. It also includes ensuring tigers are well cared for in zoos, circuses and privates reserves here in the U.S. There are an estimated 5,000 tigers in the U.S. alone, more than the global wild population. Safeguarding those animals also means safeguarding any people, especially children, who may be nearby. While there is growing awareness about the threats tigers face and what needs to be done, tigers are still in grave danger in the wild. We'll talk about what we all can do to help protect tigers and other endangered species later in the chapter.

# GIANT PANDAS

In the wild, giant pandas live in lush bamboo forests in central China, high up in the mountains. Like tigers, giant pandas are threatened by both habitat loss and poaching. They're the rarest bears on earth. There are fewer giant pandas than tigers in the wild, only about 1,800. All the giant pandas that are left couldn't even fill some high school basketball gyms. In addition to the wild giant pandas, another 300 live in zoos and other protected spaces around the world. Giant pandas have giant appetites for bamboo—they need somewhere between twenty-six and eighty-four pounds of it every day to survive! This means they can't live far from sources of bamboo (or people who bring them lots of bamboo like in zoos). That's why deforestation of bamboo forests is particularly perilous to giant pandas' survival.

LATE 1970s            2014

Information source: WWF

*The giant panda population increased by*
*more than 50 percent in about forty years.*

The most famous giant pandas in the U.S. are probably Mei Xiang and Tian Tian at the National Zoo in Washington, D.C. They're maybe most famous for being the parents of Bao Bao, their female cub born in 2013. They're also the second pair of giant pandas to live there. The first were Ling-Ling and Hsing-Hsing, given to the United States by China as gifts in 1972. When I would visit the zoo as a kid with my class or with my grandmother Dorothy—who loved the zoo as much as I did—I remember seeing Hsing-Hsing, though I

*Bao Bao celebrates her first birthday at the National Zoo.*

never got see Ling-Ling, who passed away before I moved to Washington, and I haven't yet visited Bao Bao.

All giant pandas everywhere, even outside China, belong to China. I don't know of any other species for whom that's true— where every single animal belongs to a single country (though there may be—please let me know if you know of another!). Mei Xiang and Tian Tian are two of twelve giant pandas currently living in the U.S., including four in Atlanta, three in San Diego and two in Memphis. Bao Bao is the youngest giant panda in the U.S. Visiting specific animal exhibits in zoos is an important way to show interest in a species' survival, support the vital work so many zoos do to protect certain species, and learn about the animals themselves. If visiting a zoo isn't an option for you, check out the free Giant Panda Cam on the National Zoo's website, nationalzoo.si.edu.

Although they are still endangered, giant panda conservation has seen real progress. There are more giant pandas today than there were a decade ago and significantly more than there were four decades ago. The Chinese government has made giant panda protection a priority, including by creating more giant panda reserves. The World Wildlife Fund (whose symbol is a giant panda) has partnered with the Chinese government to help the species recover. Still, more than one out of every three wild giant pandas live outside the reserves and so more work needs to be done to determine how best to protect those giant pandas. And the best approach may evolve, because while giant pandas haven't moved, people and industry are moving closer and closer to their bamboo forest homes as China's population continues to grow. We can't take for granted that the gains for giant pandas mean the threat has passed.

## POLAR BEARS

The main threat to Arctic polar bears is global warming. Arctic waters and ice are the polar bears' natural habitat. Polar bears have evolved to live in very cold temperatures, insulated by two coats of fur and a thick layer of fat to keep them warm even when they're hunting in freezing cold water or walking on very cold ice. There are somewhere between 20,000 and 25,000 polar bears living in the Arctic, spread across Canada, Greenland, Russia, Norway and the United States (in Alaska). All the earth's polar bears could fill maybe a quarter of the seats in a major college's football stadium. Unlike many bear species you may have read about, polar bears do not hibernate. Incidentally, giant pandas don't hibernate either.

Global warming affects polar bears in a few ways. As we discussed in Weather Report, the ice on which they hunt and roam is melting. This makes it harder for pregnant polar bear moms-to-be to find good spots to burrow and create ice dens where they can give birth and keep their newborns safe. Rising temperatures also make it harder for polar bears to hunt seals, their favorite food, because the seals too are desperately seeking out colder water, a search that often takes seals farther and farther away from polar bears. A number of subspecies of seals across the world are facing serious threats due to global warming and overhunting (by people, not polar bears). That means an important food source for polar bears is becoming scarcer.

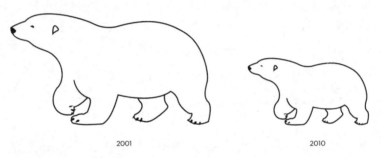

2001                                    2010

*The polar bear population in northeast Alaska and the Northwest Territories decreased by 40 percent in nine years.*

Unlike giant pandas, polar bears are common in American zoos. I remember wishing I could swim with the polar bears on hot summer days at the Little Rock Zoo as they splashed and played in the water. Unfortunately, also unlike giant pandas, polar bears have not seen a rebound in the last decade. As ice continues to melt, polar bears continue to die. The Beaufort Sea polar bear, the subspecies that lives in northeast Alaska and Canada, has gone from 1,500 to 900 bears in less than ten years.

The U.S. Geological Survey predicts that if nothing happens to reverse the melting of Arctic ice, two out of three polar bears will disappear by 2050. That means in our lifetimes, we will lose a majority of the world's polar bears. The main reason?

The same agency predicts that by 2050, sea ice in the Arctic will be totally gone.

In recent years, Arctic sea ice has been at the lowest levels ever recorded. And the structure of the ice has changed. It doesn't look like the solid cap of white we see on globes or in an atlas anymore. The remaining ice often floats

*All the polar bears in the world would only fill one-quarter of a college football stadium.*

Courtesy of Julie Larsen Maher @ WCS

in smaller and smaller chunks that are farther and farther away from each other. Imagine a game of hopscotch in which the squares were almost impossible to reach. That's the current reality for polar bears, forcing them to swim long and tiring distances. More and more polar bears are dying from drowning and lack of food, since they can't reach ice floes in time or find seals to eat. And they're having fewer babies, because when they lose weight from eating less, they also lose the ability to have children. Polar bear moms need to gain a lot of weight before they have cubs, and if they can't do one, they can't do the other. If we don't stop global warming, polar bears will slowly, surely die out in the wild.

## RHINOS

At the beginning of the 20th century, an estimated 500,000 wild rhinos lived in Africa and Asia. Over a little more than 100 years, we've lost almost 95 percent of them. Only about 29,000

Information source: Save the Rhino International

1960        1995        2010

*The African black rhino was nearly annihilated in just thirty-five years. Intensive anti-poaching and conservation efforts have started to work, and black rhinos today are coming back from the brink.*

wild rhinos are believed to be alive today, and some subspecies of rhinos are gone altogether. In 2011, both the Javan rhino in Vietnam and the western black rhino in Africa were declared extinct. In Africa, the northern white rhino is completely extinct in the wild, living only in captivity. All rhinos could be extinct in our lifetimes—unless we do something about poaching.

Rhinos are disappearing mainly because poaching has skyrocketed. In 2007, thirteen rhinos were poached in South Africa. In 2013, 1,004 rhinos were poached in South Africa. That's more than a 7,000 percent increase in less than ten years. Why? Rhino horn. In early 2015, a pound of rhino horn is worth more than a pound of gold. On the black market (the illegal market), a kilogram (or

Courtesy of Julie Larsen Maher @ WCS

*As far as I'm concerned, the perfect place for a rhino's horn is on a rhino's head.*

2.2 pounds) of rhino horn is estimated to fetch about $65,000, sometimes even $100,000 depending on the type of rhino horn. That's more than four years of in-state college tuition costs at a state university in the U.S.

Vietnam is the main market for rhino horn due to a mistaken belief that it can help cure cancer. Zero scientific evidence exists to support that claim. It's not a claim rooted in traditional medicine but a new one, which helps explain why rhino poaching has recently soared. Unfortunately, the lack of scientific proof hasn't stopped people from buying rhino horns and trying it for themselves. It's this misplaced hope for a magical cure that explains why rhino horns are more expensive than gold . . . or platinum. And, as Vietnam's economy has grown and more people have had more money to spend, sadly some of that money has gone to buy rhino horns.

If rhino poaching continues to rise (because poachers know killing a rhino means getting a lot of money) scientists estimate all African rhinos could be extinct in less than twenty years. Although poaching is the main urgent threat facing rhinos, it's not the only one. They're also losing their habitats. In Indonesia, for example, illegal coffee and rice farmers are taking over land that rhinos have long called home, killing rhinos in the process or forcing them onto land where they can't thrive and, ultimately, where they can't survive.

Thankfully, when rhinos have been threatened before by poaching and habitat loss, with careful conservation efforts, their numbers have recovered. One African subspecies, the southern white rhino, was thought to be extinct in the 19th century, but turned out not to be. In 1895, a small population was discovered and, through careful conservation efforts, thousands of southern white rhinos are living in Africa today, most of them in South Africa in protected rhino sanctuaries and parks. We know rhinos can recover—but we have to stop the poachers first.

# PANGOLINS

I confess I had never heard of pangolins until my mom and I got involved in work to save Africa's elephants, and through that work became more aware of a number of animal conservation efforts, including around the pangolin. If you saw one, you would probably never imagine they're mammals like us! Sometimes called scaly anteaters, pangolins live across Africa and Asia, eat mainly ants and termites and are covered in thick scales (their nickname is "the living pinecone"). Perversely, the scales that protect them are also one of the reasons poachers covet them.

The pangolin is one of the most endangered mammals on earth. Partly because they're nocturnal (meaning they're awake at night when most animals, including people, are generally sleeping) there aren't reliable estimates of pangolin populations. But the precarious status of pangolins couldn't be clearer. They are being killed at an alarming rate. In China alone, it's

2000                    2013

*The pangolin population in China decreased by 90 percent in thirteen years.*

Information source: Conservation International

estimated less than 2,500 pangolins live in the wild today. In 2000,
more than 20,000 did. In recent
years, thousands of pangolins have
been smuggled out of Indonesia and
Thailand, while Chinese officials
have seized thousands of pangolins
traffickers are attempting to illegally bring in from those countries
as well as from Africa.

*From this photograph it's
easy to see why pangolins are
called "living pinecones."*

Unlike rhinos, pangolins are
hunted for food, as their meat is considered a delicacy, particularly in China. Poachers also hunt pangolins so their scales can
be used in fashion accessories or so they can be stuffed and displayed as trophies. And they're yet another animal whose parts
are mistakenly believed to have medicinal value. Once again,
there is no scientific evidence that any part of the pangolin cures
anything, despite what some people believe about their scales or
blood. The pangolin has the not-so-great distinction of being the
most illegally trafficked animal on earth, meaning more pangolins than any other animal are taken out of their home countries
and across borders to be sold illegally for food, fashion and mis-
guided medicine. Because of that, pangolins are under threat
almost everywhere they've called home for a long time.

## ELEPHANTS

Elephants are the largest land mammals on earth, but their size
has not protected them from poachers who kill them for their
ivory tusks. African elephants are larger than Asian elephants,

Information source: 96 Elephants

1980                                                 2012

*The African elephant population decreased by about
two-thirds in thirty-two years.*

with differently shaped ears. Both male and female African elephants have tusks (while only male Asian elephants do). Their larger size and corresponding larger tusks have made African elephants particularly attractive to poachers. They are probably what you see in your mind when you think about elephants.

Elephants generally live in family groups led by a matriarch such as a grandmother or mother, with older male elephants living by themselves. All elephants roam over large distances (unlike rhinos), in part to be able to find the hundreds of pounds of leaves and plants the adults need to eat daily to survive. This roaming often takes elephants outside the national parks and reserves where they are more likely to be watched and protected from poachers. Matriarchs and older male elephants (called bulls) tend to be most prized—and most frequently killed—by poachers because they have the largest tusks.

When elephant mothers and grandmothers are killed, families lose more than their loved ones. They also lose all of the knowledge that matriarch gathered over decades about where to find food, shelter and water in every season throughout the year.

That means that their surviving children and grandchildren are more likely to
starve or go thirsty, particularly during droughts,
which are becoming more
common because of climate
change. There is even evidence that elephants grieve
and mourn for lost loved ones
just like humans do. Such
depth of emotion has not
remotely deterred poachers.

*Elephants are one of my favorite
animals—and I want to make sure
they're around for my daughter,
Charlotte, and future generations.*

The pile of elephant car-
casses—dead elephant mothers, fathers and children—
that poachers are responsible
for keeps climbing. In 1980, the year I was born, more than a
million African elephants were estimated to roam Africa's
savannas and forests. By 2012, that number had been slashed by
almost two-thirds, and it keeps going down as more elephants
are slaughtered. The current rate of poaching threatens the very
survival of the African elephant as well as the survival of the
plants and animals dependent on them. Elephants play a particularly important role in keeping the forests and savannahs they
live in healthy and strong. As they roam, elephants disperse
seeds vital for plants to continue to grow, and they dig water
holes that many other animals need to survive. As elephants are
dying, so too are the ecosystems around them.

Although not as valuable as rhino horn, in 2014, the price for a pound of ivory was more than $4,000, three times what it was only a few years before. Unlike rhino horn on the black market, ivory is sold legally in most places. But elephant poaching in particular is tied to the worst types of illegal activity around the world. More and more, elephant poachers are part of organized criminal networks and terrorist organizations. Arguably, elephants are easier to kill than rhinos because there are more of them and because they range over wider territory than rhinos do, which also means they're harder for rangers to protect, even inside a national park and certainly outside it. Often, poachers brutally hack off elephants' faces to get to their tusks to make the ivory easier to transport. That cruelty toward elephants helps fund the worst cruelties toward humans.

Research has linked ivory sales to terrorist groups like the Lord's Resistance Army in east Africa. That's why ivory is sometimes referred to as "the white gold of jihad," since its sale helps fund groups that threaten people across Africa and are linked to terrorists around the world. The campaign 96 Elephants (found at 96elephants.org) raises awareness about these linkages; it's named for the ninety-six African elephants poachers killed on average every day in 2014. There are a few gruesome and painful images on the site, so you may want to talk to your parents and look at it together. Understanding the link between poaching and terror helps explain why elected officials from both political parties in the U.S. have been working together to strengthen U.S. support for anti-poaching efforts. Stopping elephant poaching is vital to making sure elephants are around for generations to come. It's also an important part of stopping the terrorism that threatens communities in Africa and people everywhere. For all those reasons, in 2013, my mother and I starting working with conservation groups, countries with elephant populations, countries where there's a significant demand for ivory, law enforcement officials and others to better coordinate international efforts to stop the poaching of elephants, trafficking of ivory and demand for ivory across the world. We've made some progress, but have a lot more work to do.

# WHAT THE WORLD IS DOING (OR AT LEAST TRYING TO DO)

## *International Agreements*

CITES, or the Convention on International Trade in Endangered Species, is an agreement among different countries that determines if and when it's ever okay to ship an endangered animal or animal part from one country to another. Similar to the U.S. Endangered Species Act, CITES classifies endangered species by how close they are to extinction. It then determines how much of a threat trade—the selling of live animals or dead pieces of them—poses to a species and imposes various controls, even restrictions, intended to ensure any trade doesn't jeopardize a species' survival. Though almost every country in the world has signed CITES, illegal trade in wildlife products clearly remains a big—and sadly growing—business.

International trade of rhino horn and rhino-horn products has been banned under CITES since before I was born (since 1975). But that hasn't stopped illegal rhino-horn trafficking. In fact, more people are buying and selling rhino horns than ever before. So while CITES is very important, it alone is not enough to make sure animals are protected from extinction and supported in their recovery so that more species can have stories like the bald eagle's in the U.S.

## State Laws

What else can be done to complement CITES? Thankfully, a lot. For example, in the U.S., I favor a federal law and state laws in all fifty states banning the sale of ivory, with no exceptions. I am proud to live in a state—New York—that has banned the sale of ivory, although with some exceptions. While I wish there were no exceptions, it's a serious step forward. As of early 2015, New York is one of only two states to have taken this important step. The other is New Jersey. While two states is a start, I hope we can strengthen laws to ban the sale of all ivory and other endangered-species products—we'll talk more about this later.

## Keeping an Eye on Animals

There are also new ways to keep track of vulnerable and endangered animal populations in Africa and Asia, including new technologies like drones, the unmanned aircraft that can fly into areas considered too dangerous for humans to go—and that simply can cover more space more quickly than humans alone ever could. Drones also are less likely to attract attention from poachers or to bother animals than larger airplanes or helicopters likely would. They're now being employed to help track animals and discourage poachers—as well as to help arrest poachers who don't realize they're being watched. Although some people don't think drones should be used for any purpose, animal experts expect drones may be particularly useful in watching animals like rhinos that don't roam over large areas (unlike elephants, which do) and in areas with lots of wildlife that are particularly attractive to poachers. Early studies in Kenya found that drones helped significantly reduce poaching in certain areas.

## Protecting Rangers and Communities from Poachers

In addition to remote technologies, rangers increasingly are receiving the training and tools they need to fight against poaching and to protect themselves from poachers. But more needs to be done to support rangers on the front lines of the poaching crisis, to help save the lives of the animals they protect and, crucially, to help rangers protect themselves. Poachers use military-grade helicopters, rifles and night-vision or high-powered binoculars, as well as GPS systems to track their target animals. Everything you would see in an action movie, poachers probably have and are using. Thankfully, more and more, rangers are getting everything they need to help stop and catch poachers.

Rangers and conservation groups are also working with the communities located in and around national parks, forests and other preserves to protect animals and alert rangers to any looming danger. For example, in Namibia, the World Wildlife Fund partnered with the Namibian government and a local cell phone company to set up a free and confidential SMS hotline so that anyone could send a text message to safely alert the authorities of suspected poaching without giving their name (and possibly putting themselves in danger from poachers). Partly because of these efforts, rhino poaching in Namibia has dropped dramatically.

In Tanzania, the Wildlife Conservation Society hires people from the community around Tarangire National Park to help keep track of local elephant populations, providing cell phones so that people can easily and quickly report any suspected poaching activities. Along with partners, they also pay local villagers to protect their land for elephants to roam outside the park so that they don't have to turn to poachers for money and so it's clear that a shared future with elephants is good for them too. So far, the community has invested that money in building a primary school, where local kids learn about lots of things, including their wildlife neighbors.

In 2013, I visited Tarangire and was deeply impressed by the community's and the rangers' dedication to protecting their wildlife and themselves from poachers. I saw elephants first-hand that probably wouldn't be alive without the joint efforts of Tanzanian rangers, the local community and the Wildlife

Courtesy of Barbara Kinney/Clinton Foundation

*I loved watching the elephants at Tarangire Park in Tanzania, and I was honored to meet the courageous rangers working there to protect elephants and other wildlife.*

Courtesy of Barbara Kinney/Clinton Foundation

Conservation Society. I saw huge bull elephants and families with new babies. I met local villagers who now make a living off helping watch elephants that range outside the park—and watch for poachers who want to kill them. They were making enough money to take care of their families and send their kids to school. I met rangers who know they're more likely to make it home safely at night because they now have the tools they need to better guard the animals and themselves. I will always be grateful to the people I met and remember the elephants I saw, particularly the big matriarchs ensuring their families had enough to eat and were following safely along—I hope that I can always do as well for my daughter, Charlotte!

## Sharing the Land . . .

Sometimes it's hard for people who live in countries with large wildlife populations to support the protection and preservation of species in their area, especially if they're earning a living off the trade of endangered species and wildlife parts or illegal farming (which is a big threat to some rhinos and other species). But once people start to see that they and their families benefit from conservation efforts (like the one in Tarangire) as well as from the tourism the animals bring, hopefully they'll decide to join the fight against poachers. If working parents can make money through tourism and animal conservation to send their kids to school and support their families, the hope is that they'll be less likely to work with poachers or illegally farm the land that the animals need to live.

It's also important to help people who are farming legally and responsibly to continue doing so in a way that is good for them and for the animals they live alongside, particularly animals like elephants that cover lots of ground. Throughout Asia, the World Wildlife Fund has been working with communities so that their crops stay safe from elephants, which is good for the farmers and also good for the elephants (so people don't feel like they have to kill the elephants to protect their land). These efforts include building electric fences, teaching people how to safely drive elephants out of crop fields and even training elephants so they won't intrude on villages or their crops. The Wildlife Conservation Society and partners are working to help communities near vulnerable elephant and rhino populations improve their farming techniques so that they can grow more food and make more money off their land (making them less likely to work with poachers because they won't need the money). To learn more about this work, please visit wwf.org and wcs.org.

## Penalties

It's also important that there are strong laws and enforcement of those laws against poachers and traffickers. Once poachers or traffickers who help transport illegal wildlife and wildlife products are caught, it's crucial that they face meaningful punishment for their crimes, both as a way of standing up for what's right and to discourage future would-be poachers and traffickers. Many governments, particularly in Africa, have started passing stricter laws against poaching, with heavier penalties for convicted poachers and traffickers of illegal wildlife and wildlife products. In South Africa, a convicted rhino poacher recently received a seventy-seven-year sentence, but such strict penalties are still rare. Too often poachers aren't prosecuted or receive light sentences. China takes giant panda poaching very seriously and the strict penalties it sentences convicted poachers to—over ten years in prison is the norm—are believed to have played an important role in the decline of giant panda poaching (because no one wants to spend ten years, or longer, in prison).

## Educated Shoppers

People who buy (or who are even thinking about buying) wildlife products from endangered species need to be educated about how harmful the trinkets, potions and other things they buy really are. They need to know that pangolin scales come only from dead pangolins, that ivory comes only from dead elephants and that giant panda furs come only from dead giant pandas. A few years ago, a survey showed that the vast majority of Chinese did not know that elephants had to die for their ivory tusks to be taken. Many mistakenly thought ivory regenerated, or regrew, if someone cut it off. New Chinese ad campaigns and short movies featuring celebrities have been created to educate people that ivory only has one source—dead elephants—and that not buying ivory today will help keep an elephant alive tomorrow. They're starting to make a difference as people in China become more aware of the problem and the solution (stop buying ivory so poachers have no incentive to kill elephants). Additionally, a group of prominent Chinese business leaders recently agreed they wouldn't buy ivory or give it as a gift; hopefully others will follow their lead. Similar efforts in Japan in the 1980s helped change what people bought—and what they didn't buy. Those efforts prompted demand for ivory to go down in Japan, which helped limit poaching until the most recent epidemic started. Hopefully the new efforts (in China and elsewhere) will make a difference for Africa's elephants. Because of what happened in Japan, we know that they can.

In countries like China where pangolin is still considered both a source of medicine and a delicacy, it is important to spread the word that medicines made from pangolins don't cure diseases, and to make it not okay, not cool and not acceptable to eat pangolin meat or wear pangolin scales. These awareness campaigns, alongside improved pangolin conservation efforts in the wild and in captivity, can make a real difference—as we saw in the combined effort to save the bald eagle in the U.S. Those are only two such examples. We need public education efforts around rhino horn not curing cancer and tiger parts not curing any disease and so much more to help preserve our endangered species across the world. Some of that public education has to happen in the U.S. too.

Yes, China is the largest ivory market in the world and in many Asian countries animal parts are sold for mistaken medicinal purposes, but we need to do more in the United States as well. In particular, there are many things made from ivory and rhino horn that are marketed as antiques (often making them legal to sell)—whether statues or jewelry, chopsticks or musical instrument parts. Currently, technology does not exist to determine whether any individual ivory was taken from an animal last week or a hundred years ago (because we can't tell from ivory when an elephant was killed); much of what is billed as antique ivory probably isn't. The same is true for rhino horn. That's why I favor a full ban on the selling of ivory and rhino horn, with no exceptions, because otherwise traffickers can continue to pass off ivory from recently slaughtered elephants as antique and do the same with rhino horn.

Lots of people disagree, some because they want to be able to replace ivory in old instruments, guns or other things. What do you think? You'll have to decide whether or not you believe as I do—that a full ivory and rhino horn ban in the U.S. would help protect elephants and rhinos from being killed in Africa and Asia and remove the ability of terrorists and criminals to use poaching to fund their evil activities.

You can do a lot to help save endangered species. Help educate your family and friends about the threat of extinction facing tigers, giant pandas and other animals. Share that there is no evidence supporting medicinal claims about anything made from any part of any dead endangered animal. Help everyone around you understand that wildlife parts almost always come from dead animals. While rhino horns can regenerate, most poachers kill rhinos too. They do not carefully remove their horns. For most endangered species, there is no way to "harvest" or "pluck" their parts and they do not grow back.

Urge your family and friends who are at least thirteen to take to social media to share the (horrifying) facts around endangered wildlife products. Share why you think it's important to stop the demand for ivory and stop the destruction of elephants or any other animals you feel a connection with. This is an area where we need a lot more awareness, among everyone, of every age, around the world. For people to stop purchasing products made from dead endangered animals, we have to show them that what they may think about animal products is wrong.

Tell family and friends that no matter how "cool" a polar

bear rug might look in their den or how "attractive" an ivory bracelet might be on Grandma's wrist, the polar bear skin will look far more beautiful on an actual polar bear and the ivory far more spectacular on an elephant. Urging your family and friends to buy other fun, fascinating and beautiful things instead of buying anything made with ivory, as just one example, is an important part of stopping poaching. If fewer people want to buy things made from endangered animals' skins, tusks, horns, eyes, bones and other parts, poachers are less likely to kill animals to get those parts.

Two people helping stop demand for ivory are Nellie and Celia, both from Hong Kong. In 2013, when she was eleven years old, Nellie successfully persuaded her school to stop using ivory for educational purposes. She was also one of five kids who gathered 60,000 signatures on a petition asking Hong Kong to destroy its ivory stockpile as a strong signal against illegally trafficking ivory, something it ultimately decided to do. Through all her efforts, Nellie helped bring more awareness to the threat that elephant poaching—and ivory demand—are to elephants' survival. It's likely more people paid attention to Nellie's efforts because she was young and passionate.

Don't underestimate the power of your youth. Celia was fourteen in 2012 when she started a campaign to cut ivory demand, to urge governments to take firm action against poaching and to get former NBA

Courtesy of Katrina Shute

*Nellie helping remove ivory from her school.*

star Yao Ming involved in helping save elephants. Her tireless efforts attracted lots of media attention and support, and like Nellie, her age probably attracted more attention than if she'd been in her twenties or thirties. People wanted to support Celia and Nellie because they were young

*Celia was fourteen when she started a campaign to get Yao Ming involved in saving the elephants.*

Courtesy of Josefina Bergsten

and optimistic. One person who decided to support Celia was Yao Ming! Celia's campaign succeeded more than she could have ever imagined. Today, Yao Ming is one of the most recognizable faces of the anti-poaching and anti-ivory efforts in China.

Just like Celia and Nellie, you can speak out about the illegal wildlife trade and attend events against the illegal wildlife trade like ivory crushes and burns. At this point, you may be asking yourself, "Wait, why are we crushing and burning all this ivory?" It may seem puzzling to destroy ivory that has been confiscated illegally entering a country like the United States or China or illegally leaving a country like Tanzania or Kenya. You may be thinking, "Why wouldn't we just sell it?" Ivory crushes and burns send a very clear message that countries will not tolerate and refuse to benefit from the slaughter of elephants. It's like when illegal drugs are seized. We wouldn't say, "Let's just use them since we have them now;" we destroy the drugs. In November 2013, the United States crushed six tons of ivory it had taken from criminals who were trying to bring it to sell in the U.S. illegally. Starting in 2014, partly because of efforts like Nellie's and Celia's, Hong Kong began destroying the twenty-eight tons of ivory it had taken from criminal traffickers. You can encourage the U.S. and other countries to keep crushing ivory and destroying other ill-gotten endangered-wildlife products.

You can also support wildlife conservation efforts across the world by becoming a member of a favorite conservation group, like I did with Conservation International and others when I was a kid, or a member of your local zoo, as Marc and I now are with the Central Park Zoo (part of the Wildlife Conservation Society). Another way to show support is to sponsor animals you particularly want to help save or to give a sponsored animal as a gift. When my daughter was born, good friends gave us elephants and pygmy elephants through the Wildlife Conservation Society and the World Wildlife Fund and polar bears through Defenders of Wildlife. These were some of the most meaningful gifts we received—our daughter Charlotte's life was being honored by helping save another life somewhere in the world.

Through these organizations and others you can sponsor any of the animals in this chapter as well as many more, including various foxes, penguins, leopards, flamingos, giraffes, whales and snakes. It's okay to feel drawn more to some animals than others. As is probably clear, I

*Here is a picture I took of some of the animals friends gave Charlotte or sponsored in her honor (don't worry, I took the tags off after I took the picture).*

Courtesy of the Author

love, love, love elephants. I think they're magnificent creatures. Warm, family-oriented, resilient—so many of the qualities I most admire, elephants beautifully manifest.

The money raised through animal sponsorship or through direct donations to conservation groups helps save animals in many ways, by providing funds to communities to protect instead of poach animals; by advancing research into animals so we know how best to protect them; and by supporting park rangers and others on the front lines of protecting wildlife. Another way to help raise awareness and money is to celebrate the various animal days throughout the year.

## NATIONAL AND INTERNATIONAL ANIMAL AND ENVIRONMENT DAYS

| | |
|---|---|
| WORLD PANGOLIN DAY: | 3rd Saturday of February |
| INTERNATIONAL POLAR BEAR DAY: | February 27th |
| WORLD WILDLIFE DAY: | March 3rd |
| WORLD FROG DAY: | March 21st |
| EARTH DAY: | April 22nd |
| WORLD PENGUIN DAY: | April 25th |
| SAVE THE RHINOS DAY: | May 1st |
| WORLD TURTLE DAY: | May 23rd |
| WORLD OCEAN DAY: | June 8th |
| SHARK AWARENESS DAY: | July 14th |
| INTERNATIONAL TIGER DAY: | July 29th |
| WORLD ELEPHANT DAY: | August 12th |
| NATIONAL WILDLIFE DAY: | September 4th |
| INTERNATIONAL RED PANDA DAY: | 3rd Saturday of September |
| VISIT THE ZOO DAY: | December 27th |

Information source: WCS and Polar Bears International

Admittedly, my favorite might be International Polar Bear Day, because it falls on my birthday—February 27th.

You can probably see some of the animals in this list by visiting your local zoo or aquarium and you don't have to become a member or sponsor an animal to do so. Most zoos have free days. Zoos in colder places will be more likely to have animals from colder environments, but sometimes zoos in warmer places have them too. They're able to use ice packs, cool water pools and shade or indoor space to help animals like polar bears stay cool in the summer. This enables zoos to expose new audiences to animals from around the world. Zoos also help protect animals in their natural habitats and frequently conduct important research that helps determine which conservation efforts are most effective for various species in the wild and in captivity. Research by zoos and conservation groups is particularly important for animals like pangolins, about which we know very little, partly because they've historically had a hard time living in zoos—most have died shortly after being taken away from their wild habitats. It's also especially important for animals like polar bears that, tragically, are quickly losing their natural habitats and zoos may be one of the only ways to guarantee their survival.

Visiting U.S. national parks shows your support for the wildlife and endangered animals that live in our own country, like certain grizzly bears. The majority of America's 427 national parks generally do not charge an entrance fee, and for those that do, there are always certain free days throughout the year including Martin Luther King, Jr. Day and Presidents' Day weekend. For more information about fee-free days, please visit nps.gov. Additionally, you can join the Junior Rangers program available at over 200 national parks to help support the parks' preservation efforts and you can learn more at nationalparks.org.

Finally, if you want to do even more, particularly if you want to save the polar bear and other animals threatened seriously by global warming, help stop climate change. A big way to do that is to help people understand the many different ways climate change is hurting our planet and our future, like the shrinking of the polar bears' Arctic ice, as seen in the picture at the start of this section. As discussed in Weather Report, many small steps can together make a big difference. Encourage your families to walk or use public transportation when you can. Turn off the lights when you leave home. Encourage your schools and wherever else you might spend your time to recycle and go green. While it's your world, it's also our world. We have one earth, and our future is bound to the fate of the animals and plants with which we share it!

# Get Going!

- Never buy ivory, rhino horn, polar bear skins, pangolin scales or any other part from an endangered species
- Let people know that ivory comes only from dead elephants and tiger parts come only from dead tigers
- Tell people that having dead animals as rugs or trophies is not cool
- Tell people that there's no medical evidence any powders, potions or pills made from endangered animal parts help treat cancer, headaches or any other ailment
- Share the facts about endangered species with family and at least three friends, in person and online (if you're over thirteen)

- Support events like ivory crushes and burns
- Become a member of your favorite conservation group
- Sponsor an animal
- Celebrate each animal on its special day
- Visit zoos
- Visit national parks
- Buy baked goods made with sustainable rain forest–safe palm oil like Rhiannon and Madison from Project ORANGS
- Help prevent deforestation around the world—you can learn how from the Rainforest Alliance
- Help fight global warming by lowering the amount of $CO_2$ your family releases in daily life
- If you're thirteen or older, use social media to follow organizations (like the Wildlife Conservation Society) that protect endangered animals broadly, or follow organizations (like Save the Elephants) or celebrities (like Leonardo DiCaprio with Save Tigers Now) working to protect specific species

# IT'S YOUR WORLD

I've long believed there's a big difference between tolerance and respect. We tolerate things that aren't comfortable (like lots of mosquitoes when we want to go outside on a hot summer's night—wearing bug spray) or aren't convenient (like when there's roadwork or subway maintenance and it takes three times as long to get to school or work). Other people, other cultures, other countries shouldn't simply be tolerated, they should be respected, provided they are respectful of all people (including girls) and our shared planet. We should be able to disagree with one another without dehumanizing one another. U.S. Senator Daniel Patrick Moynihan once said, "Everyone is entitled to his own opinion, but not his own facts." So even if we disagree with one another, it's important to recognize what the facts are (like around climate change or the barriers to going to school around the world). It's also important we know what various opinions and beliefs are (like around how best to combat climate change or ensure kids get a good education), so we can make up our own minds about what we think the right answer is, whatever the question or challenge. We can—and should—respectfully disagree with others who have reached different answers from ours, even if we want (and try) to convince them of our point of view.

This is so important because we're all equally valuable and we're all connected to one another, ideas as old as time but aspirations we're far from reaching anywhere in practice, including in the United States. Did you notice any similarities across the stories you read of change-makers? Between the grandmothers with their solar panels in India and William with his backpack food program in North Carolina? Between Haile's healthy cooking and Katherine's bed net work? They all work in partnership—with family, friends and organizations close by or with NGOs and businesses across the world—to help people, communities and our world be healthier. Although I've not used many quotes or aphorisms (a fancy word for sayings) in this book, I can't help but include one of my favorites here: "If you want to go fast, go alone. If you want to go far, go together." It's from an African proverb and is a truth I have seen and experienced throughout my life. We get more done when we work together. And working together helps us support each other so we don't get discouraged by the size of a challenge or when what we try first doesn't work (and so that we try again).

We'll also get more done if we have a sense of where we want to go. What makes you angry? What do you think isn't right or fair or just? What most inspires you? What do you want to see more of in the world? The answers to those questions for you may be different than my answers, your parents' answers or your friends' answers. That's more than okay. Whatever your answers are, that's what I hope you'll tackle in your community or in our world. It might be something we've talked about in this book or it might not be and that's okay too. Everything I write about in this book I think is important—otherwise I wouldn't have included it (or written the book)—but as I said at the beginning, it definitely doesn't come close to covering all of the challenges we face in our world or all the solutions that we need even to the challenges I write about.

We have a saying in my family (yes, already, another saying):

"It's better to get caught trying." It means that if we think we can make a difference in an area we care about, we have to at least try, even if—and maybe especially if—it's not clear that we'll succeed. I'm trying to get caught trying with this book— ultimately trying to empower you with information and inspiring stories. I hope you'll all get caught trying too—and share your change-making stories on ItsYourWorld.com.

When I was in fifth or sixth grade, I started cutting up the plastic rings often used in six-packs of soda, gluing them to brightly colored construction paper (purple was my favorite) and handing them out to my parents, grandparents and grandparents' neighbors in a one-girl campaign to raise awareness about the dangers that plastic six-pack rings posed to marine wildlife around the world. I learned about that from a book— *50 Simple Things Kids Can Do to Save the Earth*. Around the same time, I learned that climate change and global warming likely posed a far greater risk to marine wildlife than uncut plastic rings did. But that didn't mean I stopped cutting up plastic rings. Not at all. I realized if I wanted to do everything I could to save our wildlife and our planet, I had to do smaller everyday things (like cutting up plastic rings) and also work for big changes (like advocating for cleaner and more efficient forms of energy). I still think that's true.

When I was reading about India before my trip with my mom in 1995, I found this quote (and the last one I'll use) from Gandhi: "The future depends on what we do in the present." I believed that when I was a teenager and I believe it even more strongly now— if only because I have twenty years of the past between then and today. The future is beginning and if we want a more equal, more healthy and more sustainable world, we all have to Get Going!

# A NOTE FROM CHELSEA

I loved working on and writing *It's Your World*. That didn't surprise me. I had thought about writing a book like *It's Your World* long before I sat down to work on it. What did surprise me was how much I loved the book tour that followed publication. I'd hoped people would come to the bookstore events, and I'd really hoped the students in the schools I visited would be engaged in the whys and wherefores of the book. What I hadn't known to hope for was how lucky I would be to hear from readers (and soon-to-be readers), parents, teachers and others about the work they were already engaged in to make a positive difference in their communities, across our country and around the world. I heard about the Walks for Water students were doing in Naperville, Illinois, and listened to students in Philadelphia present their plans to help themselves and their classmates improve their nutrition and fitness, in and out of school.

*The students at Jefferson Junior High School impressed me with their activism and passion, clearly evident in the signs they welcomed me with and the stories they shared of all the work they're doing in their community to support work around the world.*

*With Matti—in her Walk for Water T-shirt!—in Kansas City.*

Courtesy of Bari Lurie

Students and readers also shared what they hoped to do in the future—sometimes they meant tomorrow or next week and sometimes they meant later in life, in their careers. Sometimes they would tell me their dreams directly, sometimes through reaching out after an event, and sometimes through stickers. Yes, stickers. Everywhere we went, we handed out stickers that started with "I will," and then had a few lines left blank for whatever someone wanted to commit or aspire to do. We put up a board so the stickers could be shared with the community, making it clear it was more than okay to keep the stickers, and whatever might be written on them, private. I am grateful to all who filled them out and am thankful for those who chose to share them with me, their parents, their teachers and anyone who may have wandered by a school auditorium or a bookstore.

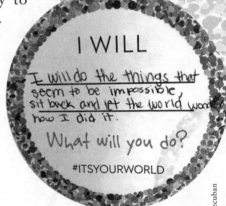

I WILL

I will do the things that seem to be impossible, sit back and let the world wonder how I did it.

What will you do?

#ITSYOURWORLD

*Wake Young Women's Leadership Academy November 12, 2015, Raleigh, NC*

Courtesy of Joy Secuban

Courtesy of Joy Secuban

*Everywhere we went, we brought a board with
stickers saying "I will . . ." that anyone could fill out
with what they wanted. Most were service related,
though some were not. At the Ann Richards School for
Young Women Leaders in Austin, there were so many
stickers, our board had to be mounted on another board
so everyone had somewhere to put their sticker—
and share their dreams.*

At the first stop on the book tour, at Mitchell Elementary
School in Chicago, where, not coincidentally, my friend Nikki
Huvelle Milberg is the principal, a student wrote: "I will work
with families affected by war." At Wake Young Women's Leadership Academy, in Raleigh, a student filled in the sentence: "I
will do the things that seem to be impossible, sit back and let the
world wonder how I did it."

I WILL
encourage
young women
What will you do?
#ITSYOURWORLD
To be
bossy

University Bookstore
November 7, 2015, Seattle, WA

I WILL
Find. Bigfoot.

What will you do?

#ITSYOURWORLD

Books & Books
October 22, 2015, Miami, FL

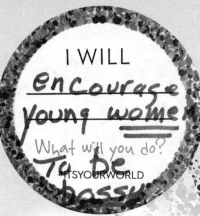

I WILL
Become a
neurologist
What will you do?

#ITSYOURWORLD

Bruce Randolph School
November 4, 2015, Denver, CO

I WILL
Talk to kids
Who don't have
Friends
What will you do?

#ITSYOURWORLD
VS

Lincoln College Preparatory Academy
November 10, 2015, Kansas City, MO

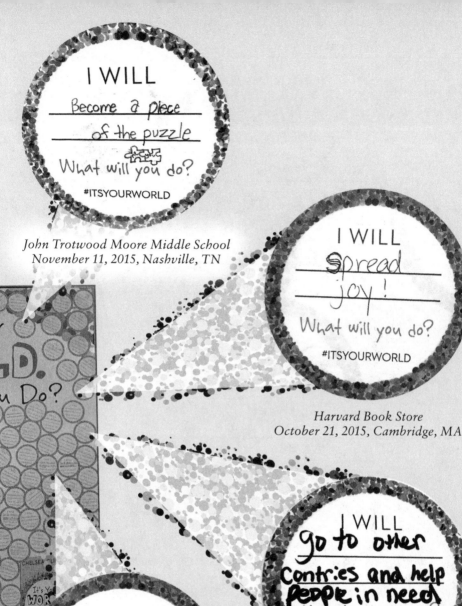

**I WILL**

Become a piece
of the puzzle

What will you do?

#ITSYOURWORLD

*John Trotwood Moore Middle School*
*November 11, 2015, Nashville, TN*

**I WILL**

~~spread~~
~~joy!~~

What will you do?

#ITSYOURWORLD

*Harvard Book Store*
*October 21, 2015, Cambridge, MA*

**I WILL**
go to other
contries and help
people in need
What will you do?
from a 6th grader
#ITSYOURWORLD

*Powell's Books*
*November 5, 2015, Portland, OR*

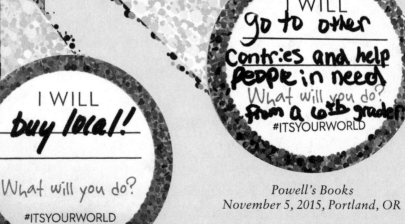

**I WILL**
*buy local!*

What will you do?

#ITSYOURWORLD

*Powell's Books*
*November 5, 2015, Portland, OR*

*I started my school visits at Mitchell Elementary in Chicago—where my friend from high school Nikki is the principal! Great to see her at work and meet some of her amazing students, including Vanessa and Xonhane.*

*In Houston, I volunteered at Houston Food Bank, our country's largest, alongside Krystal and Anthony, two members of the food bank's Student Heroes program. They led our efforts to pack meals for the Backpack Buddy program that feeds children in over 500 area schools.*

In Kansas City, at Lincoln College Preparatory Academy, as was true in so many of the schools I visited, I was asked about bullying and saw a sticker afterward that declared: "I will talk to kids who don't have friends." At Curley K-8 School in Boston, a majority of the stickers declared students' aspirations to fight, cure or solve cancer. A classmate's mom had recently passed away after losing her battle with cancer.

Courtesy of Bari Lurie

*In Boston, while at Curley K-8 School, I got to join a City Year–led service project. We made care packages and bookmarks, and talked about why the students care so much about service. As I think you can tell from the picture, in part the answer is because they love working together to make a difference.*

Courtesy of Joy Secuban

*In Raleigh, I visited the North Carolina Museum of Natural Sciences and spent time with the Girls in Science program. The day I was there, we all learned about turtles and the terrific work of a Girls in Science alum, Molly, with the Raleigh Aquatic Turtle Adoption program, which she started.*

I also heard from students and parents, friends and strangers about work they're doing or hope to do. People reached out through the *It's Your World* website, social media and directly to me, through Penguin. A friend told me his daughter now wants to be a teacher and hopes to work in countries where there are far too few teachers and girls are far too likely not to receive the same education as their brothers—or even any education at all. Through the *It's Your World* website, I learned of Marquis's terrific work in San Diego to support his school community, most recently through financial literacy programming. He thinks financial literacy is so important that he requires anyone who wants to join his NewComers Investment Club to complete a financial literacy class. I also learned about Kayla Cares 4 Kids, an organization started by thirteen-year-old Kayla to help other kids who, like her, have chronic conditions that often lead to spending some time, or even a lot of time, in the hospital. One of Kayla's goals is to donate at least one hundred items to every hospital in the U.S., to help every kid who is in a hospital on any given day still have the ability to play, create, use their imagination—and forget for a while where they are. I hope more young people will continue sharing their work with me so I can share their stories, and, hopefully, attract more attention, support and championship for their efforts to make a meaningful difference.

At El Dorado High School in El Paso, all the students mobilized to change their community—and specifically their nearby desert ecosystem. Led by dynamic students and their equally dynamic art teacher, Ms. Printz, the group committed to clean up the nearby Chihuahuan Desert. But that is only the beginning of their vision. They plan to sort all the trash they collect and wash what doesn't belong in a compost pile. They will then take those discarded—and now clean—cans, bottles,

bags, tires and more to make art. Some of that art may be large and best displayed in a park or outside their school. Some of it may be smaller and able to be displayed on a book-shelf or a desk, hung as a mobile or even used as a purse. I can't wait to go back in 2017 to see what the students have

*Here is Evan Valdez-Gibson presenting El Dorado High School's plan to turn trash from the Chihuahuan Desert into art. Can't wait to go back next year and see what they make (and how much they will have cleaned up)!*

cleaned up and what they have created.

*Meeting Isaac—now a college student at Morehouse!—in Atlanta.*

A special joy throughout the book tour was meeting so many of the amazing young people and seeing up close the work of orga-nizations I write about in *It's Your World*. In Atlanta, I met Isaac, now a student at Morehouse Col-lege, who started fighting hunger in his local community by first shar-ing beef from his family farm. He ultimately recruited thousands of people around Shreveport to help.

*At Zoo Atlanta I was lucky enough to meet and help feed giant panda twins Mei Lun and Mei Huan!*

Courtesy of Joy Secuban

Also in Atlanta, I visited the zoo to see their work with giant pandas. Since pandas are one of my daughter Charlotte's favorite animals, that visit had particular meaning. In San Francisco, I got to visit the headquarters of Kiva.org, the microlending platform I've long supported. And in Denver, I bought a cup of hot chocolate from the Girls Inc. coffee kiosk in the Rodolfo "Corky" Gonzales Branch of the Denver Public Library. Girls Inc. is one of the organizations I most admire.

Courtesy of Joy Secuban

*In Denver, I bought a cup of hot chocolate (which was delicious) from the Girls Inc. kiosk inside the Rodolfo "Corky" Gonzales Branch Library. Hope they've sold a lot more hot chocolate, coffee and goodies in the months since I visited!*

Courtesy of Bari Lurie

*Rodolfo "Corky" Gonzales Branch Library Tour November 4, 2015, Denver, CO*

Courtesy of Bari Lurie

Courtesy of Bari Lurie

*I've long admired—and supported—
Kiva, and I loved visiting their
headquarters in San Francisco and
listening to this team of seventh
graders talk about what they had
learned in their work with Kiva.*

*Cassandra came to my first event
at Barnes & Noble in New York—
I am so grateful she let me share
her incredible work on energy
efficiency and fighting
climate change!*

Courtesy of Joy Secuban

*Listening—and learning—as middle and high school students from
The Food Trust program in Philadelphia talk about all they're doing to
help their schools be healthier. Afterward, we all got to dance!*

With Haile, one of my heroes
in the kitchen and beyond. Can't
wait to see what she bakes—
and does—next!

*Courtesy of Charmaine Thomas*

Meeting William Winslow (the
Food Drive Kid) and his little
brother Alex in Raleigh. They
brought their parents too!

*Courtesy of Bari Lurie*

Here I am in front of the volleyball
net—I was on the volleyball team
at Horace Mann and think I played
in only one game the whole
of seventh grade . . .

*Courtesy of Bari Lurie*

I think Celia came the farthest—
all the way from Italy!—to join a
book event. Very grateful she took
the time to join me and even more
grateful for her ongoing work
to save Africa's elephants.

*Courtesy of Bari Lurie*

Courtesy of Joy Secuban

*With Danyel in Colorado—great to meet her and her family and hear about her continued work to support kids being healthy and proud of their heritage.*

Courtesy of Sarah Henning

*Meeting some of the youngest members of the Martha's Table community in Washington, D.C. I volunteered at Martha's Table in high school and it was great to return and see the amazing work all at Martha's Table continue to do every day.*

Although I generally avoid using quotes in *It's Your World* (and in life), sometimes I can't imagine a better way to say something that I believe than how someone else has already said it. One of my core beliefs, as I share in *It's Your World*, is that if we can do something, we have to at least try, because it's always better to get caught trying than sitting forever on the sidelines. I often think of something that Edward Everett Hale, the nineteenth-century abolitionist and minister, said: "I am only one, but I am one. I cannot do everything, but I can do something. And I will not let what I cannot do interfere with what I can do." I hope that everyone who reads *It's Your World*, looks at the website and engages with the content will be inspired to, yes, get going to follow the examples of the young people whose stories I share—or to carve their own path, wherever it may lead.

*Very grateful to all the student readers who read drafts of* It's Your World, *including from the Thalia Book Club Camp and Writopia Lab, some of whom are pictured above—thank you all again!*

# ACKNOWLEDGMENTS

The enthusiasm of my extraordinary editor Jill Santopolo helped convince me this project was worth attempting. Jill's comments and edits helped ideas come to life and unwieldy sentences to be less so. Her guidance enabled me to part ways with select content peacefully, knowing the book was stronger at the end for what it contained and what it left out. She helped me start and finish this journey and along the way I realized she'd also become my friend. Thank you, Jill.

Along with Jill, I have been fortunate to work with a terrific team at Penguin and Philomel. Thank you to Don Weisberg and Michael Green for their faith in me and belief in *It's Your World*. Thank you to Rob Farren for additional edits and suggestions and to Anne Heausler for her careful reading at the end. Thank you to Siobhán Gallagher and Talia Benamy for helping convert my various ideas, concepts and statistical snapshots into charts and graphs. Thank you to Irene Vandervoort for designing a terrific cover. Thank you to everyone else at Penguin and Philomel who helped bring *It's Your World* into the world, including Jen Loja, Adam Royce, Semadar Megged, David Briggs, Cindy Howle, Wendy Pitts, Shanta Newlin, Emily Romero, Erin Berger, Rachel Cone-Gorham, Carmela Iaria, Felicia Frazier, Jackie Engel, Daisy Kline, Mary McGrath, Leigh Butler, Helen Boomer, Amanda D'Acierno, Dan Zitt, Holly Day and Brian Geffen.

Many of the ideas in this book originated from people I've met and worked with as well as countless books, lectures, talks, podcasts, classes, seminars, discussions, conversations and reports I've read, listened to, participated in and argued about over many years. I am grateful to the extraordinary teachers I've had, from Mrs. Minor, who taught my kindergarten class, to Dr. Ngaire Woods, who supervised my doctorate at Oxford University. I am grateful to the students I've had the privilege of teaching and to all the colleagues I've worked alongside, including now at the Clinton Foundation, its affiliated initiatives and Columbia's Mailman School of Public Health. I've learned from every office, meeting room and classroom I've ever stepped into, whether I'm sitting at a desk or standing behind a lectern.

Ruby Shamir, Bari Lurie, Joy Secuban, Allie Gottlieb, Sarah Henning, Emily Young, Kamyl Bazbaz and Tara Kole helped me build on a base of ideas, provided crucial research assistance and supported the various phases and incarnations of *It's Your World*. I am grateful to each of them. I'd like to thank Ruby and Bari in particular for their early help in translating my vision for a book into a real plan, and Ruby especially for the clarity and candor that consistently characterized her suggestions and advice. Thank you to Charlene Tingle for her support and friendship while *It's Your World* took shape.

This book would not be possible without the stories that animate it and the experts whose work I draw on to help frame and explain some of the big challenges we face in our world. Thank you to everyone whose work or story is featured in the book and for reading specific passages to ensure your stories or areas of focus were accurately captured. Additionally, I am grateful to the following for reading entire chapters and for some, the entire book, and for the unvarnished commentary each provided: Cassia van der Hoof Holstein from Partners in Health; Melanie Turner from the American Heart Association; Colleen Doyle and Dr. Otis Brawley from the American Cancer Society; Dr. Howell Wechsler from the Alliance for a Healthier Generation; John MacPhee from the Jed Foundation; Dr. Mark Dybul from the Global Fund to Fight AIDS, Tuberculosis and Malaria; John Calvelli from the Wildlife Conservation Society; John Hope Bryant from Operation HOPE; Jessica Posner from Shining Hope for Communities; Dymphna van der Lans, Rain Henderson, Ami Desai, Greg Milne and Maura Pally from the Clinton Foundation; Rachel Vogelstein from the Council on Foreign Relations; Alice Albright from the Global Partnership for Education; Jen Klein from Georgetown Law School; Ann O'Leary from the Center for the Next Generation; and last, though as the saying goes, certainly not least, the brilliant Lissa Muscatine.

Additionally, I am grateful to the following people and organizations for sharing their thoughts, ideas, stories and expertise, as well as, in many cases, reviewing the passages in the book that related to their (or their kids') work: Adam Braun from Pencils of Promise, George Srour from Building Tomorrow, John Wood from Room To Read, CJ Volpe from Autism Speaks, Eric Tars from the National Law Center on Homelessness & Poverty, Barefoot College, CARE, Appalachia Service Project, New Hope for Cambodian Children, Jim Triestman, Deeanna Thomas, Campaign for Tobacco-Free Kids, Malissa Linscott, Terri McCullough from No Ceilings, Megan McIntyre, Leigh Henry, Kathi Schaeffer, Melissa Hillebrenner, Lisa Lisle, Kathleen Lane-Smith, Tia Johnson, Tammy Tibbetts, Itai Dinour, Philip Courtney, Don Cipriani, Becki Cohn-Vargas, Mario Fedelin, Lauren Howe,

Helen Nguya, Muddu Yisito Kayinga, Josh Wachs, Melanie Barber, Patricia Gentry, Leonor Montiel, Veronica Vela, Zach Maurin, Kelita Bak, Steve Patrick, Dorothy Stoneman, Jennifer Hoos Rothberg, Amy Meuers, Hilary Gridley, Kellie May, Lauren Marciszyn, John Wilson, Katherine Gerber, Amanda McDonald, Linda Mills, Imam Khalid Latif, Rabbi Yehuda Sarna, Ebony Frelix, Donna Butts, William Campbell, Tieneke van Lonkhuyzen, Leslie Lewin, Julia Porter, Angela Sheldrick, Simone Marean, Shirley Sagawa, Amy Rosen, Suzanne Taylor, Eboo Patel, Mary Ehrsam Hagerty, Hillary Schafer, Thanh Tran, Burns Strider, Jessica Church, Harold Koplewicz, Mac Winslow, Blythe Clifford, Tammy Flowers, Rosemary Gudelj, Lauren Letta, Jodi Mohney, Meagan Carnahan Fallone, Reema Nanavaty, Regina McFarland, Alison Tummon, Gustavo Torrez, Alison McSherry, Adam Rondeau, David Risher, Amanda Rosseter, Karen Tramontano, Michelle Irving, Jeffrey Rowland, Emmanuelle Peltre, Debra Duffy, Brian Feagans, Carol Moore, Annie Bergman, Meighan Stone, Carlo Dumandan, Madhuri Kommareddi, Karen Little, Jason Riggs, Jessica Hanson, Maura Daly, Murray Fisher, Pete Malinowski, Bill Wetzel, Hannah DeLetto, Chiara Cortez, Delvon Worthy, Emma Goss, Julie Schoenthaler, Lauren Su, Libby McCarthy, Luke Schiel, Maddie Macks, Nicole London, Megan Bambino, Sarah Burger, Gita Tiku, Julie Zuckerbrod, Jayne Quan, Erin McIntyre, Loren Hardenbergh, Elsa Palanza, Jackie Conrad, Izzy Rode, Nancy Lublin, Stacy Stagliano, Georgia Booth, Colleen Callahan, Charmaine Thomas, John Tucker, Walter Crouch, Deanna Congileo, Leslie Cordes, Julia Springs, Katrina Shute, Nikyea Berry, Jacqueline Pezzillo, Dave Watt, Cara Taback, Steven Sawalich, Taylor Joseph, Cecille Joan Avila, Dr. David Stukus, Janeen Manuel, Madonna Coffman, Emily Hagerman, Dana Edell, Amy Huizing, Oscar Flores, Marina Santos and Antoinette Salazar.

I want to thank everyone in Arkansas who has supported this project, many of whom supported me when I was kid, in particular Dr. Sadie Mitchell, Dr. Cheryl Carson, Lesley Andrews, Steve Barker, Herbert Ragan, John Keller, Stephanie Sims, Bobby Roberts, Dana Simmons, Shanna Jones, Terri Garner, Bruce Lindsey, Stephanie Streett and Carolyn Huber, whom I've known my whole life and loved just as long.

I am extraordinarily grateful to all of the kids who read parts of the book and provided invaluable advice on what they wanted to see more of or less of, what explanations worked and those that needed a bit more work. Thank you to Elinor Behlman, Lucas Cohen, Shira Cohen, Rohan Dash, Deirdre de Leeuw den Bouter, Rachel Eve Harris, Claire Hobson, Nathaniel Hobson, Ruby Hornik, Benjamin Kreit, Michael Lahullier, Nora Loftus, Hayden Lurie, Talia Lurie, Lulu Price, Avery Rudall-Stulberg, Jonah Samson, Jordan Samson, Justus Schmidt, Aviyam Saul Trauner, Sophia Vostrejs and Daniel Votano. Thank you to their parents for helping them all find the time.

Speaking of parents, I am grateful to my parents for their suggestions on my manuscript, for continuing to inspire me with their work in the world and most of all for their love and support on this journey.

Thank you to my husband, Marc, for reading drafts, providing insightful feedback at every juncture and taking care of our daughter, Charlotte, on Sunday afternoons when I would get caught in a swirl of thinking, writing or editing. I thought about writing this book long before I attempted to do so. Thank you to Charlotte for inspiring me already, even though she wasn't quite one when *It's Your World* was published.

This book is only possible because of all of the people mentioned above and the countless others who have inspired me with their determination to build a more prosperous, more equitable and healthier world. Any errors that remain are my responsibility alone.

# INDEX